LOVING NATURE

As the full effects of human activity on the Earth's life-support systems are revealed by science, the question of whether we can change, fundamentally, our relationship with nature becomes increasingly urgent. Just as important as an understanding of our environment is an understanding of ourselves, of the kinds of beings we are and why we act as we do. In *Loving Nature* Kay Milton considers why some people in western societies grow up to be nature lovers, actively concerned about the welfare and future of plants, animals, ecosystems and nature in general, while others seem indifferent or intent on destroying these things.

Drawing on findings and ideas from anthropology, psychology, cognitive science and philosophy, the author discusses how we come to understand nature as we do, and above all, how we develop emotional commitments to it. Anthropologists, in recent years, have tended to suggest that our understanding of the world is shaped solely by the culture in which we live. Controversially Kay Milton argues that it is shaped by direct experience in which emotion plays an essential role. Emotion is a basic ecological mechanism which connects us to our environment. It enables us to learn by alerting us to our surroundings; it helps to shape our knowledge by influencing our memories. Emotional attachments are products of learning; as we develop, we learn what to feel about particular things, and our feelings motivate our actions.

What this means, the author argues, is that the conventional opposition between emotion and rationality in western culture is a myth. The effect of this myth has been to support a market economy which systematically destroys nature, and to exclude from public decision making the kinds of emotional attachments that support more environmentally sensitive ways of living. A better understanding of ourselves, as fundamentally emotional beings, could give such ways of living the respect they need.

Kay Milton is Reader in Social Anthropology at The Queen's University of Belfast. Since the mid-1980s she has specialized in research on environmental issues. Her publications include *Environmentalism and cultural theory* (Routledge 1996) and the edited collection *Environmentalism: the view from anthropology* (Routledge 1993).

LOVING NATURE

Towards an ecology of emotion

Kay Milton

London and New York

First published 2002
by Routledge
11 New Fetter Lane, London EC4P 4EE

Simultaneously published in the USA and Canada
by Routledge
29 West 35th Street, New York, NY 10001

Routledge is an imprint of the Taylor & Francis Group

© 2002 Kay Milton

Typeset in Goudy by
Keystroke, Jacaranda Lodge, Wolverhampton
Printed and bound in Great Britain by
Biddles Ltd, Guildford and King's Lynn

British Library Cataloguing in Publication Data
A catalogue record for this book is available from the British Library

Library of Congress Cataloging in Publication Data
Milton, Kay, 1951–
Loving nature: towards an ecology of emotion / Kay Milton.
p. cm.
Includes bibliographical references and index.
1. Nature–Psychological aspects. 2. Environmental psychology. I. Title.
BF353.5.N37 M55 2002   304.2–dc21
2001045731

ISBN 0–415–25353–5 (hbk)
ISBN 0–415–25354–3 (pbk)

In memory of my friends Holly and Murphy,
who died as this book was being born.

CONTENTS

Acknowledgements   x

Introduction   1

1   **Science and religion**   8

Science, religion and nature protection 9
Science, religion and magic 11
Science, religion and common sense 12
The natural and the unnatural 15
The personal and the impersonal 19
The emotional and the rational 21
The way forward 23

2   **The naturalness of ideas**   26

Persons, non-persons and nature protection 27
Representations, metaphors and knowledge 31
Personhood as a natural idea 33
Innate learning mechanisms 34
Persons and the theory of mind 36
An assessment 37

3   **Knowing nature through experience**   40

Experience and constructionism 40
Perception and knowledge 42
Perceiving persons 44
Getting to know nature 48

4   Enjoying nature   **55**

Conservation and the enjoyment of nature 56
The naturalness of emotion 58
Biophilia and domain-specific emotions 60
Enjoying nature through experience 62
Emotion, perception and memory 64
Emotion and self-perception 66
Emotions in their social setting 68
Learning to enjoy nature 70

5   Identifying with nature   **73**

Identification and deep ecology 74
Identification and identity: Part 1 77
Other bases of identification 78
Emotions, feelings and consciousness 79
Emotions, personhood and identification 81
Identification and self-realization 83
Personhood and the enjoyment of nature 86
Identification and identity: Part 2 87

6   Valuing nature: meaning, emotion and the sacred   **92**

Value in anthropology, psychology and philosophy 93
Value and meaning 95
Meaning and emotion 98
Emotion and the sacred 101
Sacredness, identity and self-realization 105

7   Protecting nature: wildness, diversity and personhood   **110**

Protecting nature's independence 112
Protecting diversity and personhood in nature 115
Diversity and personhood in harmony 118
Diversity and personhood in conflict 123

8   Protecting nature: science and the sacred   **129**

Emotion and rationality 130
Emotion, rationality and capitalism 134
Science and scenery 135
A tale of two mountains 139

CONTENTS

Conclusion   147

Notes   152
References   159
Index   173

ACKNOWLEDGEMENTS

Many people have helped in the research and writing of this book in various ways: by welcoming me as a participant in their activities and by submitting to interviews, by providing pre-publication material and other documentation on particular issues, by allowing their published material to be used, by providing helpful comments on the initial book proposal, on earlier drafts of chapters, parts of chapters and, in one case, the whole manuscript, and by giving encouragement and inspiration through discussion of ideas. They are, in no particular order, John Stewart, Harvey Whitehouse, Maruška Svašek, Tim Ingold, Paul Richards, Roy Ellen, Ben Campbell, James Carrier, John Knight, Eeva Berglund, Terre Satterfield, Galina Lindquist, Alf Hornborg, my fellow participants in workshops and seminars at the Universities of Kent, Manchester, Aberdeen, Copenhagen, Stockholm, and Queen's University Belfast; participants in international conferences at the Findhorn Foundation in Scotland, the Jagiellonian University in Kraków and Queen's University Belfast; Kenneth C. Steven and the National Poetry Foundation, Alastair McIntosh, Alison Johnson, Andrew Johnson; Bob Brown, Barbara Young, Graham Wynne, Gwyn Williams and Mike Clark, and their colleagues at the Royal Society for the Protection of Birds (RSPB); staff and volunteers at the Ulster Wildlife Trust; staff at the Environment and Heritage Service in Northern Ireland and members of Northern Ireland's Council for Nature Conservation and the Countryside.

INTRODUCTION

I believe . . . that our overriding anthropological purpose should be to reach
a general understanding of the kinds of beings we humans are.

(Ingold 2000b: 25)

As I write this Introduction, President George W. Bush is on his first visit to Europe
since taking office. A few days ago, speaking to European heads of state in
Gothenburg, he explained why he was refusing to ratify the Kyoto agreement on
climate change. People gathered on the streets of the city to protest against his
policies on the environment, and against capitalism's relentless drive for economic
growth against the wider interests of humanity and the natural world. Meanwhile,
a television documentary gave public exposure, for the first time in Britain, to
research which indicates that global warming could take place much more quickly
than previously predicted.[1] In the second half of this century, the Amazon rainforest could dry out enough to succumb to fires, releasing its vast store of carbon. The
resulting dramatic rise in temperature could warm the oceans sufficiently to release
their store of methane, causing another sharp increase. The result could be a 'global
catastrophe', mass extinctions and hardship beyond our imagination. The researcher
hopes that his work will be a warning rather than a prediction of doom, that we shall
be sufficiently motivated to take action to avert this disaster. The international
record on environmental protection suggests that we should not be optimistic.

Why isn't everyone an environmentalist? Why do some people care more about
the future of the natural world than others do? Why do some people actively protect
nature while others, by indifference or intent, are prepared to see it destroyed?
These questions, in some form or other, constantly puzzle those engaged in
campaigning, negotiating and lobbying for a more environmentally benign society.
They are also interesting to an anthropologist, for they are questions about cultural
diversity. They ask why people think, feel and act differently towards nature and
natural things. How should we set about answering these questions? Anthropologists, in recent decades, have adopted a constructionist approach to cultural
diversity. They have assumed that our perspectives on the world, the knowledge
we hold, our assumptions and desires, are determined by the cultural context in

1

which we live. This means that we learn about the world from our fellow human beings, through exposure to *their* cultural perspectives. Our own understandings are constructed out of the messages we receive from those with whom we associate (relatives, teachers, friends, colleagues), and from the many cultural products we encounter in our everyday lives.

This book addresses the questions in a more radical way. This is not to deny that what we become depends, to a large extent, on the social and cultural contexts in which we live, but to ask how this process works. How does an individual human being learn to relate to the world in a particular way? How does a particular combination of thoughts and feelings, assumptions, goals, values and motivations emerge out of the intensely personal experience of living in the world? I suggest that, to find a satisfactory answer to these questions, we need to go beyond social and cultural contexts and see each human being as an individual organism living in an environment and developing through their engagement with what they encounter in that environment. This approach follows the lead of Tim Ingold, who drew on the work of environmental psychologists and ecologists, such as Gibson and von Uexküll, to argue that human beings come to understand the world by perceiving it directly, and not only through the medium of cultural interpretation (Ingold 1992).

In this book, I also draw on other disciplines – psychology and cognitive science, ecology and philosophy – to gain an understanding of how human beings operate, how we pick up information from our surroundings, how our knowledge of the world is generated, how we come to feel about things, to value things, as we do. The book is necessarily speculative; it presents arguments, not definitive statements. I assume that these other disciplines, like anthropology, are dedicated to understanding what kinds of beings we are, and that something might be gained by engaging in debate with them, even though, or perhaps because, there are points of disagreement (see Ingold 2000b).

The very general questions of how people come to think, feel and act as they do could have been addressed in relation to any area of human life. Like many anthropologists, I could have studied the variable patterns of human social relationships, the emergence of power structures, sexual identities or ritual traditions. But this book focuses instead on how people relate to nature and natural things. There are two main reasons for this. First, the questions arose out of my own research on environmental issues. This research, conducted mainly in the UK and Ireland since the mid-1980s, has involved participation in the activities of groups engaged in protecting nature and natural things from the damaging effects of other human activities. The questions of why more people do not share these concerns, and why more do not actively commit themselves to the defence of nature, are constantly present. They are implicit in the planning of campaigns, in the writing of recruitment leaflets, press releases and educational materials. They arise whenever nature protectionists seek to persuade others that nature matters. So my attention was continually drawn to this particular area of cultural diversity, to the obvious fact that each individual thinks, feels and acts differently towards nature.

Second, the reason why I chose to conduct research on environmental issues in the first place is that nature matters to me. It worries me deeply that my own species, and particularly my own broad cultural tradition of western capitalism, has created ways of living that damage and destroy the natural world. So I share the desires of those I have worked with, that more people should care about nature and natural things and make their protection a priority. In other words, I share their desire for change and I want to help bring that change about. The most useful contribution that anthropology can make is to improve our understanding of why we are as we are, of what makes us think, feel and act the way we do, in the hope that such understanding will provide a basis for informed change. I am aware that this declaration of interest might raise doubts, in some readers' minds, about the objectivity of the analysis presented in this book, but all analyses are motivated by commitments of some kind (whether to the pursuit of knowledge, or career, or some other cause), and it is more honest to declare them than not to do so.

From the beginning of this exploration into what makes people care about nature, it has been clear that emotion would be a central factor. This was self-evident, given that caring is an emotional response. I have been constantly aware, throughout my research, of the passion that drives efforts to protect nature and natural things. Nature protectionists frequently speak of their feelings for nature, their enjoyment of it, their distress at its destruction, their fears for its future. So I have assumed that feelings are the prime motivators of human activity, and have sought to understand how they motivate. This inevitably led to an investigation of what emotions are and how they operate in human life, and this in turn has given the book a theoretical purpose which I had not initially envisaged: to develop an approach to emotion which is different from that which has prevailed in anthropology and the other social sciences in recent years.

This is not the place for a detailed analysis of social scientific approaches to emotion, nor is it necessary, since good summaries already exist (Lutz and White 1986, Lupton 1998, Williams and Bendelow 1998, Williams 2001). Briefly, studies of emotion appear to fall between two poles. At one extreme are the 'essentialist' or 'positivist' models which emphasize the biological nature of emotions. At least some emotions are assumed to be universal and inherited rather than learned, and explanations for them are sought in our evolutionary past (for instance, Tooby and Cosmides 1990). At the other extreme are the constructionist approaches which treat emotions as cultural products (Harré 1986). It is assumed that rules about what to feel are learned by growing up in a particular culture (Hochschild 1983). Most analytical models fall between these two extremes, treating emotions as outcomes of various combinations of biological and cultural factors. In sociology and anthropology, recent studies of emotion, as of other phenomena, have tended towards the constructionist pole (Lutz 1988, Lutz and Abu-Lughod 1990, Lupton 1998).

Leavitt (1996) observed that the existence of these two poles highlights the dual nature of emotions. On the one hand, they are feelings, experienced as bodily states by individual human beings. On the other hand, they are expressed and interpreted often in social situations; they have meanings which are culturally variable.

3

The problem with essentialist or positivist approaches to emotions is that they emphasize the feelings but tend to ignore the meanings, whereas constructionist approaches focus on the meanings at the expense of the feelings. Thus both kinds of approach fail to take account of the special nature of emotions, the fact that they consist of both feelings *and* meanings (Leavitt 1996: 515). The challenge for anthropologists, sociologists and other scholars interested in emotion has been to develop an approach which addresses this dual character. One solution has been to treat emotions primarily as social phenomena (Parkinson 1995, Hochschild 1998, Lyon 1998). It is recognized that emotions are internal bodily states, experienced by individuals, but, it is argued, they arise in social situations, when individuals interact with each other. Emotions are constituted by, and in turn help to constitute, social relationships.

The approach developed in this book is slightly different. Drawing on the work of Damasio (1999), I argue that emotions operate primarily (though not exclusively) in ecological relations rather than social relations. In other words, emotions operate in the relationship between an individual organism and its environment; they are induced when an organism interacts with objects in that environment. For most human beings, much of the environment happens to be social and much of their interaction is with other human beings. But my point is that our environment is not essentially or primarily social; it is simply an environment, consisting of things other than ourselves with which we interact. If this distinction seems trivial, its importance will become clear in Chapters 4, 5 and 6, where emotional responses to nature and natural things are discussed.

I have assumed that emotions are the prime motivators, but not that they are the sole basis of human activity. Our actions are based, not only on what we feel, but also on what we know and think about the world. This raises the question of how feeling is related to thought and knowledge. There is a strong convention in western culture that emotion is opposed to thought, or at least that it impedes rational thought (Lutz 1988, Barbalet 1998) which is considered essential to sound knowledge and understanding. This convention features prominently in public discourses about nature protection. Quite often, one side in an environmental conflict will accuse their opponents of acting irrationally, on the basis of their emotions. Usually, though not always, it is nature protectionists who are accused, often by commercial developers or politicians, of being too emotional in their attitudes to nature. Whenever I have encountered such accusations they have struck me as being, themselves, irrational or unreasonable. They seem to imply that commitments to some things, like trees, landscapes and non-human animals, are emotional, while commitments to other things, like profit and progress, are rational. I have often suspected that this distinction between different kinds of commitment is logically unsound, and one of my purposes in this book is to test this impression by exploring the relationship between emotion and rationality in discourses about nature protection.

In doing so, I am following an established tradition. Barbalet (1998) identified three views on the relationship between emotion and rationality in the work of philosophers, social scientists and other scholars. First, there is the conventional view, that emotion and rationality are opposed, that emotions distort reason and prevent its proper operation. This view is most prominently represented in social science in the work of Weber, and derives, in philosophy, from the work of Descartes and Kant (Barbalet 1998: 33–8). Second, there is what Barbalet calls the critical approach, which holds that emotion supports reason by giving it direction; it makes rational thought and action possible by identifying desires, goals, purposes, preferences (Barbalet 1998: 38–45). This view is derived, in philosophy, from the work of Hume (1911 [1740]), and is supported in contemporary scholarship by Frank (1988), de Sousa (1990), Oatley (1992) and Damasio (1994, 1999). Finally, there is the radical approach, also detectable in the work of Hume, but most prominent in the work of James (Barbalet 1998: 45–54). In this view, emotion and rationality are continuous. Emotion does not just support and enable rational thought, it constitutes it, in that rationality is, itself, a feeling (James 1956 [1897]). The arguments presented in this book move from a critical approach (in Chapters 4 and 5), in which I draw on the work of Damasio to show how emotion enables the development of perception and knowledge, towards a radical approach (in Chapter 6) in which the distinction between emotion and meaning is questioned.

Before proceeding, it is important to clarify, as far as possible, the scope of this book. Much of my research has been with organizations dedicated to nature conservation, which means, in particular, the protection of biological diversity (or 'biodiversity': ecosystems, habitats, species and subspecies) and landscape (scenic beauty). Nature conservation generally depends on an 'anthropocentric' view of nature, one in which nature is valued for its benefits to human beings. But this book covers a broader field which includes nature conservation, and which I refer to as 'nature protection'. This encompasses all protective approaches towards nature and natural things.[2] It includes deep ecology and concerns for the rights and welfare of non-human animals and other natural entities (trees, forests, ecosystems, nature in general, Mother Earth). Such concerns are generally 'ecocentric' or 'biocentric'; nature and natural things are assumed to have value in and of themselves, independent of any benefits they may have for human beings. Although my research has been primarily among nature conservationists, I have encountered many among them who express more ecocentric views, and have participated in many discussions of the relationship between conservation and other forms of nature protection. There is also a great deal of literature on deep ecology, ecocentrism, animal rights, and so on, on which I have drawn. The book explores what turns people into nature protectionists, and examines some of the ways in which they act on their concerns.

Much harder to define is the geographical or cultural scope of the book. This is a problem faced by all social scientists whose research is not confined within clearly bounded units. My field research has been conducted mainly in the UK and Ireland, but the people I have encountered identify with a broad community of nature protectionists engaged in discourses which range freely across national and cultural boundaries. My understanding of nature protection has been shaped, not only by my field research, but by contributions to and products of these transnational and transcultural discourses – by documents produced in international arenas such as the Rio Earth Summit and the European Union, by books, articles and websites circulating in a global context. This is not to deny that the character of nature protection varies in different countries and regions (see Jamison *et al.* 1990), where it is shaped by laws, political structures and cultural traditions. But communication about nature protection transcends these boundaries, and local events – the conflict over logging in Oregon, efforts to prevent a quarry from scarring a Scottish mountain – have distant effects through their incorporation into a global discourse. The term 'deep ecology' was first used by a Norwegian, but there is nothing specifically Norwegian or Scandinavian about the range of ideas, feelings and practices to which it now refers. Concerns for the rights and welfare of non-human animals are probably expressed more often and more strongly in the US, Canada and the UK than on the continent of Europe, but this does not make them specifically American, Canadian or British concerns.

In describing the broad context of my main subject matter, I have adopted the common if not very satisfactory solution of referring to 'western' countries, society(ies) and culture(s).[3] The label is unsatisfactory because it could be taken to imply that the west is a sealed container, whereas in fact the opposite is the case; the west has no clear boundaries, and it is in the nature of market capitalism and liberal democracy, which characterize the west, to break down whatever boundaries there are. The only reason I refer to nature protection in a western context is because I do not wish to assume that any generalizations I make about it are universally applicable.

In fact the book contains three levels of analysis. Running throughout the first six chapters there is the discussion about how human beings, as individual organisms, come to think and feel as they do, not only about nature and natural things, but about whatever they encounter in their environment. Clearly, this discussion is intended to be general, to apply to all human beings everywhere. Also running through the first six chapters is a discussion of how nature protectionists come to think and feel as they do about nature and natural things. It is this discussion which refers to a broadly western context. Finally, in illustrative material throughout the book, but mainly in Chapters 7 and 8, I describe particular techniques, events and debates in the practice of nature protection. I treat these as most anthropologists treat ethnographic material: as specific instances which illustrate more general arguments, and from which cautious generalizations may be made.

Introductions usually end by summarizing what is to come. I shall do this very briefly, saving a more detailed outline for the end of Chapter 1. Two of the main ways in which people in western societies relate to nature and natural things are through science and religion. More specifically, for my purposes, nature protectionists talk and write about nature in ways that can be described as broadly scientific or broadly religious. In Chapter 1, I discuss the relationship between science and religion, as it has been understood by anthropologists and other specialists, as a vehicle for thinking about how nature protectionists relate to nature and natural things. This discussion generates three distinctions: between natural and unnatural ideas, between personal and impersonal understandings of nature, and that discussed above, between emotion and rationality.

These distinctions set the scene for the remainder of the book. Chapters 2 and 3 consider how people come to know nature as they do, as personal or impersonal, and examines whether these understandings are 'natural' (in the sense of being biologically predetermined) or learned through experience. Chapters 4 and 5 focus on emotion, on how people in general and nature protectionists in particular come to feel as they do about nature and natural things. Two 'kinds of loving' – enjoyment of and identification with nature – are examined in a discussion which shows how emotion (or feeling) and understanding (or knowledge) support each other. Chapter 6 draws the theoretical arguments together by discussing how nature and natural things are valued, a process in which, I suggest, emotion and understanding are difficult to distinguish. In the final two chapters, the emphasis is more ethnographic. I draw on my own research and the work of other anthropologists to show how understandings of emotion shape the practice of nature protection in western societies.

1

SCIENCE AND RELIGION

The hope that science could replace religion as a way for human beings to cope with the world . . . was really a hope that 'nature' could replace 'God' as a source of inspiration and understanding. Harmony, permanence, order, and an idea of our place in that order – scientists searched for all that as diligently as Job, with their unceasing attention to the 'web of life' and the grand cycle of decay and rebirth. But nature, it turned out, was fragile.

(McKibben 1990: 76–7)

For as long as I can remember, I have been surrounded by people who take an active interest in the protection of nature and natural things. During the past fifteen years, when environmentalism has been my main research interest, I have spent many hours reading reports, policies and campaign literature produced by nature protection authorities and NGOs, and engaged in debates about these documents. I have attended many formal and informal gatherings at which nature protection has been discussed, and had many conversations with nature protectionists about their activities. I have also, in the pursuit of work and pleasure, been an enthusiastic consumer of books, magazines, television programmes and, more recently, websites, aimed at increasing public concern for nature. One of the clear impressions gained from all this exposure is that nature protectionists relate to nature in ways that can be described, broadly, as 'religious' or 'scientific'. These two idioms do not, by any means, exhaust ways of relating to nature, but they are prominently expressed in discourses about nature protection. This observation creates an interesting possibility. Debates about the differences between religion and science have arisen repeatedly in anthropology and related disciplines throughout the past century. Perhaps this academic discourse could provide an appropriate vehicle for thinking about how nature protectionists relate to nature, a way of identifying key ideas that might help us to understand how people engaged in the protection of nature come to think, feel and act as they do towards the objects of their concern.

In this chapter, I explore this possibility by analysing what anthropologists and other specialists have written about the relationship between science and religion. There are three tasks to be accomplished. First, I need to show that both scientific and religious ways of relating to nature are present in discourses about nature protection; this task occupies the next section. Second, I need to identify those ideas about science and religion that might be useful in explaining what motivates nature protection. This task, which occupies most of the chapter, takes the form of a discussion of what has been written about science, religion, their relation to each other and to other kinds of cultural perspective (magic and common sense). Three pairs of contrasting or opposed concepts emerge from this discussion: natural and unnatural ideas, personal and impersonal understandings of nature, and emotion and rationality. Finally, I need to suggest ways in which these oppositions might be relevant for understanding nature protection. These thoughts are drawn together in the final section which identifies the issues to be addressed in the following chapters.

Science, religion and nature protection

My starting point is the observation that nature protectionists relate to nature and natural things in both scientific and religious ways. This means, essentially, that they talk and write about nature, and act towards it, in ways that conform to commonsense understandings of what science and religion consist of. In the following sections it will become important to indicate how anthropologists and other scholars have defined science and religion, but for the present I am using these labels rather loosely and taking their meanings for granted. I am assuming that 'science' will conjure up in most readers' minds a body of knowledge generated through systematic observation, knowledge which is seen as authoritative because of the controlled manner in which it is generated. And I assume that 'religion' will suggest a concern with ultimate meanings as a basis for moral rules, rules which are often, though not always, believed to be sanctioned by a sacred authority, in the form of a divine being or beings.

The close relationship between science and some forms of nature protection is so taken for granted that it is difficult to describe it without seeming to state the obvious.[1] Problems in nature are defined as such on the basis of scientific knowledge. We know about pollution, ozone depletion and climate change because scientists have told us about them. Science explains how these problems have arisen and what might be done to solve them. Some nature protectionists, those whom I shall refer to throughout this book as 'nature conservationists' (or simply 'conservationists'), employ a scientific model of nature as an array of living and non-living things and substances which interact with one another. Many of the terms which conservationists use to describe the components of nature – species, ecosystem, habitat, biodiversity – come from science. According to science, biodiversity is good for the future of life on earth because, in accordance with Darwinian theory, the greater the variety of living things there are, the greater the chance that some will adapt and survive in a changing environment. Some conservationists describe this as the most important reason for conserving nature, a point to which I shall return in later chapters. Science indicates what specific organisms need for their survival, enabling conservationists to define objectives for the preservation and restoration of species and habitats.

In summary, the main function of science in nature protection is to be used as an arbiter of truth. Even though scientific knowledge is open-ended and constantly changing (see below), it is treated by environmental activists and policy makers as the main authority on the state of nature, and therefore as the most reliable foundation on which to base decisions. Its importance as a basis for decision making rests on the belief – one that has often been questioned by social scientists – that science can provide impartial knowledge (Berglund 1998: 193), a point to be explored further in Chapter 8.

The role of religion in nature protection is harder to describe, perhaps because religion is a less precise concept than science. Some branches of nature protection have features which are generally associated with religion. In some of the most influential writing (for instance, Carson 1956, Seed *et al.* 1988, Macy 1991, Spangler 1993),[2] the sustenance of life on earth is presented, both explicitly and implicitly, as a sacred purpose, and the protection of nature as a spiritual commitment to that purpose. This is particularly so for those who see the modern development of technology, based on science, as the main cause of environmental destruction, and who seek fundamental changes in the way people in western society relate to nature. Deep ecologists, who fall within this broad category, have argued that science and technology have 'disenchanted' nature, destroying the sense of respect and awe with which it was once treated. They seek a 're-enchantment' of nature, a restoration of respect and the establishment of harmony in human–nature relations (Barry 1999: 17). Some turn to non-industrial societies for models of a more appropriate relationship with nature (for instance, Manes 1990: 28, Ereira 1990); often these are hunter-gatherer cultures in which nature is 'enspirited' (Callicott 1982: 305), in which relationships between people and their environments are governed by moral obligations on both sides (see Tanner 1979, Scott 1989).[3]

As well as some of the ways in which protectionists relate to nature having what might be called religious characteristics, organized religion has featured in discourse on nature protection, both as an object of criticism and as a positive influence. White (1967) is among many who have held Christianity at least partly responsible for western society's exploitation of nature, and who have compared it unfavourably, in this respect, with other religions. Recognizing the powerful influence of religion in the lives of many people, nature protectionists have sought to enlist religious world views in the promotion of an environmental ethic (Tucker 1997). This approach was exemplified in the World Wide Fund for Nature's Network on Conservation and Religion (WWF 1986), which brought religious leaders together to discuss ways in which their various doctrines could support the cause of conservation. Religious leaders and church organizations have also, on their own initiative, expressed their concern for nature and sought to define their role in its protection, often against the background of broader national and international discussions such as the Rio Earth Summit in 1992 (see, for instance, Gottlieb 1996: 636ff.).

10

It is tempting to oversimplify the relationship between science and religion in nature protection by suggesting that, while science provides the knowledge on which actions are based, religion provides their moral justification. Some of the discussion among nature protectionists is along these lines. For instance, Callicott (1994) argued that science should form the basis for environmental ethics with religion playing a supporting role, while Taylor (1997) argued that scientific knowledge cannot provide people with moral values (cf. Yearley 1992: 144), and that religion provides the only sound basis for moral motivation. But many nature protectionists value ways of knowing nature other than science, and there are other bases for morality besides what is conventionally regarded as religion (Barry 1999: 38ff.). These issues will be addressed in the following chapters. The remainder of this chapter focuses on the relationship between science and religion, as a vehicle for thinking about ways of relating to nature.

Science, religion and magic

'Is magic a kind of science or a kind of religion?' Through this question, some thirty years ago, I and my fellow anthropology undergraduates were introduced to one of the discipline's early debates. The quest, which remains central to anthropology, was to reach a better understanding of human culture by comparing the familiar with the exotic. Magic was the exotic. It had no place in our everyday lives; it was something that only societies distant in time or space took seriously. Religion and science, in contrast, were familiar. Both had figured prominently in our formal education, were featured in the media, and had inspired films and popular fiction. For some of us, religion was a personal commitment.

The main protagonists in that early debate were Tylor, Frazer and Malinowski. For Tylor and Frazer, magic was a pseudo-science. Its status as such depended on two features of magical thought: like science it was logical and systematic, but unlike science it was fallacious. It had the character of science but not its truth. In Tylor's words, it was 'a sincere but fallacious system of philosophy, evolved by the human intellect by processes still in great measure intelligible to our own minds' (Tylor 1871, vol. i: 122). For Frazer, the principles of magical thought were:

> excellent in themselves, and indeed absolutely essential to the working of the human mind. Legitimately applied they yield science; illegitimately applied they yield magic, the bastard sister of science. It is therefore a truism, almost a tautology, to say that all magic is necessarily false and barren; for, were it ever to become true and fruitful, it would no longer be magic but science.
>
> (Frazer 1994: 46)[4]

Malinowski also recognized a degree of similarity between magic and science (Malinowski 1948: 67), but saw their differences as more fundamental than their similarities. For him, they operated in different cultural contexts and fulfilled different functions. Science belonged to the realm of practical, everyday tasks, where it provided solutions through empirical observation and rational thought. But this kind of knowledge was not adequate for all situations. There were problems it could not solve – how to cure a particular illness, how to ensure safety on a sea journey. These gaps in knowledge created emotional stress which magic relieved by providing a set of ready-made beliefs and practices (ibid.: 70). It thus operated, according to Malinowski, in the same way as religion, whose purpose was to relieve the emotional stress created by extreme situations (ibid.: 67). But the similarity between religion and magic rested, not only on the type of problem they solved, but also on the type of solution they provided. Both provided escapes 'by ritual and belief into the domain of the supernatural' (ibid.). This placed them, in Malinowski's view, in the realm of the sacred, in clear opposition to science, which belonged to the realm of the profane.

Our task as undergraduates was to understand the arguments of Tylor, Frazer and Malinowski, their points of agreement and disagreement, how they reached their conclusions. We were not expected to provide a definitive answer to the question of whether magic is a kind of science or a religion, but to understand why it was a question worth asking. I fear that in my naivety, like many young students, I missed the point. The familiarity of science and religion and the strangeness of magic concealed what, with hindsight, seemed quite obvious: that the question was asking as much about the nature of science and religion as it was about the nature of magic.

Of course, it is significant that Tylor, Frazer and Malinowski also saw magic as the most problematic of the three concepts. Magic, as the relatively unfamiliar phenomenon, confined to the margins and the history of western society, needed to be investigated in a range of non-western cultures before its place in the broad scheme of things could be determined. Science and religion were at least familiar if not easy to define, given the diversity of opinions about them. Because they were familiar, they could be used as fixed points against which the unfamiliar could be measured. In the work of all three analysts, science and religion were placed apart, on opposite sides of a dividing line (see Figure 1.1). The work of Tylor, Frazer and Malinowski may not be representative of early anthropological thought (Durkheim and Weber, for instance, identified continuities between science and religion; see Tambiah 1990), but it demonstrates that an opposition between science and religion was present and, to some extent, taken for granted in the formative development of anthropology. The precise nature of that opposition will come under scrutiny below.

Science, religion and common sense

Malinowski's famous essay on *Magic, science and religion*, originally published in 1925, began with a bold declaration: 'There are no peoples however primitive without religion and magic. Nor are there, it must be added at once, any savage races lacking either in the scientific attitude or in science' (Malinowski 1948: 1).

(a) Tylor and Frazer   **(b) Malinowski**

Figure 1.1 Models of science, religion and magic

But later in the essay he seemed to draw back from the view that science is universal in human culture. His 'minimum definition' of science as 'a body of rules and conceptions, based on experience and derived from it by logical inference' (ibid.: 17) was so broad, he acknowledged, that it would not satisfy most epistemologists, and might equally apply to an art or craft. He occasionally used the broader term 'rational knowledge' in favour of 'science', and admitted that 'whether we should call it *science* or only *empirical and rational knowledge* is not of primary importance' (ibid.: 18, emphasis in original). Thus he both obscured and hinted at a distinction which has since become important in the analysis of culture: the distinction between science and common sense.

The phenomenon which Malinowski cautiously labelled 'science' (and, less cautiously, 'rational knowledge') is now more widely referred to as 'common sense' (Horton 1967, Atran 1990). Inevitably, anthropologists mean different things by 'common sense'. In general, it is assumed to include people's everyday knowledge. But does this knowledge consist only of 'manifestly perceivable empirical fact' (Atran 1990: 1), or is it 'what the mind filled with presuppositions . . . concludes' (Geertz 1983: 84)? And where, in any case, should the line be drawn between presupposition and perceivable fact, if it should be drawn at all? These questions will be addressed in Chapters 2 and 3.

'Science', meanwhile, through the influence of philosophers, historians (Popper 1965, Kuhn 1970) and practising scientists (Wolpert 1992), is now more narrowly defined than it was by Malinowski, though again, definitions vary. Most would agree that science is a systematic search for knowledge, characterized by induction (verification through observation) and reduction (explanation of phenomena in terms of their progressively smaller components). It is open-ended (Horton 1967), it continually generates new knowledge and it employs a rigorous methodology (Wolpert 1992: 2). According to this view, science has to obey rules which do not constrain common sense.

In more recent debates about science and religion, common sense has replaced magic as the 'middle ground' (Richards, P. 1997: 109), the connecting territory through which the similarities and contrasts between science and religion are identified. Horton took this approach in his (1967) comparison between western science and African religious thought. He described both kinds of knowledge as 'theory'; they seek to explain what lies behind commonsense observations. The understanding provided by common sense leaves a great deal unexplained. Why do some people suffer greater misfortune than others? Why do crops sometimes fail? Theory fills this gap by positing an ordered universe, in which the observable world, with its puzzles and anomalies, is the outcome of a limited number of general principles (Horton 1967: 51). Theory 'places things in a causal context wider than that provided by common sense' (ibid.: 53). Where common sense seeks the obvious and immediate cause, theory searches further afield. Common sense tells us that the crop failed because of a storm, but we need theory to explain that the storm was caused by witchcraft, or an angry god, or by unseasonal temperatures produced by carbon dioxide emissions.

What then distinguishes religious from scientific theory? In Horton's view, the key difference is that scientific theory is open to alternative explanations whereas religious theory is closed (Horton 1967: 155ff.). In religious thought, established theories are accepted truth; it would be inappropriate to question them. It follows from this that religion protects its established ideas (ibid.: 167). The failure of rituals to have the desired effect does not cause people to lose faith in their efficacy. A body of religious theory contains ready-made explanations for failure. Science, on the other hand, not only requires established ideas to be abandoned if they fail, but also requires them to be tested systematically through experiment (ibid.: 172).

Atran also treated common sense as the middle ground between scientific and religious, or in his word 'symbolic', thought. Common sense is the means by which people come to know the world through the rational interpretation of information received through their senses. It constitutes a core of basic knowledge on which theory depends (Atran 1990: 265). Like Horton, Atran presented science and symbolism as kinds of speculative theory which employ different rules. Science seeks to understand the unknown in strictly rational ways, by providing evidence which can be confirmed or refuted using the same universal cognitive properties that produce commonsense knowledge – the powers of observation and inductive interpretation. Symbolic thought, in contrast, is not constrained by rationality (Atran 1990: 250), so it cannot be relied upon to produce truthful propositions. Symbolism has no means of testing the truth of its beliefs, and so depends, for its authority, entirely on faith (ibid.: 217). Scientific and symbolic thought are thus 'diametrically opposed' in their relation to common sense. Science seeks to augment 'the rational processing of empirical reality' while symbolism bypasses it (ibid.: 220). On this basis it seems reasonable to ask how symbolism can be grounded in common sense at all, given its non-rational nature. The relationship, in Atran's analysis, is one of opposition and contradiction. Symbolic thought challenges common sense in specific, non-random ways (ibid.: 219–20), and is dependent on it in the sense that the counter-intuitive is always dependent, for its meaning, on the intuitive (ibid.: 265).

The continuity, noted by Horton and Atran, between science and common sense was forcefully denied by Wolpert.[5] He pointed out that scientific facts and ideas are often at odds with commonsense observations and expectations. For instance, we perceive white as a single colour, but science reveals that it consists of all the colours of the spectrum (Wolpert 1992: 4). He also observed that common sense is often vague and inconsistent (ibid.: 15–16), whereas science is precise and rigorous. A crucial difference, he argued, is that science is a 'self-aware' endeavour, in that scientists always know when they are doing science; common sense, 'almost by definition', is unconscious (ibid.: 18). Finally, the purpose of common sense is to be useful in everyday life, while the purpose of science is abstract understanding, detached from practical goals (ibid.: 16). Hence it is important, in Wolpert's analysis, to distinguish science from technology. The latter can be based on science but is directed towards purposes which are not themselves scientific (ibid.: 25).

Where does religion fit into Wolpert's model? Its relationship with common sense is unclear, but he was quite explicit about its incompatibility with science. Religion provides moral guidance and offers 'unquestioning certainty' (Wolpert 1992: 144) on matters which would otherwise be difficult to understand. Even scientists, when they have revealed the most fundamental principles governing the operation of the universe, have to accept that something remains unexplained. Why *those* principles, and where did they come from? This inevitable gap in understanding leads some scientists to accept religion, but in doing so they have to live with an uncomfortable juxtaposition. Religion means believing in entities (spiritual beings, for instance) whose existence can be neither demonstrated nor falsified. Thus religious knowledge will inevitably conflict with scientific knowledge, and scientists can only hold religious beliefs, and remain true to their science, by setting that conflict aside (ibid.: 146–7).

The material discussed above suggests at least four distinct analytical models of the relationships among science, religion and common sense (see Figure 1.2). Lines are drawn and connections made on the basis of different criteria, but in all of them (as in those depicted in Figure 1.1) science and religion fall on opposite sides of an analytical divide; the sense of opposition between them could hardly be clearer.

The natural and the unnatural

Historians and philosophers have often commented on the rarity of science (McCauley 2000). Notwithstanding its current widespread acceptance, science is said to have arisen only twice in human history – in ancient Greece and early modern Europe, and possibly just once if the latter instance is assumed to be a continuation of the former. Religion, in contrast, is assumed to have arisen in more or less every known human society. The above discussion warns that such claims should be treated with caution. Our perception of the rarity of anything depends on how we define it. Malinowski employed a very broad concept of science which made it as common as religion. Wolpert and others, by separating it from technology and common sense, have made it rare. Religion too has been subjected

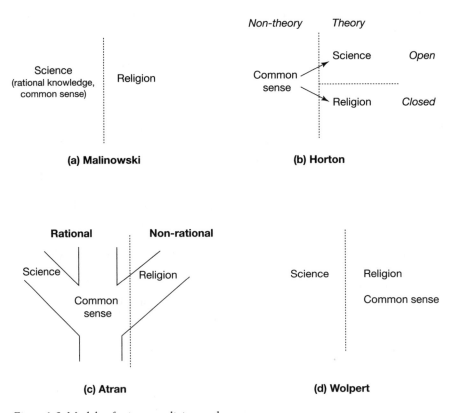

Figure 1.2 Models of science, religion and common sense

to various definitions (Tylor 1871, Durkheim 1971 [1915], Horton 1960, Goody 1961, Spiro 1966) which have affected anthropologists' perceptions of its distribution. Depending on how these definitions are viewed, the relative rarity of science *vis-à-vis* religion can either be dismissed as an artefact of analysis or treated as an interesting observation worthy of attention. The former view makes undeniable sense, but as a starting point it would leave us with little to say. The latter view, adopted by a number of anthropologists and other social scientists, has produced some interesting ideas on the opposition between science and religion.

One way of explaining why religion is common and science is rare is to argue that religion is natural (Guthrie 1993, Boyer 1994a) and science is unnatural (Wolpert 1992). How should the terms 'natural' and 'unnatural' be understood in this context? Religion and science are both components of human culture. Does it make sense to suggest that some parts of culture are more natural than others? To answer this question we should recognize that 'nature' has several meanings. In one sense, perhaps its most common in western discourse, it refers to whatever lies outside culture (Ellen 1996: 110–11, cf. Berglund 1998: 105). In terms of this meaning, it is clearly illogical to suggest that some cultural phenomena may be more natural than others. But nature can also refer to the inner essence of things (Ellen 1996: 111–12), as in the expression 'human nature'. On this understanding, one cultural phenomenon might be more natural than another if it is more closely related to what makes us human, to what we all hold in common as human beings. Conversely, it could be seen as less natural if it depends more on variable factors, such as personal experiences (including experiences of particular cultural institutions). I suggest that any debate about the naturalness or unnaturalness of cultural phenomena is most accurately seen as a debate about human nature and human experience (often expressed as 'nature and nurture') rather than nature and culture. What confuses the issue, apart from a failure to recognize the different meanings of 'nature', is that human experience and its products are often described as 'culture', while attributes of human nature are often described as 'noncultural' (for instance, Boyer 1994a: 3). Thus the discourse tends to slip into the language of a nature–culture dichotomy, even though it cannot logically assume such a dichotomy.

So, the debate about the relative naturalness of religion and science is about the extent to which these *cultural* phenomena are products of human *nature* rather than human experience. The question of what human nature is and how it finds expression in culture is, itself, a matter of intense debate, and will be discussed more fully in Chapter 2. The naturalness of religion has been linked to the operation of human cognition and memory. Boyer (1994a, 1996) argued that human beings are cognitively predisposed to develop particular kinds of religious beliefs. The starting point for his analysis was the observation that similar beliefs recur in a wide range of cultures:

> In most cultural environments, one finds representations concerning the life-like and human-like features of non-living or non-human objects: trees that protect people in exchange for sacrifices, animals that have marriage ceremonies or funerary rituals, mountains that breathe, rivers that talk, statues that listen or divining wands that predict future occurrences, not to mention gods who have meals and fall in love or spirits who live in invisible villages.
>
> (Boyer 1996: 83, cf. Sperber 1975)

He cited evidence from studies of cognitive development in children (for instance, Keil 1979, 1989) which indicate that human beings are predisposed to recognize certain ontological categories and associated principles. We 'naturally' distinguish living from non-living things, persons from artefacts, events from abstract objects (Boyer 1996: 84–7). We also 'naturally' identify the criteria which distinguish these things; we attribute intentions and feelings to persons but not to artefacts, for instance. Boyer did not attribute the emergence of this 'intuitive ontology' entirely to human nature – experience is also a contributory factor (see Chapter 2), but the central point of his analysis is that our learning is biased; we are naturally predisposed to understand the world through particular kinds of ideas.

17

Religious beliefs violate these intuitive ideas; they break the rules of our natural ontology. They attribute intentional action to inanimate objects, and human capacities to animals and invisible beings. The consistency of these violations is striking. Religious ideas do not simply violate ontological principles; they do so in similar ways in many human cultures. Boyer explained this recurrence in terms of another natural predisposition: to remember certain kinds of counter-intuitive ideas. It is because religious ideas break ontological rules in particular ways that we find them memorable, and because they are memorable, they are easily transmitted and are therefore persistent and widespread components of human culture.[6]

Boyer's model could be seen as a comment on the relationship between religion and common sense, one that comes very close to Atran's analysis discussed above. Commonsense knowledge, according to Atran, consists of certain 'cognitive universals', 'plain thinking about the world' in terms of ontological categories whose 'actual realization . . . depends upon the fragmentary and limited experience available to us'. It is 'just the way humans are constitutionally disposed to think of things' (Atran 1990: 2). In Atran's analysis, the relationship of religious beliefs to common sense consists in the non-random ways in which they depart from it, ways which dramatically contradict basic commonsense assumptions, making the beliefs particularly memorable (ibid.: 219).

Ideas about the unnaturalness of science are more contentious and less developed than ideas about the naturalness of religion. One view, advanced by McCauley (2000), is that scientific ideas could be seen as unnatural in that they are difficult to master. Nevertheless, Atran argued that science has a natural foundation in common sense, whereas Wolpert described scientific ideas as unnatural, being 'entirely counter-intuitive and against common sense'. Against this view, we could pose the argument put forward by Boyer and others, and outlined above, that certain kinds of counter-intuitive ideas are natural if their counter-intuitiveness makes them more likely to be remembered and transmitted.[7] Some scientific ideas might well fit this model. Science tells us that human beings share a common ancestry with apes, that the apparently stable and solid land masses are moving, and that the scattered universe was once small and dense. If persistence and widespread distribution are signs of naturalness, these ideas seem to pass this test very well. The theories of evolution, continental drift and the 'big bang' origin of the universe are at least as familiar in western societies as are many religious ideas. The theory of evolution is so well established that creationists in the United States have tried with fifty pieces of legislation to prevent it from being taught in schools, and have so far failed (Jones 1999: 1).

This discussion suggests that the division between science and religion may not be as clear as it appears; both religion and science could be said to contain the kinds of ideas that some analysts have described as 'natural'. And yet the sense of opposition between science and religion has, as we have seen, remained strong right from the early development of anthropology through to the current debate. Do we have to conclude that it is based on an illusion, or does it have some other foundation? The discussion in the following section focuses on a more conventional way of dividing religion and science, in terms of personal and impersonal understandings of the world. It is important to point out that, although the adjective 'personal' usually indicates the kind of agent that holds a view or performs an action (an individual rather than an organization), I use it in this book to refer to a particular way of understanding and relating to nature. A 'personal' understanding of nature assumes it to be composed primarily of 'persons', while an 'impersonal' or 'non-personal' understanding assumes it to be composed primarily of 'non-persons' – objects and mechanisms that have no thoughts or feelings.

The personal and the impersonal

Religion is based on the assumption that events in the world are caused by intentional agents (persons) while science assumes that the world is explicable in terms of impersonal objects and mechanisms. This has been seen by many as a fundamental aspect of the opposition between religion and science. It entered anthropology as part of the magic–science–religion debate at the end of the nineteenth century. Its reasoning is clear from the following passage by Frazer, who defined religion as 'a propitiation or conciliation of powers superior to man':

> all conciliation implies that the being conciliated is a conscious or personal agent, that his conduct is in some measure uncertain, and that he can be prevailed upon to vary it in the desired direction by a judicious appeal to his interests, his appetites, or his emotions. Conciliation is never employed towards things which are regarded as inanimate, nor towards persons whose behaviour . . . is known to be determined with absolute certainty. Thus in so far as religion assumes the world to be directed by conscious agents who may be turned from their purpose by persuasion, it stands in fundamental antagonism to magic as well as to science, both of which take for granted that the course of nature is determined, not by the passions or caprice of personal beings, but by the operation of immutable laws acting mechanically.
>
> (Frazer 1994: 48)

That religion assumes a world of personal agents is widely accepted among anthropologists and other scholars. Accordingly, many definitions of religion, like that proposed by Frazer, either explicitly or implicitly refer to beliefs in 'beings' of some kind (see, for instance, Goody 1961, Spiro 1966). But there are different views on what forms the basis of these beliefs. Guthrie (1993) treats them as anthropomorphic; they attribute human characteristics to non-human phenomena (see also Kennedy 1992). In his view, religious beliefs arise out of a tendency to see human-like features in our environment ('faces in the clouds') and to attribute events, on a human model, to intentional causes. Lawson and McCauley (1990) see religious beliefs as originating in a more general theory of agency which

19

interprets events in terms of intentions. Human agency is not, in their view, the starting point of this theory, but forms a special category within it.[8]

The idea that science is necessarily or essentially tied to an impersonal understanding of the world is more contentious and less widely accepted. For Tylor, writing a century ago, the role of science in the evolution of human culture was to replace ideas about personal forces with ideas about impersonal forces (see Tambiah 1990: 50). According to McCauley (2000), this role has continued and is likely to do so well into the future. But Horton separated the development of impersonal theory from the development of science. He based his view on the observation that 'the extensive depersonalization of theory' happened spontaneously, not only in Europe, but also in China, whereas science arose only in Europe, where its growth 'accompanied' the depersonalization of theory (Horton 1967: 70). The fact that science did not develop in China suggests that impersonal theory is not dependent on science.

Horton also argued that science is not dependent on impersonal theory. He described western psychology as a science which employs both personalized (e.g. psychoanalytic) and non-personalized (e.g. behaviourist) theories. But he also acknowledged that science has 'progressed greatly through working in a non-personal theoretical idiom' and admitted to the view that 'it is this idiom, *and this idiom only*, which will eventually lead to the triumph of science in the sphere of human affairs' (1967: 70, emphasis added). Interestingly, Wolpert, who, as we have seen, defined science rather narrowly, does not regard psychoanalytic theory as scientific (Wolpert 1992: 129ff.).

One of the most forceful advocates of impersonal science is Kennedy, who sought to purge science in general, and the study of animal behaviour in particular, of the tendency to explain things with reference to intentions and other subjective states of mind. For instance, he argued that it is inappropriate to describe an animal as searching for something, because this refers to the animal's presumed state of mind. He advocated a more neutral language which describes only observable behaviour (1992: 164). He also rejected the metaphoric use of subjective language, as in Dawkins' (1976) concept of 'the selfish gene'. Such metaphors, in his view, indicate that unconscious assumptions of a personalized world are operating, assumptions which he sees as incompatible with science.

Dennett is equally committed to 'the objective, materialistic, third-person world of the physical sciences' (Dennett 1987: 5), but argued that 'the intentional stance', the assumption that the behaviour of others is governed by intentions, is a useful strategy in the scientific study of non-human animals. While Kennedy saw the intentional stance as undermining objectivity in science, Dennett saw it as entirely consistent with objectivity: 'It is important to recognize the *objective* reality of the intentional patterns discernible in the activities of intelligent creatures' (ibid.: 28, emphasis added). This approach is supported by many scholars of animal behaviour, exemplified by Goodall (1990: 11ff.), who have explicitly interpreted the behaviour of animals in terms of subjective states of mind, and whose work fuels the continuing debate about 'personalism' in science.

20

In view of this debate, it might be appropriate to revise the proposition that opened this section along the following lines: religion takes a personal understanding of the world for granted, whereas in science this understanding, though held by some, is widely opposed. Thus, although the distinction between personal and impersonal understandings of the world does not divide religion from science quite as clearly as many assume it does, it can still play an important role in an analytical comparison between them. The important difference, as we have seen, lies in the attitude taken towards personal theory. In religion it is the normal taken-for-granted way of thinking about the world; in science it is problematic, contentious and deeply divisive.

It is worth adding that the opposition between personal and impersonal understandings of the world plays a role in the debate about the naturalness of religion and the unnaturalness of science. It has been argued that a personal understanding of the world is more natural, in the sense that it is human nature to think in this way. Guthrie (1993) explained our tendency to anthropomorphize as an evolutionary advantage. The most important agents in a human being's environment are other human beings; they are more likely than anything else to represent potential danger or salvation, conflict or co-operation. So it is in our interests to assume that any phenomenon whose cause is not immediately obvious might be human in origin. When the assumption turns out to be well founded, it can be of considerable benefit, alerting us to circumstances which could aid or hinder our survival. Overall, Guthrie argued, the evolutionary benefits of perceiving a human influence in events outweigh any disadvantages; thus anthropomorphism has become part of our natural way of perceiving the world (1993: 62ff.). It is for this reason, according to Kennedy (1992: 5), that anthropomorphism is so difficult to eliminate from science.

If the personal understanding of the world (based on anthropomorphism or a general theory of agency) is the more natural, it makes sense to claim that any perspective which opposes it and seeks to replace it with something else is unnatural. Although it is misleading to suggest that this is true of all science, there is clearly a strong tendency within science to oppose personal theory. By the reckoning of theorists such as Lawson and McCauley (1990) and Guthrie (1993), science is unnatural in this sense.

The emotional and the rational

One further perceived contrast between science and religion is highlighted in the literature, one that is embodied in the dichotomy between rationality and emotion. This dichotomy, which is often said to characterize western culture, is thought to derive from Descartes' distinction between mind (or soul) and body (Winter 1996: 34). Rationality is seen as a property of the mind, emotion as a property of the body. The anthropological literature on science and religion gives the strong impression that science is seen as rational and religion as emotional. Although the converse, that religion is non-rational and science unemotional, does not necessarily follow, this is often implied and sometimes stated explicitly.

The association of science with rationality is clear in some of the models discussed earlier. As we have seen, Malinowski equated science with 'rational knowledge' (Malinowski 1948: 18) and Atran argued that science elaborates on common sense in strictly rational ways; it seeks to augment the rationality of common sense (Atran 1990: 220). The rationality of scientific knowledge depends on its empirical basis – its need for evidence and its requirement to change in the face of new evidence; it would not be rational to go on believing what is contradicted by evidence. Conversely, the robustness of religious beliefs despite contrary evidence confirms the non-rational nature of religion, leading Atran to argue that religious or symbolic thought is not constrained by rationality, that it bypasses commonsense rationality (see above).

The association of religion with emotion is also clear in Malinowski's model. He argued that religion and magic fulfil emotional needs. In particular, he suggested, they enable people to cope with the sense of helplessness that threatens to overwhelm them when the options for practical action run out (1948: 60). The idea of religion as a last resort in the face of failure has remained strong in more recent models. For instance, Worsley suggested that religious movements take place when other kinds of action are either not feasible or have been tried and have failed (Worsley 1957). In his sociological account, the emotional component, the psychological need to find an alternative to failure, remains implicit. Burridge presented a more explicitly psychological model: when traditional ways of maintaining personal integrity and self-respect are failing, millenarian movements provide alternative routes to redemption (Burridge 1969). In this way, religion provides an escape from an emotionally intolerable situation.

A different kind of association between religion and emotion is suggested by those who claim that religion is based on particularly direct emotional experiences (Otto 1950, Schleiermacher 1988), feelings of awe, transcendence, love, fear, unmediated by reason. This view has been criticized as a hindrance to understanding (Lawson and McCauley 1990). By claiming that religious experience is different from other human experiences, its advocates imply that it cannot be understood through normal social scientific approaches; they place it beyond the scrutiny of science (Gaskin 1984, and see Guthrie 1993: 205, n.3). Geertz sought to overcome this dilemma by formulating a concept of religion which locates it within the general study of culture while retaining the idea that religious experiences are special. All culture, he argued, consists of symbols, and religious symbols act in a way that creates particularly strong emotional experiences: 'powerful, pervasive, and long-lasting moods and motivations' which seem 'uniquely realistic' (Geertz 1973: 90).

Guthrie linked the view that religion is based on emotional experiences with its dependence on a personal view of the world. Our perceptions are, he argued, largely unconscious. Therefore we may experience feelings towards what we perceive without being conscious of the object of those feelings; this makes the emotions appear unmediated by knowledge or reason. Religious experiences are emotional, he suggested, because our unconscious perceptions are anthropomorphic. We unconsciously perceive human-like qualities in our environment, and the feelings that strike us as religious experiences 'stem from the unconscious suspicion that we are in the presence of something alive or humanlike' (Guthrie 1993: 203). It is because the world is assumed to be governed by personal forces that it provokes emotional responses. An impersonal world does not, in Guthrie's view, have the same emotional force (ibid.: 246, n.128).

If religion is emotional, is science necessarily unemotional? In the light of discussion in the previous section, Guthrie's argument would lead us to expect an ambiguous answer to this question. As we have seen, some scientists, particularly scholars of animal behaviour, adopt an intentional stance, and explain their subject matter as the actions of personal agents. According to Guthrie, these scientists might be expected to experience a greater emotional involvement with their work than those who employ an impersonal view of the world. The reality is more complex. As Alison Richards observed, 'Scientists think and feel about their work using the same psychological apparatus as the rest of us' (Richards, A. 1997: 1). This unsurprising observation was made in the context of a series of radio interviews with scientists, interviews which make clear that the extent of scientists' emotional involvement with their work depends neither on their area of study nor on their adoption of a particular intellectual stance (Wolpert and Richards 1988, 1997). Theoretical physicists, chemists and mathematicians are no less passionate about their work than are animal behaviourists or anthropologists. Nevertheless, there is a widespread suspicion of emotion in science, based on the requirement for scientific observation to be free of bias, and the frequently noted assumption (for instance, Lutz 1988, Toren 2001) that emotion creates bias.

The way forward

This chapter began with an observation, that both scientific and religious ways of relating to nature are present in discourses about nature protection. From this observation came a suggestion, that the academic discourse about the relationship between science and religion might contain ideas that would help us to understand how nature protectionists relate to nature and natural things.

The discussion presented in this chapter has focused on three prevailing opinions:

1   religious ideas are natural while scientific ideas are unnatural;
2   religion is characterized by a personal understanding of the world while science is characterized by an impersonal understanding;
3   religion is characterized by emotion and science by rationality.

The simplest way of using these opinions as a model for understanding nature protection would be to suggest that nature protectionists relate to nature in two contrasting ways: one which is 'natural' assumes that nature is composed of personal agents, and is characterized by emotional commitment, and one which is unnatural assumes that nature is composed of impersonal objects and mechanisms, and is characterized by rationality. But to do this would be to ignore the findings of the analysis presented in this chapter: that the three opinions are, in fact, contested, that the criteria they use do not differentiate, in any simple and consistent way, between science and religion. These findings should warn us that, while the distinctions between natural and unnatural ideas, between personal and impersonal understandings of nature, and between emotion and rationality, may indeed be important in nature protection, they should be treated independently and not in the form of two packages. So, what I take from the analysis in this chapter is the suggestion that each of these distinctions, taken on its own, points to something worth looking at within the discourse of nature protection. This suggestion is followed up in the remainder of this book. Here I comment briefly on how this is done, taking each distinction in turn.

The relationship between emotion and rationality is a matter of some debate in nature protection discourse, and will be addressed in detail in Chapter 8. They are often, but not always, perceived as incompatible. There are many instances in which a detached rationality, unbiased by emotion, is claimed to be the proper basis for decisions, but there are also many contexts in which nature protectionists openly express an emotional commitment to their cause, and in which emotional responses to nature are considered appropriate. A love of nature is a perfectly respectable credential for nature protectionists and is more or less taken for granted in many contexts. What we see is not a consistent opposition between emotion and rationality, but an ongoing debate about the role of emotion in decision making. There is a parallel debate in social and cognitive science. The Cartesian split between body and mind, emotion and rationality, has been challenged by neurological evidence which indicates that emotion is essential to decision making (Damasio 1994, 1999). In Chapters 7 and 8, I consider the role of emotion in nature protection, both as a motivation for action and as an instrument of power. But it is important to base this discussion on an understanding of what nature protectionists mean by a love of nature and of how they develop the emotional attachments that fuel their concerns. These issues are addressed, through an analysis of different perspectives on emotion, in Chapters 4 and 5, and through a discussion, in Chapter 6, of the relations among emotion, value and motivation.

Of the three distinctions, that between personal and impersonal understandings of nature corresponds most closely to meaningful divisions within discourses on nature protection. This is not to say that it necessarily marks off camps or factions – though there are contexts in which it can do this – but that it defines different ways of knowing and representing nature, which come into play in the discourse. Some of the ways in which this takes place are described in Chapter 7. First it is important to consider how these different understandings of nature come to exist in the first place, why they are part of our broad cultural repertoire and, more specifically, of how nature protectionists understand the world. Chapters 2 and 3 address these issues by considering how people come to know nature as they do, and by setting this problem within the wider context of how understandings of the world are generated in human minds.

An important part of this wider context is provided by the remaining distinction, between natural and unnatural ideas. This is of a different order from the other two, because it refers, not to the content of our understanding of the world, but to the process whereby we acquire that understanding; it suggests that some kinds of ideas come more easily to the human mind, and/or are more easily retained and transmitted, than others. Ideas that are natural in this sense, it has been argued, are more persistent and widespread than others. If this is correct, it could have important implications for any political discourse, any discourse in which participants seek to influence the thoughts and actions of others. It implies, for instance, that arguments composed of natural ideas will take a greater hold in people's minds than others, and might therefore be more effective in influencing their actions. If so, it would benefit any campaigner to understand the difference between natural and unnatural ideas, and to use natural ideas wherever possible.

But as we have seen, this distinction depends on the more fundamental one between human nature and human experience (or 'nature and nurture'). It only makes sense to distinguish natural from unnatural ideas if it also makes sense to distinguish human nature and human experience as sources from which knowledge can be derived. Only then would it be possible to argue that some ideas are derived more from human nature than from human experience or vice versa. The identification of specific ideas or kinds of ideas as natural or unnatural is yet a different problem. This only becomes possible if we can distinguish empirically between the effects of human nature and human experience on cognition, and measure those effects. These conceptual and technical issues are matters of intense debate in anthropology and cognitive science, and are discussed further in Chapter 2 with reference to the question of how people come to know nature as they do.

It is important to stress one point before moving on. Chapters 2 and 3 are about ideas and knowledge, how people in general, and western nature protectionists in particular, come to understand nature as they do. From Chapter 4 onwards the book focuses primarily on emotion or feeling as a way of relating to nature and natural things. This division is imposed partly by the material being discussed; knowledge and emotion have generally been treated separately by scholars, and to have attempted a more integrated analysis of their work would have resulted in confusion. This division in the literature may well be a product of the Cartesian model, which splits mind from body, thought from feeling, rationality from emotion. I hope it will become clear, in subsequent chapters, that my intention, as indicated in the Introduction, is not to perpetuate this model but to question it.

2

THE NATURALNESS OF IDEAS

So we all make – my mental processes make for me – this beautiful quilt.
Patches of green and brown, black and white as I walk through the woods.
But I cannot by introspection investigate that creative process. I know
which way I aim my eyes and I am conscious of the *product* of perception,
but I know nothing of the middle process by which the images are formed.
(Bateson and Bateson 1987: 92, emphasis in original)

Like most children, I spent my early years in happy ignorance of Cartesian science.
I took for granted that the non-human animals who occupied my world were
essentially the same as the human ones. How could it be otherwise? Like us, they
did things, they had purposes, they had lives. If anyone had told me that some
scientists think of animals as nothing more than soulless machines, I would have
answered confidently, 'They are wrong'. My conviction sealed my destiny. I turned
away from biology, which I loved, because my school's Advanced-level programme
would have required me to kill and dissect mice and insects. I stayed with the only
species which could be studied, or so it seemed, without its members being abused.
Ironically, anthropology later taught me, through its doctrine of cultural relativism,
that my understanding of non-human animals is a cultural construct, one of many
possible versions of reality, which may or may not bear much relation to what
animals are really like.

Gregory Bateson argued that 'if we were aware of the processes whereby we form
mental images, we would no longer be able to trust them as a basis for action'
(Bateson and Bateson 1987: 89). I take a less pessimistic view. If anything destroys
trust in our mental images, it is the social scientific convention that they are cultural
constructs. If we investigate how they are formed, we might be able to conclude
that there is some truth in them, and so trust them more. So I consider it desirable,
as well as interesting, to ask how people come to think of animals as non-human
'persons', or as resources, or as mechanical systems driven by instinct, and why
some personify nature when others think of it as an impersonal system governed
by laws. This is the task for this chapter and the next, to address the question of
how particular ways of understanding nature and natural things come about, how

26

they arise in human consciousness and so become a part of western culture and of western discourses on nature protection. I shall focus primarily on personal understandings of nature, because they have attracted more attention from theorists in anthropology and cognitive science, perhaps because, in an academic world dominated by impersonal science, the personification of natural things appears as a curiosity in need of explanation. And yet, ironically, as we shall see (and as already suggested in Chapter 1), personal understandings of nature appear, for whatever reason, to come most easily to mind.

In this chapter, I examine the view that personal understandings of nature as personal might, themselves, be 'natural'. I explore the concept of natural ideas discussed in Chapter 1 as a way of explaining how particular ways of knowing nature come about. In Chapter 3, I examine an alternative view, that personal understandings of nature are products of widespread, probably universal, human experiences, rather than being innate products of our evolution. It is important to begin by describing what is meant by personal and impersonal understandings of nature and how these are expressed in discourses on nature protection.

Persons, non-persons and nature protection

I suggested at the end of Chapter 1 that the distinction between personal and impersonal understandings of nature corresponds to meaningful divisions within discourses on nature protection. And so it does, but not in a simple and straight-forward way. Strathern (1988) and others have pointed out that in western culture a 'person' is generally seen as a single, irreducible entity, quite literally an 'individual' or 'indivisible identity', separate from others of a similar kind.[1] As such, a person can be described as having a range of characteristics, but three criteria seem to be used more explicitly and more widely than others to represent personhood in western discourse: the capacity to act autonomously and intentionally, the capacity for emotional experience, and moral worth. The relationship between emotional experience and personhood will be discussed in later chapters; here I focus on the other two criteria.

In the debate about the relationship between science and religion, discussed in Chapter 1, persons are defined as conscious agents who act intentionally; their actions are understood in terms of their beliefs, desires and intentions. This way of understanding action is referred to by psychologists as a 'theory of mind' (Leslie 1987) and is assumed to be a universal feature of human cognition which is acquired in some way (to be discussed below) during early childhood. In terms of this definition, personal understandings of nature assume it to be governed primarily by intentional beings, while impersonal understandings assume that nature is reducible to non-intentional processes. Personhood in this sense may be located at different levels within nature. For instance, the whole of nature might be governed by a divine will, or its component processes might be determined by gods, spirits, human beings and other animals acting intentionally. Alternatively, nature might, at least in theory, be seen as ultimately purposeless and mechanistic at all these levels: there is no all-encompassing divine power, no gods or spirits, and the actions of human and non-human animals are determined by impersonal mechanisms such as genes and natural selection.

In terms of this understanding of personhood, western understandings of nature are hardly ever one thing or the other. Many people believe that nature as a whole is an impersonal system but take for granted the personhood of human beings and many other animals. There are also, no doubt, many who believe that a divine power, acting intentionally, has an influence on all things, including our everyday actions, implicitly diminishing the intentionality of human agency. It is also important to recognize a common finding of ethnographic research, that individuals often appear inconsistent in their views. Beliefs are taken up or expressed within specific situations and change from one context to another. The impersonal scientific model advocated by Kennedy (1992), which reduces human and animal activity to mechanistic processes, is a stance adopted for particular explanatory purposes. In general, scientists who adopt this stance in their work still think of their own actions (including the act of adopting the impersonal stance) as intentional. And outside their work, they almost certainly treat other human beings, and often non-human animals as well, as if they have beliefs and intentions.

Representations of personhood in terms of moral worth are particularly important in nature protection, where the central concern is how nature should be treated. Does it matter if we treat nature and natural things as we wish, or do they have some kind of right to be treated with moral consideration? In general, persons are seen as having a different moral status from other objects. We are expected to feel our strongest moral obligations towards those objects that are most obviously persons, usually our fellow human beings, and many non-human animals have a degree of moral status sanctioned by law in most western countries. But some nature protectionists argue that we hold moral responsibilities towards other things as well, such as plants, species, ecosystems, life in general and the planet as a whole. In recognizing moral obligations towards these things they are implicitly according them rights, thereby defining them as the kinds of things that can have rights, in other words, as persons.

This interpretation is supported by the fact that those who advocate the moral rights of non-human things, and seek a philosophical basis for such rights, do so by identifying what human beings, as archetypal persons, hold in common with these other objects of concern. In the case of non-human animals, the important questions are whether they are sentient, can suffer pain, have the capacity for emotional experience, and so on (see e.g. Singer 1976, Regan 1983, Garner 1993, Clark 1997). Such questions are easy to pose, if not to answer, in terms of western notions of personhood. The concept of a person as an individual, an irreducible entity, makes it appropriate to compare a human being with a non-human animal. They are the same kind of thing – a living individual – so it is easy to imagine them having the same kind, if not the same degree, of moral worth. This comparability, which will be discussed more fully in Chapters 3 and 5, also signals a correspondence between the two representations of personhood. Things that are known

28

to have beliefs and desires and to act intentionally are generally assumed to be capable of suffering, if only through the frustration of their intentions. It therefore makes sense to suppose that we hold moral obligations towards intentional agents.

This kind of reasoning is harder to apply to entities such as ecosystems and nature as a whole. Nevertheless, those who advocate moral rights for such things do so in terms that seem to imply a comparison with the human person. Deep ecologists, for instance, extend their understanding of 'self' to apply to a wide range of environmental entities, and argue that moral worth depends on the capacity for 'self-realization' (Devall and Sessions 1985, Mathews 1991). Plants, species, ecosystems, and life in general, are thought to be capable of 'unfolding in their own way' (Fox 1989, 1995) and, deep ecologists argue, should be allowed the freedom to do so. Some would no doubt contend that 'self' does not necessarily imply a concept of personhood, though I think this argument is difficult to sustain – a point made more fully in Chapter 5. Those who suggest that species, ecosystems and nature as a whole are capable of 'self-realization' do not usually go so far as to claim that such entities have beliefs and intentions, and at this point the correspondence between the two representations of personhood breaks down. Although it makes sense to argue that beings with beliefs and intentions should be objects of moral concern, it is far from clear that all objects of moral concern can be assumed to have beliefs and intentions.

It is now possible to clarify the ways in which the distinction between personal and impersonal understandings of nature correspond to meaningful divisions within the discourse on nature protection. First, it distinguishes different ways of relating to non-human animals. Some nature-protectionist arguments define nature and natural things primarily as resources, as things whose value depends on how they benefit others. Non-human animals are valued as sources of food, clothing, medicines and aesthetic pleasure. They are also valued as components of 'bio-diversity' (see Grubb et al. 1993: 76), the variety of life, which provides a resource for evolution, the raw material on which natural selection depends. In resource-based arguments, the personhood of non-human animals, though not explicitly denied, is not relevant. Such arguments contrast with those in which the person-hood of animals is given priority, specifically those arguments used to promote animal rights and welfare, in which an animal's value in and of itself takes precedence over its value for others.

Not surprisingly, there are many occasions on which these distinct kinds of arguments are positioned on opposite sides in environmental debates, but there are also situations in which they can serve the same purpose. For instance, resource-based arguments used to be paramount in the campaign to conserve whales. The International Whaling Commission (IWC) was established in 1946 to provide for the conservation of whale populations as a commercial resource. The scientific evidence of over-exploitation was sufficient to ensure strict controls on commercial whaling from the mid-1970s. By the 1980s, due partly to the efforts of Greenpeace, moral arguments had become prominent in anti-whaling campaigns and were influential in securing a moratorium on commercial whaling from 1986. Moral arguments stress the personhood of whales, drawing attention to the similarities between whales and human beings, in their intelligence, their social organization, their capacity for emotional experience, and so on (WDCS 1991). Paradoxically, such arguments have been responsible for promoting whales as a different kind of resource, through the rapid growth, in the 1990s, of whale watching as a tourist attraction. The relationship between person-based and resource-based attitudes to animals, in the context of nature protection, will be discussed more fully in Chapter 7.

The distinction between personal and impersonal understandings of nature is also reflected in the ways in which other entities, such as plants, ecosystems, life in general and the global environment, are represented by nature protectionists. For instance, the Earth is often portrayed as an integrated system of interacting living and non-living things and substances. As indicated above, for some this system is directed by divine will, while for others it is an impersonal ecosystem which operates according to consistent but purposeless laws. The difference between these views, and its moral implications, can be illustrated using Lovelock's Gaia theory. The central idea of this theory is that the condition of the Earth is 'actively made fit and comfortable by the presence of life itself' (Lovelock 1979: 152). In other words, living organisms keep the planet in a condition able to support life. This theory, named after the Greek earth goddess, was not intended to imply personhood; it was meant purely as an explanation of how the Earth's ecosystem works. But it has proved susceptible to interpretation as a purpose-driven system, implying the involvement of a divine will (Lovelock 1988: 203ff.). If Gaia is seen as an impersonal system, its implications for human activity are purely practical. It tells us simply that our actions will have certain consequences, that by damaging one part of the biosphere we are endangering other parts. But if Gaia is an intentional system, our relationship with the Earth becomes personal, imbued with moral significance. If we act in our own interests, and against the interests of the system as a whole, we prevent Gaia from fulfilling her intentions, we impede her self-realization.

The assumption of moral worth in things which are neither human nor animal characterizes those branches of nature protectionism described briefly in Chapter 1 as having religious qualities. They include those that seek a 're-enchantment' of nature (Barry 1999), and which draw their inspiration from non-western cultures in which nature is thought of as 'enspirited'. They represent natural things in explicitly personal terms: 'The planet, our mother, Grandmother Earth, is physical and therefore a spiritual, mental and emotional being. Planets are alive, as are all their by-products or expressions, such as animals, vegetables, minerals, climatic and meteorological phenomena' (Allen 1996: 364). This way of representing nature directly conflicts with the impersonal representations employed by many scientists, and often, in practice (though not necessarily in theory), with the representation of natural things as resources. In mainstream western discourse, natural things are represented *primarily* as resources, and science is treated as the main arbiter of truth, the most reliable basis for decisions (see Chapters 1 and 8).

Those perspectives which personify nature are marginalized by this emphasis on resources and science. Even when their ideas form a coherent political philosophy, as in the case of deep ecology, they are given no chance of providing a practical alternative to mainstream politics (Barry 1999: 27). I shall argue, drawing on the work of cognitive scientists and anthropologists, that what is marginalized in mainstream western discourse is a more fundamental understanding of personhood, one that is based on direct perception and which underlies the two representations described above.

Representations, metaphors and knowledge

At the end of Chapter 1, I suggested that personal and impersonal understandings define different ways of knowing and representing nature within discourses on nature protection. The distinction between knowing and representing is an important one that needs to be clarified. Representations are essential components of discourse; we need to represent things in order to communicate our ideas about them. When nature protectionists speak of the Earth as 'mother', when they describe non-human animals as sentient beings worthy of moral consideration, when they refer to Gaia as a superorganism whose interests might conflict with our own, they are using representations, interpretations constructed in the process of conveying a message. Discourses on nature protection are packed with representations of its objects of concern, just as cultural discourses in general are packed with representations of the things about which people communicate.

Anthropologists have always tended to see some representations as non-literal. They have understandably assumed that statements such as the Nuer's 'twins are birds' (Evans-Pritchard 1956), and the Kalam's description of cassowaries as their sisters and cross-cousins (Bulmer 1967, 1979), are not intended to be taken literally. This quality of non-literality is usually described as symbolism or metaphor, terms that are often treated by anthropologists as more or less synonymous (Leach 1976). This is how Einarsson described the attribution of personhood to non-human animals in his analysis of the rhetoric used in anti-whaling campaigns: 'One of the most powerful metaphors is that of anthropomorphism, changing what people in Western culture ordinarily classify as non-human and without self-evident rights into moral objects of sympathy and concern' (Einarsson 1993: 78). In a similar way, representations of the Earth as mother, or as Gaia, might be described as metaphor, as non-literal representations.

Although metaphors or symbols are non-literal, we do not think of them as lies. If they were not thought to contain a degree or kind of truth, they would not be effective as representations. So when the Nuer say that twins are birds, we assume they mean that twins have something of the essence of birds. When scientists refer to 'selfish genes', we assume they are intending to convey something about how genes behave, and when the Earth is described as mother, we assume this means that the Earth embodies something of the essence of motherhood. But what, exactly, is that something? Anthropologists have spent a lot of effort trying to

31

clarify what particular symbols mean (e.g. Douglas 1957, Turner 1967, Willis 1975), and have frequently concluded that it is in the nature of symbols to be ambiguous. So to describe a representation as a symbol or metaphor is to imply, not that it is untrue, but that its truth is problematic, that its relationship with what it represents is not straightforward but open to interpretation.

The constructionist perspective, which has dominated anthropology and sociology for the past three decades, applied this model to the analysis of culture in general. Cultures were seen as systems of symbols, and their analysis as an interpretive science 'in search of meaning' (Geertz 1973: 5). Culture was assumed to consist, not only of the mechanisms through which people communicate, but also of things that exist in people's minds: ideas, values, norms, knowledge, 'folk models' (Holy and Stuchlik 1981). Indeed, since the 1960s, the term 'culture' has often been used to refer primarily to mental phenomena (Goodenough 1961, Kay 1965).[2] Knowledge in the mind has been cast in the form of 'mental representations' (Sperber 1985), making it, like other representations, an object of interpretation. In this way, constructionist anthropology typically questions the meaning, not only of representations used in communication, but also of knowledge in the mind.

I would argue that meaning is not a property of knowledge in the mind, nor indeed of the representations used in communication, but that it is generated in the relationship between that knowledge and those representations. To illustrate: on encountering the phrase 'Mother Earth', I might take it literally (the Earth is my mother), or I might take it metaphorically (the Earth embodies something of the essence of motherhood), or I might take it as nonsense (the Earth has nothing of the quality of motherhood). The manner in which I interpret this representation – its meaning, in other words – will depend on the extent to which it resonates with my knowledge of the Earth. Whether I take it as literally true, as symbolic, or as straightforwardly untrue, depends on how I know the Earth. The representation 'Mother Earth' has no meaning independent of my (or someone else's) knowledge. Nor can my knowledge be described as literally true, metaphoric or false, because my knowledge does not represent the Earth, it simply *is* the Earth as I know it (cf. Ingold 2001).

This point may be clarified by returning to Einarsson's analysis of the rhetoric used in anti-whaling campaigns. For him, the representation of whales as persons worthy of moral concern was a metaphor because it did not resonate with his own knowledge of them as 'natural resources' (Einarsson 1993: 73). He acknowledged, as would any anthropologist, that others might know whales differently (ibid.: 82, n.1) and consequently did not treat the personification of whales as a straightforward lie. But neither was he willing to assume that it was intended and understood as literally true, even by people engaged in anti-whaling campaigns. This, I suggest, misrepresents the representation. I would want to ask of his analysis: Why does this so-called metaphor work? Why is it effective in generating public support for the campaign against whaling? It works because it resonates with people's knowledge of whales, it corresponds with what they know whales to be like.

It is misleading to describe it as a metaphor, because for the participants in the anti-whaling campaign it is a literal representation.

This argument points the way to a better understanding of discourses on nature protection. The meanings of the countless personal and impersonal representations of animals, plants, ecosystems, the Earth and nature in general, depend on how participants in the discourse *know* these things.[3] To understand the discourses, we need to understand the knowledge; we need to ask how and why people come to know nature and natural objects as personal or impersonal. Recent and current debates in anthropology and cognitive science, on the issue of how knowledge is generated and sustained, suggest some possible answers to this question.

Personhood as a natural idea

One possible way of understanding how people come to know nature as personal is suggested by those theories, discussed in Chapter 1, which claim that religious ideas are natural. If, as is often assumed, religion depends on the understanding that events in the world are caused by intentional beings, then religion, effectively, personifies nature: 'in claiming gods exist, it attributes human characteristics to nature . . . religion makes nature humanlike by seeing gods there' (Guthrie 1993: 177). Personal understandings of nature and natural things do not necessarily see gods in nature, but they do see persons there – intentional beings and/or beings worthy of moral concern. Perhaps those theories which claim to explain religious ideas might also explain other personifications of nature and natural things. And if religious ideas can be explained as 'natural', perhaps these other personifications of nature make sense as products of natural predispositions.[4] Whatever features of our universal human nature have led us to create and sustain religious ideas might also lead us to think of non-human animals as persons, or to personify nature in general as Gaia or Mother Earth (concepts which are, in any case, often described as religious).

The discussion in Chapter 1 indicated two senses in which ideas are described as 'natural':

1   if they are part of an 'intuitive ontology' (Boyer 1996) through which we understand the world (or, in Atran's terms, part of our common sense);
2   if they are easily remembered and transmitted.

The relationship between these two senses of naturalness, in the literature on human cognition, is not simple. In the first sense, naturalness has to do with how ideas arise, how we come to know things. In the second sense, it has to do with how ideas are retained, how memory and communication operate. We might expect these two senses of naturalness to coincide empirically – ideas which form part of our intuitive ontology will also be easy to remember and transmit. On the other hand, it could be argued that the first sense makes the second sense redundant. If an idea is part of our intuitive ontology we have no need to remember it, or to communicate it to others; it is simply there, as part of what everybody 'naturally' knows.

In Boyer's analysis of religion, the two senses not only do not coincide but actually conflict. He argued that religious ideas are memorable precisely because they *violate* our intuitive ontology in particular ways (Boyer 1994b, 1996). In other words, he claimed the naturalness, in the second sense, of ideas which are clearly *un*natural in the first sense. This line of reasoning seems, to me, to introduce unnecessary complications into an already complex subject. We can discuss what makes ideas easy to remember and to communicate without needing to call them natural. Boyer's argument that they are counter-intuitive in particular ways is one suggestion. Ideas might also become memorable by being continually reinforced through experience (McCauley 1997), or by being generated or transmitted in highly emotional circumstances (Whitehouse 1996, McCauley 1997); this point will be taken up in Chapter 4. I am also doubtful about the usefulness of the first concept of naturalness, and shall explain why in the course of this chapter, but for the moment it provides a vehicle for thinking about personal understandings of nature. It raises the question of whether personifications of nature and natural things are part of an intuitive ontology, part of what we 'naturally' know about the world.

Innate learning mechanisms

What grounds are there for recognizing the existence of an intuitive ontology, for accepting that some ideas about the world are more natural than others? This question focuses attention on what is often called the 'nature–nurture' debate (mentioned briefly in Chapter 1), about whether cultural phenomena (in this case knowledge) are produced by mental processes that have evolved through natural selection, and which are therefore 'innate'[5] or 'genetically specified', or learned through experience. In fact, few participants in the debate would explain cognition in terms of either one or the other. Most take for granted that both innate mechanisms and experience are involved in the production of knowledge; the question is, how much and what kind of influence does each of these factors have? At the very least, evolution has provided us with the cognitive equipment that enables us to learn. But is this 'general purpose' equipment that leaves us free to learn anything, or is it more restrictive equipment which makes us more likely to learn some things than others (see Whitehouse 2001)? The proposition that some ideas are more natural than others clearly implies the second of these alternatives. It implies that we are naturally equipped with mechanisms that determine, at least to some extent, the content of our knowledge.

The debate over whether our innate learning mechanisms are general or restrictive has centred on the issue of 'domain specificity'. It is difficult to make sense of this debate because 'we lack an explicit and well-articulated account of what a domain is' (Hirschfeld and Gelman 1994: 21). According to Hirschfeld and Gelman's 'fairly uncontroversial characterization', a domain is 'a body of knowledge that identifies and interprets a class of phenomena' (ibid.). In other words, domains are present in the mind but refer to things in the world; they are sets of ideas about particular ontological categories, such as 'physical objects, artifacts, living kinds, and persons' (Boyer 1994b: 401). Broadly speaking, domain-specific learning mechanisms, often referred to as 'modules' (Fodor 1983), are those through which we come to know what distinguishes these categories, for instance, that animate objects are self-propelling and that persons have beliefs and intentions, while inanimate objects and non-persons do not have these characteristics. This implies that domain-specific learning mechanisms determine something of what we know, rather than just our ability to know something. When such mechanisms are assumed to be innate, it makes sense to think of the ideas they produce as 'natural'. There is also a widely held assumption that innate domain-specific learning mechanisms still need to be 'initialized' (Sperber 1994: 48) or 'triggered' (Boyer 1996: 86) by stimuli in the environment.

Since the mid-1980s, evolutionary psychologists and those conducting research on cognitive development have reached a broad agreement that our innate learning mechanisms are, at least to some degree, domain-specific. The view that 'human reasoning is guided by a collection of innate domain-specific systems of knowledge' (Carey and Spelke 1994: 169) is now quite widely held.[6] Cosmides and Tooby argued that domain-specific mechanisms ('modules') are, for various reasons, more likely to have evolved than general mechanisms (Cosmides and Tooby 1994: 89ff.). In their view, such mechanisms determine ideas about the world:

> The new research on domain-specific reasoning in cognitive develop-
> ment indicates that the human mind is permeated with content and
> organization that does not originate in the social world. *This content was
> placed in the mind by the process of natural selection . . .* At a minimum,
> children's cognitive mechanisms were selected over evolutionary
> time *to 'assume' that certain things tend to be true* of the world and of
> human life.
>
> (Cosmides and Tooby 1994: 106–7, emphasis added)

Within anthropology, the view that learning mechanisms are innate and domain-specific has been advanced, in particular, by Sperber (1994) and Boyer (1996). Like Cosmides and Tooby, Sperber regards domain-specific mechanisms, or modules, as evolved adaptations to a previous hunter-gatherer existence. He suggested that cognitive modules evolved to handle particular domains within the environment of our hunter-gatherer ancestors, enabling them to know that environment in a way that assisted their survival. Boyer sees domain-specific learning mechanisms as central to the idea of an intuitive ontology, and supported the view that this ontology is a product of evolution: 'There are good evolutionary arguments for assuming that natural selection would have equipped human minds with a variety of domain-specific conceptual categories, each carrying strong prior assumptions about its domain of application' (Boyer 1996: 86).

Persons and the theory of mind

In order to address the question of how we come to know nature as personal, we need to consider what kinds of domain-specific learning mechanisms lead us to distinguish persons from non-persons. Cognitive scientists have tended to assume (in accordance with one of the representations of personhood discussed at the beginning of this chapter) that persons are defined as intentional beings with beliefs and desires, that their actions are understood in terms of a theory of mind. The mechanism that is claimed to produce knowledge of persons is referred to as the 'theory of mind module' (Leslie 1994), the 'innate structure dedicated to interpreting behaviour in terms of beliefs and desires' (Gopnik and Wellman 1994: 280). Like other innate cognitive modules, it is assumed to need experiential input in order to operate: 'Intentional explanations of behaviour could not appear if the social environment of the child did not include people acting on the basis of intentions' (Boyer 1994a: 291), but once triggered by experience, 'it creates mandatory interpretations of human behaviour in mentalistic terms' (Gopnik and Wellman 1994: 280).

As these quoted remarks indicate, the theory of mind module is assumed to generate an understanding specifically of *human* behaviour. In order to explain how personal understandings of non-human nature arise, we need to consider how a theory of mind module might produce personifications of non-human animals and other natural entities. In theory, there seem to be two obvious possibilities. First, the theory of mind module could be triggered initially by some characteristic(s) not specific to human beings but shared by a wide range of human and non-human things (such as self-propulsion). This would produce a very broad application of the theory of mind in which a whole range of things might initially be assumed to have beliefs and intentions. This application would later be modified through other learning processes, so that the theory of mind (and, with it, the concept of personhood) would eventually be applied more selectively.

This hypothesis seems to offer a possible explanation for the personification of non-human animals. It seems quite plausible that a theory of mind module might be triggered by characteristics which we share, for instance, with other mammals, so that a child might begin by assuming that self-propelling objects that are warm and have faces also have beliefs and intentions. This might later be narrowed down, as a result of particular environmental stimuli (such as school biology lessons in the Cartesian tradition), to 'only human beings have beliefs and intentions'.[7] Alternatively, again depending on environmental stimuli, the initial broad application might be retained, and other mammals, as well as human beings, would continue to be seen as persons.

But it is most unlikely that the personification of other, and particularly more inclusive, entities could arise in this way. Even if it is possible to imagine environmental stimuli that could trigger such a broad initial application of a theory of mind – one that would allocate beliefs and intentions to trees, forests, ecosystems and nature in general – we could hardly think of it as a domain-specific mechanism.

Research on cognitive development indicates that children distinguish clearly, from an early age, between living and non-living things (Keil 1989), reinforcing the point that such a broad initial application of a theory of mind looks implausible.

The second possibility is that a theory of mind could be triggered initially by experience of human or human and animal behaviour, and later extended, through other learning processes, to other things. So a child would begin by thinking only of humans, or humans and some other animals, as having beliefs and intentions, and might later, depending on particular environmental stimuli, come to think of other entities in this way. This kind of conceptual change is often referred to as 'mapping across domains' (Carey and Spelke 1994), a process in which phenomena belonging to one domain are understood in terms of the characteristics of another.

There might be good reasons for expecting a theory of mind to be extended in this way. The main evolutionary benefit of such a theory is that it enables us to anticipate the behaviour of others, it provides us with expectations of what they will do. People in any society need to predict the behaviour of their fellow human beings, and many, particularly hunters and pastoralists, also need to anticipate the behaviour of non-human animals. It is also essential, in many societies, to predict phenomena such as rainfall, drought, flooding, disease, and so on. If predictability is somehow closely related, in the evolution of domain-specific cognition, to the emergence of a theory of mind, then the personification of natural entities is exactly what we would expect. This could explain the persistence of anthropomorphism or animism in science, much of which is concerned with making and testing predictions about the behaviour of animals, plants, genes, substances, particles, continents, weather patterns, and so on. Anthropomorphism might be difficult to shake off, as Kennedy (1992) found, precisely because personification is our 'natural' idiom of prediction; when we need to predict, we naturally tend to personify.

An assessment

At this point I feel I should summarize the argument presented above, which has become more complex than intended. It began with the suggestion that, given the general assumption that religion depends on personal understandings of nature, and given the view (discussed in Chapter 1) that religious ideas are natural, an explanation for personal understandings of nature and natural things might be found in the proposition that some ideas are more natural than others, that it is in our (human) nature to know certain things about the world. The concept that most closely fits this proposition, in the contemporary debate about human cognition, is that of innate learning mechanisms (modules) that are domain-specific, mechanisms which guarantee that, given the right environmental stimuli, we shall know the differences among the kinds of things in our environment. One such mechanism, a 'theory of mind module', could, according to the line of reasoning presented above, be partly responsible for personifications of nature – only *partly* responsible, because other cognitive processes (such as mapping across domains) and experiential input are involved as well.

Thus, by examining the general proposition that some ideas are more natural than others, I have arrived at a more specific one, that personifications of nature are produced, in part, by a theory of mind module, a domain-specific learning mechanism dedicated to understanding behaviour in terms of beliefs and intentions. If such a mechanism is innate – a product of our biological evolution – then it makes sense to say that some personifications of nature are more natural than others. Those that arise directly from the triggering of a theory of mind module are, in a sense, waiting in the mind ready to spring to our attention when the appropriate environmental stimuli come along; they are a part of our intuitive ontology. I have acknowledged that personifications of non-human animals could be seen as arising in this way. Other personifications of nature (such as Gaia and Mother Earth), it could be argued, are unnatural (or less natural), because they are not waiting in the mind to be triggered by environmental stimuli. They are not part of our intuitive ontology but emerge from a manipulation of that ontology, by taking the principles that define one domain and applying them to another; in this case, by taking the principles that define persons and applying them to non-persons.

However, I am less convinced than some that it is possible in practice to tell the difference between natural and unnatural (or more and less natural) ideas, to tell which ideas need merely to be triggered by environmental stimuli and which emerge in other ways. Many cognitive scientists would probably argue that studies of cognition in children (for instance, Carey 1985, Keil 1989), and particularly in infants (for instance, Spelke 1991, Gopnik et al. 2000) indicate that some ideas must be innate. Infants appear to know things without having had enough experience to have learned them. But how can we tell how much experience is enough? The way in which experience works on cognition is just as open to interpretation as the way in which our evolved human nature works on cognition. Insofar as they are seen as alternative or complementary influences, we cannot make claims about the effects of one without knowing the effects of the other. Boyer's (1996) claim that we are genetically predisposed to understand the world through an intuitive ontology appears to be based on his assumption that certain kinds of knowledge are 'under-determined by experience'. But how can this assumption be valid when we do not know what experience is capable of determining?

This means that evidence of early cognitive abilities in children will always be open to different interpretations (Gopnik and Wellman 1994: 282). However young children may be when they show signs of being able to distinguish living from non-living things, persons from non-persons, and so on, we cannot know how this knowledge has arisen, whether it has developed through experience or simply been triggered by it. Because of this uncertainty, the argument that some ideas are more natural than others can only be circular (cf. Ingold 2001). The task of identifying natural ideas begins with their distribution; ideas that are apparently universal or at least extremely common (like religious ideas and personifications of nature) are candidates for naturalness, they are taken to be part of a common human inheritance, products of our evolution. Ideas which are rare (like scientific theories) are taken to be unnatural or less natural. But although we can speculate about the cognitive mechanisms involved, we currently have no means of observing them, and so no independent test of the naturalness of ideas.

Thus far, my efforts to understand how people come to personify nature and natural things have produced a hypothesis which cannot be tested: that some such personifications are part of an intuitive ontology, and are caused when innate domain-specific learning mechanisms are triggered by environmental stimuli, while others are produced by some other combination of environmental and cognitive factors. The fact that a hypothesis cannot be tested does not make it wrong, but it leaves us free to follow other lines of enquiry, one of which seems to arise 'naturally' from the material discussed above. So far I have considered attempts to describe the mental equipment (or 'cognitive architecture') used to generate knowledge. But cognitive scientists and anthropologists all appear to agree that experience is an equally necessary part of the process; even so-called 'natural' ideas do not arise without it. So it seems appropriate to ask what can be said about experience as a contributor to the production of knowledge. Instead of asking what kinds of mental equipment cause us to personify nature, we can ask what kinds of experience generate personifications of nature and natural things. This is the task for the next chapter.

3

KNOWING NATURE
THROUGH EXPERIENCE

If the doors of perception were cleansed, everything would appear to man
as it is.

(William Blake, *The Marriage of Heaven and Hell*,
Cohen and Cohen 1960: 62)

Experience is the impact of the environment on the individual (cf. Brewer 1998:
205). So by focusing on experience, we direct our attention to the relationship
between the individual and their environment. It is within this relationship, as
Ingold has pointed out (2001), that development of an individual, including
development of their knowledge, takes place. In the model discussed in Chapter
2, the impact of the environment on the development of at least some of an
individual's knowledge is restricted; it merely triggers ideas that are already present
in the mind, placed there by natural selection. The suggestion that some ideas are
more natural than others thus restricts the ways in which individuals are assumed
to experience their environment. What we need is an approach that leaves the
nature of experience more open to investigation. This does not mean abandoning
all assumptions about our natural cognitive equipment – as noted above, it is quite
clear that evolution has equipped us to learn things – but it does mean avoiding
the assumption that particular ideas are innate.

Experience and constructionism

Broadly speaking, it has fallen to anthropologists to study how experience generates
knowledge of the world. In recent decades, their main analytical tool for doing so
has been the constructionist model of culture, mentioned briefly in Chapter 2. In
this approach, knowledge is assumed to consist of mental representations or
'constructs', transmitted through social interaction. Some of these constructs will
be more or less complete conceptualizations of various parts of the environment,
transmitted through formal education in the form of scientific theories, religious
or political world views, stories about the past and moral codes. Some will be
transmitted in bits and pieces which coalesce, in individual minds, to form ideas

40

of varying degrees of complexity. For instance, it has been claimed that women were 'constructed', in western thought, as subordinate to men, through exposure to a wide range of mutually reinforcing cultural messages, which include the story of Adam and Eve, media representations of women as home makers rather than breadwinners, the predominance of men in senior management positions and political roles, and the constant use of the word 'man' to refer to humanity in general. In a similar way, some cultural conventions combine to construct non-human animals as persons (children's toys and stories, cartoons, advertisements), while others combine to construct them as resources (meat eating, farming, hunting, medical research). As we saw in Chapter 1, nature in general is constructed as personal, in the sense of being governed by intentional agents, by many religious beliefs and practices, and as impersonal by many, but not all, scientific beliefs and practices.

But there is a problem with the constructionist model as a tool for analysing people's knowledge of the world. Ingold (1992) pointed out that constructionism imposes a barrier between the environment and our understanding of it. In the constructionist perspective, the environment can *only* be understood through cultural constructs, and these constructs are acquired from others, in the ways described above, in the course of social interaction. Each individual constructs their own knowledge of the world out of what has been communicated to them by others. And because what people communicate is their own constructed knowledge, constructs are only ever derived from other constructs or, as Steward put it, 'culture comes from culture' (Steward 1955: 36). This means that the role of the environment itself (independent of cultural construction) in the production of knowledge is not merely restricted (as it is in the approach discussed in Chapter 2), but denied altogether. It cannot even contribute information, for information is meaningful and the unconstructed environment is assumed to be meaningless chaos.

The way in which the constructionist model denies the unconstructed environment a role in the production of knowledge is by assuming that the only experience relevant to this process is *social* experience. It implies that learning is always mediated by social interaction. This is understandable, given that human beings, generally speaking, are born into societies and remain in them throughout their lives, and given that anthropology and the other social sciences are concerned specifically with the understanding of social life.[1] But to assume that learning is always socially mediated is to ignore an obvious fact: that human beings are as capable as any other animal of picking up information directly from their environment. If we were not able to do this, we would not be able to learn from each other. In order to learn from social interaction, we have to be able to treat it as a source of information. And if we can do this, there is no reason why we should not be able to treat our non-social environment – consisting of all the non-human things with which we engage – as a source of information. This means that, in order to examine what kinds of experience generate what kinds of knowledge, we need to consider a human being's relationship with their total environment, not just their social environment.

Perception and knowledge

Efforts to understand how knowledge develops within this relationship were pioneered in psychology by Gibson (1950, 1966, 1979) and Neisser (1976), and more recently in anthropology by Ingold (1992, 1993, 1995, 2000a). Central to this work are the assumptions that we gain knowledge of our environment through perception, and that perception is a skill which is learned rather than something that just happens to us (Gibson 1979: 239, Neisser 1976: 52).

Both Gibson and Neisser described perception as a process of 'information pickup' (Gibson 1979, Neisser 1976). For Gibson, this concept replaced traditional theories of perception which he saw as unsatisfactory for various reasons. One of the flaws in these theories, which he felt resulted from psychology's reliance on laboratory experiments, was the tendency to treat the sense organs on their own, as if disconnected from the rest of the body, as receptors of information. To understand the visual system it was not sufficient, in Gibson's view, to consider how the eyes work. It was also necessary to consider that the eyes are positioned on a head that turns, on a body that moves within an environment (1979: 245). Visual perception, and indeed all perception, is achieved by the whole individual, not only by their sense organs.

Gibson was also concerned to dispel the dualistic image of perception as a process in which information received through the body is processed by the mind. For Gibson, awareness and attention are not located at a centre within the nervous system, but pervade the whole system (1979: 246). In fact Gibson described the process of perception with little reference to the mind, claiming that 'the theory of information pickup does not need memory' (ibid.: 254).[2] His accounts of perception are dominated by detailed descriptions of the information present in the environment. This information takes the form of 'affordances' (ibid.: 127ff.) – possibilities that the environment holds for the individual; a building affords shelter, a path affords access, another human being affords conversation, and so on. Clearly, a single object might hold many different affordances, an observation which led Neisser to ask how, if mental processes are not involved, does the perceiver select, from the full range of possibilities, those affordances which are relevant? Gibson did not see this as a problem. He regarded the perceiver's attention as being directed by the activities in which they are engaged. A bench affords rest to a tired walker, and height to a child who wishes to see over a fence. The relevant affordance is not selected, it is given in the nature of the perceiver's activity (see Ingold 1992: 44).

Neisser, like Gibson, believed that perception is 'a matter of discovering what the environment is really like' (Neisser 1976: 9), of picking up information from the environment rather than imposing meaning upon it. However, he argued that mental processes must be involved because perception *trans*forms as well as *in*forms the perceiver (1976: 11, cf. Brewer 1998). If this were not the case it could not be a learned skill. He described perception as a cyclical process (Neisser 1976: 20ff.). The perceiver anticipates receiving specific information from the environment.

Their anticipations direct their attention, alerting them to particular affordances; the walker anticipates a resting place, the child anticipates something that will provide extra height. They notice that the bench affords these things because their anticipations have prepared them to pick up this information. The information received modifies the perceiver's knowledge and affects future anticipations. The next time the walker decides to pass this way, he will know about the bench; he will be better tuned to his environment and will be able to plan his rest from the start.

Perceptual skill is the foundation of all knowledge. It enables the perceiver to move around in the world, to understand language, to recognize others and to read their moods and intentions. Of course, we do a lot more than perceive; we think about what we know in countless different ways. The information we pick up from our environment and the knowledge we use to anticipate its affordances can be detached from the perceptual context and thought about, manipulated, elaborated upon, and so on. This ability to detach and manipulate our knowledge is extremely important. Neisser described it as 'the fundamental operation in all so-called higher mental processes' (1976: 133); it creates our memories, our mental images, our language, our theories and explanations, our religious and political ideologies, our moral guidelines. The ability to detach and manipulate information is also essential to the act of perception itself, as Neisser described it. The anticipations that guide our perception, which he referred to as 'anticipatory schemata', sets of ideas that make us ready to receive particular information, are mental constructs (ibid.: 20). We create them ourselves out of the information we receive from our environment.

In view of this, it is important to clarify how this way of understanding the production of knowledge differs from the constructionist model of culture discussed above. After all, the information we use to construct anticipations of particular things need not come from past experiences of those things themselves. It is very often communicated to us in the course of social interaction. We anticipate what a new place is like before arriving there because we have been told about it, seen it on television, read about it, and so on. In other words, our anticipations are constructed on the basis of our social experience, which is exactly what the constructionist model assumes. But there is a crucial difference. The constructionist model implies that we could not understand our environment, that we could neither anticipate nor pick up information, without this social experience. It implies that social interaction is the only source of meaningful information about the world. Neisser's (and Gibson's) account of perception implies that someone deprived of social interaction would still gain a full practical understanding of their environment, because that environment is its own source of meaningful information. This view is supported by those rare cases of children who have grown up and learned to survive outside human society in the company of non-human animals (see e.g. Armen 1976).

It is important to emphasize another point. Although I have distinguished here between social and non-social experience in order to clarify how Neisser's account differs from the constructionist model, this is in fact a misleading distinction, because it has no bearing on the perceptual process. Perception works in the same way in all contexts. The cycle of anticipation, information pickup and modification of future anticipations is the same whatever we happen to be experiencing, whether we are walking through a city, watching a film about it or listening to someone talking about it. Although our anticipations are mental constructs, our environment and the information we receive from it are not.[3] They are discovered through perceptual engagement with our surroundings, which is the condition in which we and all other perceiving organisms normally live (see Ingold 1995 and 2000a).

It should be clear that Neisser's understanding of cognition, as grounded in direct perception of the environment, differs radically from that discussed in Chapter 2, in which it was suggested that some ideas are innate, placed in our minds by natural selection. Nevertheless, his account says something about what our innate cognitive abilities are like, for he suggested that we cannot even begin to perceive unless we are able to anticipate: 'The newborn infant opens his eyes onto a world that is infinitely rich in information: he has to be ready for some of it if he is to engage in the perceptual cycle and become ready for more' (Neisser 1976: 63).[4] Neisser described innate learning mechanisms in very general terms, suggesting simply that what babies know is 'how to find out about their environment, and how to organize the information so it can help them obtain more' (ibid.). He saw his own view of cognitive development as having something (but not everything) in common with that of Piaget, which depended on the assumption that learning mechanisms are not domain-specific (Karmiloff-Smith 1992: 7, Whitehouse 2001). Neisser's account of how knowledge develops may be summarized as follows: we begin life with a very general ability to pick up information from our environment; we become more skilled in doing so, more closely attuned to our environment and more able, therefore, to move around in it effectively, as we learn to anticipate what it affords us.

Perceiving persons

At the end of Chapter 2, I defined the task for this chapter by asking what kinds of experience generate personifications of nature and natural things. In the light of the ideas discussed above, it is now clear that 'personification' is an inappropriate term. It implies that we make nature and natural things *into* persons, that we *construct* them as persons. According to the ideas advanced by Gibson and Neisser, we *discover* the personhood of nature and natural things by perceiving their person-like affordances. One consequence of this view is a different way of thinking about the theory of mind, the understanding that a person has beliefs and intentions. Rather than being part of a natural, intuitive ontology, present from the start and ready to spring into operation when the appropriate environmental stimuli are encountered, a theory of mind becomes an 'anticipatory schema', a set of ideas developed over time, based on past perceptions and guiding future ones, enabling us to improve our skill in perceiving persons. This view is supported by evidence that a child's theory of mind develops over a number of years (see Gopnik and Wellman 1994, Leslie 1994).

But this is a relatively minor adjustment. The proposition that our knowledge of the world is grounded in perceptual experience of our total environment has far more fundamental consequences than this for our understanding of personhood. In order to examine those consequences, we need to consider what the perceptual experience of a developing human being is like. An important part of this experience is the perception of self. Gibson pointed out that, as we perceive our environment, we also perceive ourselves (1979: 240). This is not to say that we focus attention on ourselves, though we often do that as well, but that we perceive our environment in relation to ourselves and ourselves in relation to our environment. These are not two separate processes but simultaneous effects of the same process. The information we receive as we move through our environment gives us precise knowledge of our location and circumstances, and at the same time makes us aware of ourselves as physical bodies and agents. As our perceptual skills develop, we discover what we are and what we can do.

Neisser elaborated on this by suggesting that engagement with the environment generates different kinds of self-perception (Neisser 1988). He argued that there are at least five kinds of self-knowledge, two of which are produced by direct perception and three of which depend at least partly on reflective thought processes (ibid.: 36). Only the two that depend on perceptual experience alone are relevant here. The kind of information described above, about ourselves as bodies and agents in an environment, specifies what Neisser called 'the ecological self'. Perceptual experience also specifies what he called 'the interpersonal self'. The following passage describes this concept quite clearly:

> The interpersonal self is the self engaged in immediate unreflective social interaction with another person. Like the ecological self, it can be directly perceived on the basis of objectively existing information. Again like the ecological self, most of the relevant information is essentially kinetic, i.e. consists of structures over time. In this case, however, the information – and the state of affairs that it specifies – come into existence only when two (or more) people are engaged in personal interaction. If the nature, direction, timing, and intensity of one person's actions mesh appropriately with the nature/direction/ timing/intensity of the other's, they have jointly created an instance of what is often called *intersubjectivity*. The mutuality of their behaviour exists in fact and can be perceived by outside observers; more importantly it is perceived by the participants themselves. Each of them can see (and hear, and perhaps feel) the appropriately interactive responses of the other. Those responses, in relation to one's own perceived activity, specify the interpersonal self.
>
> (Neisser 1988: 41, emphasis in original)

45

Neisser cited studies of infancy, and particularly of mother–child interaction, to support his claim that intersubjectivity is perceived directly. He stressed that the information picked up in such contexts is about the ongoing relationship, not just about the interacting partner. He drew a parallel between the development of the ecological self, through perception of one's interaction with the physical world, and development of the interpersonal self, through perception of interaction with other persons (ibid.: 43).

This division of the perceived self into two different kinds introduces an element of innate domain-specificity into Neisser's account of cognitive development. He had indicated earlier that he saw interpersonal perception as a special case, by suggesting that we have innate mechanisms for anticipating information provided by facial and bodily expressions: 'Babies are innately prepared to perceive smiles or frowns, soothing tones or harsh inflections, as indications of what significant others will do next' (Neisser 1976: 191). In describing the interpersonal self, he suggested that these innate mechanisms are species-specific: 'We take the expressions and gestures and vocalizations of other people as evidence of an ongoing intersubjectivity because, being human, we are genetically programmed to do so just as they are' (Neisser 1988: 41–2). This is very similar to the kind of proposition discussed in Chapter 2, that innate learning mechanisms produce knowledge about specific domains of our environment and are triggered by experience of those domains. In this case, Neisser is effectively suggesting that we have innate mechanisms which prepare us to learn about persons, and that those mechanisms are triggered by interaction with other human beings.

More importantly for my own purposes, Neisser's claim that the interpersonal self is perceived only in relation to other human beings makes it impossible to understand non-human persons (Gaia, Mother Earth, gods, spirits, non-human animals) as anything other than mental constructs. If we are not perceiving ourselves as persons in relation to these things, then we are not perceiving them as persons. Their personhood must be constructed through other mental processes, by detaching the information picked up from human interaction and attaching it to other things, in other words by 'mapping across domains' (see Chapter 2). If this is how it works, then anthropologists have probably been correct in assuming that many cultural representations are symbolic or metaphoric rather than literal, and Einarsson's (1993) interpretation of whales as symbolically constructed objects of moral concern (discussed in Chapter 2) is probably appropriate. But as I have already pointed out, this kind of interpretation can contradict what people clearly know to be true. Anti-whaling campaigners do not construct whales as symbolic persons, they know that whales are persons because they perceive them as such. If they did not, they would not object so strongly to their being killed. And the effectiveness of their representations of whales as persons, in gaining public support for their cause, depends on the extent to which others also take them literally, the extent to which they also know that whales are persons. We can only begin to understand this knowledge if we assume that personhood can be directly perceived in non-human things.

I must make clear what I am saying here. I am not suggesting that we have no innate mechanisms that prepare us to perceive persons. I am not even suggesting that we have no innate tendencies to perceive specifically human and human-like features. I am aware that biologists frequently claim the opposite (for instance, Dawkins 1998: 87) and, while I would treat such claims with scepticism, I am not qualified to argue against them. I am suggesting that our perception of personhood in the environment is not restricted to information picked up from human beings. I am suggesting, effectively, that there is no dividing line between the ecological self and the interpersonal self, that an understanding of personhood, of ourselves and others as persons, develops within our relationship with our total environment, not just within our relationships with our fellow human beings.

This means that our perceptions of personhood must be guided by anticipations of something other than purely human characteristics. Bird-David (1999) suggested that this something is a kind of responsive relatedness, and developed this idea using material drawn from her work among Nayaka hunter-gatherers of South India. Drawing on Gibson's understanding of learning as the 'education of attention' (1966: 51, 1979: 254), she showed how Nayaka focus their attention on events in their environment rather than things: 'Their attention is educated to dwell on events. They are attentive to the changes of things in the world in relation to changes in themselves' (Bird-David 1999: 74). They attend to what things in their environment do rather than to what they are. Animals and other objects which actively engage their attention – stones which 'come towards' or 'jump on' them, elephants which 'walk harmlessly' or 'look straight into the eyes' (ibid.: 74–5) – are perceived as having a kind of personhood.

The sort of environmental knowledge expressed by the Nayaka, which Bird-David referred to as 'relational epistemology', has been identified many times by anthropologists, particularly in hunter-gatherer cultures. For instance, Tanner (1979) and Scott (1989) have described how the Cree hunters of Quebec understand their relationships with the animals they hunt. The animals are seen, not as victims, but as active participants in the hunt, deciding when, and whether, to offer themselves to the hunters (see Milton 1996: 126–9). Hallowell (1960), Callicott (1982) and many other writers have noted that indigenous hunters of North America describe, not just animals, but a wide range of other natural phenomena as 'persons', including trees, rocks, winds, the sky, and so on (Callicott 1982: 305). But the perceptual basis of these ideas has not been fully understood (Bird-David 1999: 71). In the constructionist tradition, they were always described in terms of the attribution of personhood *to* these things, rather than the perception of personhood *in* these things. This is because, in the western, modernist tradition, personhood is part of what something *is*, an individual; in relational epistemology, personhood emerges out of what something *does* in relation to others.

The suggestion that personhood is perceived in what things do is fully borne out by hunter-gatherers' own expressed ideas. Callicott (1982) pointed out that personhood, in indigenous American cultures, depends on life, and that life is indicated by the presence of power, which in turn is indicated by movement and change. So personhood can be perceived in something that moves or changes.

I am inclined to agree with Bird-David (1999) and Ingold (1999) that relational epistemology is not specific to hunter-gatherers but common to all human cultures. It is a product of universal perceptual experience. As such, it ensures that people everywhere are quite likely to perceive a kind of personhood in non-human as well as human things. It is important to stress that, in suggesting that our understanding of personhood emerges in our relationship with our total environment, I am not intending to deny the significance of human relationships. For the vast majority of human beings, information picked up from human relationships contributes more to their understanding of personhood than information picked up from relationships with non-human things. This is why 'person' is often used as a 'species concept' (Carey and Spelke 1994: 188, and see this volume, Chapter 2, n. 6). But this is because other human beings generally relate more closely, more responsively to us than do non-human things, not because they are human. It is responsive relatedness that constitutes personhood, not humanness.

It is also worth acknowledging, in view of the arguments discussed in Chapter 2, that this understanding of personhood is not inconsistent with the concept of innate, domain-specific learning mechanisms. We could have such mechanisms which prepare us to learn about interactive relationships, those in which others (human and non-human others) engage our attention and relate to us. One such mechanism could indeed be a theory of mind module, which, whenever interactive relationships are perceived, is triggered into action as an anticipatory schema to alert us to what others might do. This could be what happens, but, as pointed out in Chapter 2, we cannot know that this is what happens because we have no way of identifying innate ideas. But the important point is that, whatever innate cognitive mechanisms we possess, and however they are used in perception, the domain of personhood is not an ontological domain (human beings, mammals, animate objects, or whatever), but an experiential one (responsive relatedness). It is produced by the many ways in which the human and non-human things in our environment actively relate to us, as we actively engage with them.

Getting to know nature

I suggest that relational epistemology forms the basis of all cultural perspectives in which objects and entities are understood in personal terms. We use it whenever we think of each other, non-human animals, plants, spirits, gods, ecosystems, the Earth, nature in general, or even cars and computers, as responsive agents. This is not to deny the obvious fact that cultural perspectives on personhood vary enormously. This is only to be expected. Human beings everywhere experience interactive relationships, but those relationships involve many different partners and kinds of interaction.

In western societies, in particular, information is picked up in a huge range of contexts. For instance, information about non-human animals comes from our pets and other domestic animals, from birds, mammals and insects in our streets, gardens, fields and wild areas, from visits to zoos, all of which provide opportunities for direct perception of the animals themselves. But it also comes from what people tell us, from what we read, from films, television, the internet, in other words from cultural discourse and its material apparatus. Perception takes place in these cultural contexts in exactly the same way as it does in real-life encounters with animals, but the quality of the information received varies a great deal. Much of it comes from representations created in the process of communication. Clearly, our knowledge of some things is more dependent on representations than our knowledge of others. Many people in western society have direct experience of cats and dogs, but relatively few have direct experience of whales. Very few of us have direct experience of how the Earth looks from space, though many of us have seen the photographs. For information about the largest and smallest of natural processes, like the formation and development of the universe and the behaviour of atoms and particles, most of us are entirely dependent on representations created by scientists, journalists and religious specialists. Whether we judge that information to be literally true, metaphoric or simply false depends on a range of factors, including what we know from past experience about the object being represented and about the authority of whoever is representing it.

All this means that, despite the public availability of huge amounts of information, the development of knowledge is an intensely private process, because every human being's perceptual experience is unique. This makes it extremely difficult to make even broad generalizations about how and where people locate personhood in their environment, about how they come to know nature as personal. Notwithstanding this difficulty, I offer the following observations in an attempt to address, in the light of the arguments presented in this chapter, the question posed at the beginning of Chapter 2: How do personal and impersonal understandings of nature and natural things arise in the minds of people brought up in western societies, and so become a part of their culture and of western discourses on nature protection?

Personhood in animals

It is easy enough to see why many non-human animals are often perceived as persons. The 'mutuality of behaviour' which, Neisser pointed out (1988: 41), characterizes human interaction and helps to specify the interpersonal self is routinely observed in the interactions between non-human animals of the same species, where it appears just as interpersonal, just as self-specifying. Two cats engaged in a stand-off, or two stags locking antlers in a struggle for dominance, are using sounds and gestures whose meanings we have to guess at, but it is plain that they understand each other (Neisser 1988: 42), and that they pick up from the exchange information about their relationship which influences their future interactions. Such mutuality of behaviour is also evident across the boundaries between species, for instance, in an encounter between a predator and its potential prey, and the understanding gained from the encounter (assuming that the potential prey survives) can certainly affect their future actions. Information on the inter-subjectivity generated in interaction among non-human animals is available, not only to those who directly observe them, but also to those who watch films about them. Wildlife documentaries often emphasize (some would say 'exaggerate') the personhood of their subjects by giving them names or by following the lives of particular animals to create what is often called a 'wildlife soap opera'.[5] Such techniques of representation are designed to engage the audience by reinforcing the sense of personhood gained from direct perception of the filmed behaviour. Whether it does so, of course, depends on the kinds of factors mentioned above, the past experiences of the viewer and the perceived credibility of the film makers.

In addition, and perhaps more important for our perception of their personhood, the intersubjectivity created when people interact is also experienced with the non-human animals with whom we associate most closely. My cats watch me and mew as their feeding time approaches, and rub against my legs as I open the tin. I have no difficulty understanding this behaviour. Its meaning is as clear to me as when a human friend says, 'I'm hungry'. Bird-David (1999) and others have pointed out that our sensitivity to the personhood of non-human animals depends on the intensity with which they engage our attention and respond to what we do. Subsistence hunters know a great deal about what animals do and why, and so have a particularly strong sense of their personhood (Ingold 1994). Scientists studying animal behaviour think of them more as persons the more familiar they become with them (Kennedy 1992: 26–7). In Britain, supporters of fox-hunting complain that anti-hunt campaigners, whom they see as urban-based, do not really know the animals they seek to protect. Rural dwellers, on the other hand, and particularly livestock farmers, know foxes as adversaries who engage their attention and impinge on their lives by killing lambs and chickens. The sense of personhood is as strong in the farmers' image of the fox as it is in the anti-hunt literature, but for the farmers, foxes forfeit their right to moral concern, as do human criminals, through their destructive behaviour.

Personhood in natural processes

Human beings cannot survive without engaging with their environment, and relational epistemology is an inevitable consequence of this fact. Nature does not just do things, it does things to *us*. It provides what we need, by feeding us directly or providing the conditions that make our crops grow. It provides everything that industrial society needs to create its complex material culture. It also, of course, frustrates our efforts and destroys what we produce, often in dramatic and devastating ways. Given that we cannot avoid engaging with natural processes, given that such processes impact on our survival and livelihood, it is not surprising that people in many societies perceive personhood in the earth, the wind, the sun, the rain and nature as a whole. Relational epistemology is thus the foundation of religious ideas. Guthrie (1993) was right to connect religion with other forms of animistic thinking, but wrong to suggest that there is anything anthropomorphic about it. Religion does not make nature *human-like* by seeing gods there, it perceives personhood in processes and events which actively and inevitably engage people's attention and concern. Religion is common, I would assume universal, simply because human beings everywhere, like other organisms, must pay attention to what nature does. We employ our theories of mind in order to anticipate what it might do next, and we perform rituals of propitiation and conciliation in the hope of persuading it to do what we want.

Where does this leave ideas which imply the personhood of nature and natural processes, ideas about Gaia as a purpose-driven system, about Mother or Grandmother Earth? Such ideas often explicitly mimic those of non-western cultures and pre-Christian Europe. Neopaganism, which has grown in popularity in Britain during the past few decades, has, according to Luhrmann (1993), been fuelled 'by the growing political power of environmentalism'. As Luhrmann asked, 'Why now? What encourages this nature-drenched mythology to flourish in the contemporary world?' (ibid.: 222). I suggest that it is because we are increasingly aware of nature's responsive relatedness to our own actions. Ironically it is science which, for the most part, seeks to understand nature as an impersonal system, that has created this awareness. We know, as a result of scientific monitoring, that human activities are responsible for changes in climate, ozone depletion, pollution and the extinction of species. Not only does nature do things to us, we do things to nature, and nature responds in ways that impact on us. We are engaged in an interactive relationship with our environment. It has always been so, but now, thanks to science, we know more about it than we ever have.

The result of this knowledge has been, for some nature protectionists and other environmentalists, an increasing sensitivity to the human-like features of nature and natural processes, and a greater tendency to represent nature in personal terms. This is not confined to those branches of nature protectionism that are seen as having religious qualities. Conservation scientists often refer to species and ecosystems as 'suffering', and person-based arguments even appear occasionally in statements produced by central authorities and international organizations (see Milton 1996: 208–9). As indicated in Chapter 2, such arguments are important in establishing a moral case for concern about nature, and represent personhood primarily in terms of its moral status.

Impersonal nature

This discussion would be incomplete without some attempt to consider how nature and natural things come to be seen as impersonal. Whatever we do in the world, we are in a state of continual perceptual engagement with our environment, but of course we do not engage equally with everything. Some things engage our attention and actively relate to us while others are simply there. Consequently, in any society, the likelihood is that only some things will be perceived as persons. In western culture the perception of personhood in the environment is undoubtedly deeply affected by the conventions of science. Although not all science depersonalizes nature (see Chapter 1), impersonal perspectives on nature are extremely common in science. The reason for this, I suggest, is that the most popular mode of explanation in science is what Dawkins called 'hierarchical reductionism':

> The hierarchical reductionist . . . explains a complex entity at any particular level in the hierarchy of organization, in terms of entities only one level down the hierarchy; entities which, themselves, are likely to be complex enough to need further reducing to their own component parts; and so on.
>
> (Dawkins 1986: 13)

In fact, there is nothing specifically scientific about this principle. Religious explanations break down nature into the forces – usually personal forces – that drive its component processes. But leaving religion aside, what kinds of entities could possibly be explained by a hierarchical reductionist in terms of personhood? Only those whose constituent parts are persons. Most obviously, these include human and animal societies. For social scientists, whose speciality is the study of human societies, explanations in terms of personhood (and particularly in terms of beliefs and intentions, a theory of mind) are the norm.[6] However, the social sciences are often excluded from the domain of 'proper' science by virtue of their qualitative (and therefore supposedly imprecise) methodology. Animal societies are studied by ethologists, and it is in precisely this field of biology that explanations in terms of personhood have held their own (Dunbar 1985, Goodall 1986).

It is difficult to think of other entities studied by scientists which have persons as their constituent parts. Of course, scientists also study the objects we routinely perceive as persons, but the principle of hierarchical reductionism immediately carries explanation to levels below that at which personhood is perceived. We perceive personhood in those entities that relate responsively to us, and, in western culture, this usually means whole individuals. Apart from occasionally, for the purposes of artistic expression, we tend to see ourselves as relating to each other, not to each other's component parts – heart, lungs, liver, and so on. Nevertheless, the pervasiveness of relational epistemology is demonstrated by the fact that, despite the efforts of Kennedy (1992) and others to eliminate animism from science, the language of personhood is reproduced at the lower levels, through concepts such as 'the selfish gene' (Dawkins 1976).

Understanding why science depersonalizes nature is not the same as understanding why such ideas are so widespread and well established in western culture. Following Bird-David (1999) and Ingold (1999), I have suggested that relational epistemology develops out of universal perceptual experiences, and it appears to be sufficiently tenacious to survive rigorous scientific training. So why is it that impersonal, scientific views of nature are treated in mainstream western discourse, including discourse about nature protection, as the soundest basis for decision making? Why is it that, as Ingold pointed out, 'within the context of the modern state and its political, economic and educational institutions, relational ways of knowing have lost much of their authority' (Ingold 1999: 81)?

I think part of the answer lies in a powerful alliance between science and economics. If they are to survive in any environment, human beings have no choice but to treat nature and natural things as resources. Where relational epistemology is the conventional way of thinking about nature, this means treating persons as resources; it means taking what we need from the personal powers that drive nature, from God, the spirits or the animals. In many societies, taking from others is an act with serious moral implications, and cultures in which relational epistemology dominates have different ways of dealing with these. In some, the need to take from nature is rationalized in terms of what Bird-David has called a 'cosmic economy of sharing' (Bird-David 1992) which permeates human as well as human–environment relations. Nature gives generously and unconditionally as a parent gives to their child (Bird-David 1993), and there is a general assumption that people will share unconditionally with each other. In other societies, the need to take from nature establishes a reciprocal relationship, in which gifts are offered to nature in return for continued sustenance (Tanner 1979). In peasant Christian societies, such return gifts are accompanied by elaborate ceremonies of praise and thanksgiving. By depersonalizing nature, science removes the sense of moral responsibility towards it. Instead of taking from persons, we are taking from impersonal things and substances, so the need for cultural conventions to discharge that responsibility disappears. Thus science serves capitalism very well by making the exploitation of nature morally acceptable.

Everyone living in a modern industrial state is surrounded by representations of nature and natural things as impersonal. We are also surrounded by representations of things (human beings, other animals, plants, nature in general, trains, cars and computers) as persons. Which of these representations we treat as literal, which as metaphoric and which as straightforwardly untrue depends on what our enormously varied and complex perceptual experience of the world has taught us. The persistence of relational epistemology, 'deeply embedded in the experience of everyday life' (Ingold 1999: 81), alongside modernist ways of knowing, grounded in science and sustained by economics, creates a tension between personal and impersonal understandings of nature. This tension, I suggest, lies at the centre of many contemporary moral issues. It creates dilemmas for individuals and debates between individuals. It certainly fuels many of the environmentalist concerns about contemporary western society. Within this context, as I shall demonstrate in Chapter 7, it shapes some of the practices and debates that characterize discourses on nature protection.

In this chapter I have presented what might be called an ecological understanding of knowledge. I have argued that the ways in which an individual human being comes to understand nature as they do emerges out of that individual's perceptual experience of their (social and non-social) environment. I have done this partly because the question of how we come to know our environment interests me as an ecological anthropologist and as an ethnographer of environmental discourse. But as I have explained in the Introduction, I also have a theoretical purpose, to develop an ecological approach to emotion, which is presented in the next three chapters. As we have seen, ecological approaches to perception are well established, through the work of Gibson, Neisser, Ingold and others. An ecological approach to emotion, though it is hinted at in the work of some scholars, has so far failed to emerge from the dominance of biological, cultural and social models. The analysis of perception and cognition in this chapter serves as an approximate model for the treatment of emotion presented in the following chapters. It also sets the scene for one of the main sub-texts of this book: an exploration of how emotion relates to the operation of knowledge and rational thought.

4

ENJOYING NATURE

Out there should have been a bounce of otter
Something playing on its back with storm, rolling into waves,
As liquid as water. But though I waited
Small and wooden there beneath the wind
Only the seaweed wrapped in mocking coils around my feet
And the gulls clattered about laughing.

In the end I learned that otters were just accidents
At times I least expected them
Unrehearsed visitations, turning my world upside down.
(From *Otter Hunting* by Kenneth C. Steven (1993: 15),
published by the National Poetry Foundation)

A few years ago, a nature-conservationist friend of mine was birdwatching on the shores of a lake in County Fermanagh, Northern Ireland, when he saw an otter. He had seen them many times before, but the experience always thrilled him. In his excitement he flagged down a passing car and asked its occupants if they had ever seen an otter, and would they like to? Alas, they did not share his enthusiasm; they had indeed seen otters before and thought them nothing to write home about. They drove on, leaving my friend to return, deflated, to his abandoned telescope, from whose field of view the otter had departed.

It is self-evident that nature protectionists feel strongly and positively about nature and natural things. It is equally clear that some people feel differently. Why is it that, for some of us, the sight of an otter turns our world upside down while others do not even wish to know about it? Why are some people deeply distressed at the destruction of woodlands or the invasion of wilderness by industrial development, while others are unmoved by these things? In this chapter and the next, I consider how nature protectionists come to feel as they do about nature. I shall address this problem both by broadening it and by narrowing it down. I shall broaden it by considering how emotions in general arise and come to be associated with objects. It is important to pay attention to this process if we want to understand how people feel about particular things. As in the previous chapters, answers will be sought in the work of psychologists, anthropologists and other specialists. I shall narrow down the problem by focusing on two types of emotional response – two kinds of loving – commonly expressed in discourses on nature protection. In this chapter I consider how people come to enjoy nature, and in Chapter 5 I consider how nature protectionists identify with nature and natural things.

Emotions are often assumed, in western culture, to be internal and private. This assumption, which has influenced the academic discourse on emotion, has tended to make descriptions of emotion appear unconvincing. Ethnographers who describe how people feel are sometimes criticized for having presumed too much (Leavitt 1996). How do I know what nature protectionists feel? The fact that I consider myself one of them could be both an advantage and a disadvantage.[1] On the one hand, I think I know what they feel because I feel it myself, and I do not have the problem faced by many ethnographers, of translating from an unfamiliar system of expression. On the other hand, this might make my account appear suspiciously subjective. I might be accused of simply describing my own feelings and assuming that others feel the same. My decision to focus on enjoyment of nature and identification with nature is an attempt to avoid this difficulty, since these feelings are explicitly articulated in discourses about nature protection. Nature conservationists, who are concerned primarily with the protection of biodiversity and natural landscapes and habitats, often discuss their enjoyment of nature. Identification with nature and natural things is most explicitly developed in the work of deep ecologists, but is also important in motivating those concerned with the rights and welfare of non-human animals, and those concerned with the conservation of biodiversity. In this chapter and the next, I draw on what nature conservationists, deep ecologists and other nature protectionists say, do and write, to present what I hope will be a believable analysis of their emotional responses to nature.

Conservation and the enjoyment of nature

Over the past ten years I have attended around 200 meetings and conferences held by nature conservation organizations, mainly in the UK. The participants in these events include professional conservationsts working for NGOs and statutory agencies, and others who are sufficiently interested in nature conservation to give their time to further its cause. On such occasions, away from the official business, the conversation often turns to experiences of nature. Many of these are part of everyday life. A fox had crossed someone's garden that morning, someone else had stopped on the way to check on a peregrine's nest in a nearby quarry, the first swallows of the spring were returning, a bank of primroses was in full bloom. Others are more dramatic encounters with the rare, the spectacular and the simply beautiful; a Himalayan sunset, whales off the coast of British Columbia, a golden eagle in Scotland last summer. The excitement of these experiences is relived in the sharing of them, sometimes with a competitive edge and, I suspect, a degree of exaggeration.

Conservationists spend much of their time seeking out encounters with nature. Many of them choose to live in rural areas, where such encounters are a daily occurrence. Those who live in towns and suburbs try to attract wildlife into their gardens. There is a general expectation that holidays will extend enjoyment of nature beyond the everyday. The disclosure that someone is going whale-watching in Alaska or birdwatching in Thailand elicits expressions of envy and interest in what they hope to see. There is never a shortage of advice from those who have been before, about where the 'best places' are and what to look out for. Time spent in nature is seen as intrinsically worthwhile; no excuse is required for it. In contrast, time spent away from nature is assumed to be impoverished and, to some extent, wasted. Conservationists obliged to admit, on being asked, that this year they will be taking a 'normal' seaside holiday, or visiting a city, do so in a slightly apologetic tone, usually with an explanation – it is 'for the children' or for those members of their family more interested in culture than in nature.

It is because they enjoy nature, many conservationists claim, that they seek to protect it, so an important part of their mission is to persuade others to share their enjoyment. Simon Barnes, writing in *Birds* magazine, gave readers a resolution for the new millennium – to enjoy more: 'Stop to enjoy the gulls wheeling over the playing-field or rubbish-tip: applaud their mastery of the air' (Barnes 2000: 17). A speaker at a meeting in Belfast began his lecture with a photo of a meadow, glowing with the colours of wildflowers. 'This is why I'm a conservationist,' he said, 'because I want there to be places like this.' In the literature of conservation campaigns, a love or enjoyment of nature is often invoked to define a boundary – 'Those of us who love wildlife and the countryside' – establishing an emotionally united community of insiders, and encouraging others to join.

If I were to seek comparisons for conservationists' enjoyment of nature, I would suggest that, superficially, it resembles the emotional experiences of sports fans. The exhilaration of a good wildlife sighting is similar to the excitement felt when a favourite hero scores a goal or wins a race. Conservationists live on their memories of emotional experiences in nature, and relive them many times over, in much the same way as sports fans live on and relive the memories of famous victories. If this comparison appears to trivialize conservationists' love of nature, note that I am comparing the emotional experiences, not the issues. Indeed, one of the ways in which opponents seek to undermine the case for nature conservation is by arguing that it is just a hobby, no more worthy of consideration than any other. By promoting the enjoyment of nature, conservationists have, to some extent, brought this argument upon themselves. Nevertheless, most conservationists see their mission as much more than a hobby; they are concerned for the future well-being of humankind, perhaps the future of life on earth. This is why it is so important that others should feel as they do about nature: 'The future of the planet depends on your enjoyment' (Barnes 2000: 17).

Of course love has its down side, which is also important in motivating and communicating the conservationist cause. The damage to and destruction of nature is experienced as a personal loss which provokes anger and sadness. Mark Jerome

Walters, writing in *National Wildlife*, described the sadness felt by ornithologist Herb Kale and entomologist Harry Lange, at the extinction of the species they had studied and loved – the dusky seaside sparrow and the Xerces blue butterfly (Walters 1999). Conservationists exhort us to feel this loss, not only for ourselves but for our fellow human beings, and particularly for future generations. 'Extinction is for ever', declared a conservationist slogan of some years ago (before science and *Jurassic Park* had begun to suggest otherwise).

The main way in which conservationists try to persuade others to share their feelings about nature is through education. They assume that knowing about nature will create enjoyment of nature and concern for its future, that when people know what *they* know, they will also feel as they feel. In other words, they see a close relationship between knowledge and emotion, in which knowledge generates emotion. This means, of course, that knowledge cannot be the same as emotion. In order to examine the relationship between them, to discover whether knowledge does indeed generate emotion, we need an analytical approach that keeps them conceptually distinct.

As mentioned in the Introduction, anthropological and sociological studies of emotion in recent decades have been characterized by a constructionist perspective in which people's emotional responses are understood primarily as cultural products (see, for instance, Harré 1986, Lutz 1988, Lutz and Abu-Lughod 1990). As Lyon (1998) and Leavitt (1996) have pointed out, this effectively places emotion within the same realm as knowledge and ideas, making it difficult to distinguish from these phenomena. So it would be inappropriate to begin this investigation from a constructionist position.[2] In psychology, alongside constructionism, is a range of approaches in which knowledge and emotion are clearly distinguished, enabling their relationship to be examined. I should emphasize that, in avoiding a construc-tionist approach, at least initially, I am not intending to ignore the social context in which emotion is generated. I shall give it the attention it deserves later in the chapter.

The naturalness of emotion

One of the most influential models of emotion within psychology is that developed originally by William James (1884). He saw emotion as a process with two main components: changes that take place in the body – for instance, in heart rate and glandular activity, and the subjective experience of those changes. This subjective experience is what we normally think of as 'feeling', and this, for James, was the essential component of emotion. Following James, the view that emotions are composite processes has become widespread among psychologists. Drever suggested the following definition: 'a complex state of the organism, involving bodily changes of a widespread character . . . and, on the mental side, a state of excitement or perturbation, marked by strong feeling, and usually an impulse towards a definite form of behaviour' (Drever 1952, quoted by Lazarus 1991: 36). Izard's later definition covered more or less the same ground: 'a complex process with neural, neuromuscular/expressive, and experiential aspects' (Izard 1991: 42).

It is not surprising, given the widespread view that emotion is, at least in part, a physiological process, that debate has focused on the extent to which emotions are innate – part of our evolved human nature (Darwin 1965 [1872]). Despite some dissenters (Mandler 1975, Ortony and Turner 1990), there is considerable support among psychologists for the view that *some* emotions are part of our natural inheritance. These are often referred to as 'primary' or 'basic' emotions. Ortony and Turner pointed out that the existence of basic emotions is usually proposed in order to explain 'some routine observations about emotions': that some emotions appear to exist in all cultures and in some non-human animals, that some are associated with characteristic facial expressions and that some appear to carry survival advantages (Ortony and Turner 1990: 316–17). Panskepp (1992) argued that additional and convincing evidence for basic emotions is provided by neuroscience. Different emotions appear to be processed by different genetically determined systems in the brain. This is supported by the fact that selective brain damage can result in the loss of particular emotions (Damasio 1999).

Although many psychologists accept the existence of basic emotions, there is little agreement about how many there are and how they should be labelled. Kemper (1987: 266) identified sixteen different lists of basic emotions in the work of psychologists published between 1962 and 1985. The number of emotions listed varied between three (Sroufe 1979) and eleven (Emde 1980), and the only ones agreed upon by all were fear, anger and pleasure (or joy). Different labels were used for what could be seen as the same or very similar emotions; for instance, happiness/ pleasure/joy/enjoyment, interest/curiosity and anticipation/expectancy. But this lack of consensus is not seen as a problem, given that evidence is still being accumulated. Panskepp, who identified four basic emotions – fear, rage, panic and expectancy (1982) – warned that 'all taxonomies must remain open-ended until the brain is better understood' (Panskepp 1992: 555), and Izard, while identifying ten basic emotions (1991: 49), admitted that his approach 'is open to the question of the number of basic emotions and the best labels for them' (1993: 562).

Although the classification and labelling of basic emotions varies among psychologists and, no doubt, among non-specialists in countless other cultural contexts, I do not feel uncomfortable with the assertion that there are such things as basic emotions. This might appear inconsistent with the position taken in Chapter 2, where I questioned whether it is useful to treat some ideas as innate, as part of our evolved human nature. In fact there is no inconsistency, for, as I have made clear, I am explicitly trying to avoid treating emotions as if they were ideas.[3] But if basic emotions are not ideas, what are they and why do we have them? One possibility is that they are learning mechanisms, devices for helping us to discover what the world is like. As we shall see, this view is supported by what psychologists have written about the relationship between emotion and perception.

If basic emotions are learning mechanisms, it seems appropriate to ask the same question that has been asked of innate cognitive modules: Are they general purpose mechanisms or are they domain specific? Do they simply equip us to feel joy, sadness, fear, and so on, or do they predispose us to have these feelings about particular things in our environment? Tooby and Cosmides argued that emotions have evolved to enable us to cope with specific situations. They suggested that common present-day emotional responses to particular things, such as fear of snakes, grief over the death of a relative and jealousy over a lover's infidelity, are the result of our ancestors' repeated exposure to these situations (1990). A similar view has been expressed by Wilson in his 'biophilia hypothesis'. It is worth considering his model in more detail because it appears, at first sight, to suit my purpose very well, referring as it does to feelings about nature.

Biophilia and domain-specific emotions

From infancy we concentrate happily on ourselves and other organisms. We learn to distinguish life from the inanimate and move toward it like moths to a porch light.

(Wilson 1984: 1)

Taken literally, 'biophilia' means the love of life or of living things (Soulé 1993: 439). But in Wilson's formulation, and in the debate that has developed around it, biophilia is, in at least two senses, a more general concept than its literal interpretation would suggest. First, it is used to refer to responses, not just to living things but to a broader category of phenomena which Wilson described as 'life and lifelike processes' (Wilson 1984: 1). Second, the term 'biophilia' is used to indicate, not just a *love* of life and lifelike processes, but a 'tendency' or a 'need' to 'focus on' or 'affiliate with' these phenomena (Wilson 1984: 1, Kellert 1993: 42). These terms do not necessarily imply love at all, and could refer to any number of ways in which human beings relate to other living (and lifelike) things. Accordingly, biophilia often refers both to people's positive responses to nature (Ulrich 1993: 74), and to their distinctly negative responses (Kellert 1993: 42). Although biophilia is often used to describe ways in which people behave towards nature, its strongest connotations are emotional, the assumption being that behaviour expresses emotion. Wilson himself referred to biophilia as an 'emotional affiliation between human beings and other organisms', and suggested that it can occupy 'several emotional spectra: from attraction to aversion, from awe to indifference, from peacefulness to fear-driven anxiety' (Wilson 1993: 31).

The biophilia hypothesis is the suggestion that our tendency to respond emotionally to life and lifelike processes is innate, that our emotional responses to nature have a genetic basis. So the hypothesis can be supported by finding reasons why particular emotional responses to nature might have evolved. Such reasons are easier to find for some responses than for others. A fear of snakes, spiders and thunderstorms could have evolved because those who avoided these things would have been more likely to survive than those who waited to find out whether or not they were dangerous. But the reasons why a love of nature and natural things might have evolved are less obvious. It has been suggested that aesthetic appreciation of landscapes is linked to the recognition of suitable habitats, that the landscapes we now find the most attractive are those which contain the kinds of features that would have provided what our ancestors needed to survive (see Heerwagen and Orians 1993, Ulrich 1993). Other suggestions appear more speculative. A sense of wonder at the complexity and diversity of nature might have encouraged the kind of explorations that enabled our ancestors to gain control over natural processes. Deep attachments to individual animals or trees might have conferred the sort of well-being that is thought to be gained, in contemporary western society, from companion animals (Kellert 1993).

The biophilia hypothesis provides nature protectionists with a potentially powerful argument. It suggests that nature, and particularly the presence of other living things, is important for our emotional health (Heerwagen and Orians 1993: 168, Wilson 1993), that the destruction of nature deprives us of countless opportunities for emotional fulfilment, that the extinction of other species is, in some ways, the extinction of our own emotional experience (Nabhan and St Antoine 1993). Walters described each extinction as 'a unique voice silenced' and asked, 'What is the psychological and emotional toll of this growing silence? Have we even begun to grasp the price extinction will extract from future human emotion, spirit and creativity?' (Walters 1999). By invoking biophilia, conservationists are able to hold up the threat of an emotionally impoverished future. Such a future could be bleak indeed if, as some have argued, emotions are central to our understanding of ourselves as individual and social beings (Denzin 1984, Damasio 1999) and to our sense of morality (Foucault 1983: 238). I shall return to the role of emotion in the development of a concept of self in Chapter 5.

This brief description of Wilson's model indicates that it is not one hypothesis but several. First, there is the general idea that we have an innate tendency to respond emotionally to living and lifelike things. In the language of basic emotions theory, this seems to be saying that we have an innate tendency to take an *interest* in living and lifelike things. 'Interest' has been identified by psychologists as a basic emotion (Tomkins 1962, Izard 1977, 1991, Emde 1980), and Wilson's use of the phrase 'focus on' (1984: 1) suggests precisely this kind of response. But note that, in Wilson's hypothesis, the domain referred to, like the domain of 'personhood' explored in Chapters 2 and 3, is not an ontological domain but an experiential one. Wilson's phrase, 'life and lifelike processes' goes beyond the biological definition of life and implies the inclusion of anything that might be perceived as living or lifelike. As we have seen in the discussion of personhood, almost anything might be perceived as being alive or as somehow directed by living processes, especially things that grow, move or change in some way. Thus, as a statement about human–environment relations, this general version of the biophilia hypothesis makes sense, but does not say very much. It simply suggests that we tend to take an interest in things that change in our environment, and these are precisely the things which we expect to capture our attention. I shall return to this point below.

The biophilia model also incorporates a number of more specific hypotheses, that particular emotions have evolved in association with particular things in our environment; that we naturally fear snakes, that we naturally fear spiders, that we naturally love rich green landscapes, and so on. The main objection to these is one that has often been raised against the idea of domain-specific cognitive modules (Sperber 1994), that they seem to deny the cultural and individual variation that is known to exist. Things that provoke intense fear or pleasure in some individuals or in some cultures provoke a less intense response, or an entirely different response, in others. Even where poisonous snakes are common, people do not necessarily fear snakes in general, but learn routinely which are dangerous and which are not (Diamond 1993: 265). Some people feel at home in forests while others are intimidated by them, mountain landscapes please some but make others feel claustrophobic, and so on. Wilson's answer to this is also similar to those given by advocates of domain-specific cognitive modules, that biophilia, rather than causing us to have particular emotional responses, predisposes us to learn or to resist learning such responses (1993: 31). In other words, we are not compelled, by our evolved human nature, to fear snakes; rather, what we learn from experience is biased by our nature, so that we find it easier, on encountering snakes, to fear them than to love them.

Since I have already addressed the question of domain-specificity in some detail in relation to cognitive mechanisms, it seems unnecessary to do so again in relation to emotions, mainly because the arguments will be the same. I suspect that it is no easier to tell, empirically, whether an emotional response to a particular object is innate or has been learned, than it is to discover this about particular ideas. More importantly for my purpose, even the strongest supporters of domain-specificity do not deny that experience is necessary for innate mechanisms to operate. Just as an innate theory of mind is assumed by some cognitive theorists to spring into action when we encounter other human beings, so a natural fear response is assumed by some to be activated when we encounter a snake, or some kind of representation of a snake. But the point is that the encounter still has to take place. It is also clearly the case that we come to fear, hate, love and enjoy a great many things to which our ancestors could not have been exposed, and that these particular emotional responses cannot be innate. All this suggests that if we want to understand how people come to feel as they do about particular things, we need to consider their experience. In seeking to understand how people come to enjoy nature in the ways described at the beginning of this chapter, it seems appropriate to consider what those who do so have had to say about their own experiences.

Enjoying nature through experience

Consult the autobiography of any prominent, influential environmentalist; the chances are that their lives, particularly their early lives, have been rich in direct, personal experiences of nature. Sir Peter Scott, who founded the Wildfowl and Wetlands Trust (WWT) and co-founded the World Wide Fund for Nature

(WWF), could not remember a time when he was not interested in animals, and was already a committed naturalist at the age of 5 (Scott 1990: 13). Gerald Durrell, who pioneered the captive breeding of endangered species, lived as a child on the Greek island of Corfu, where he 'would spend hours squatting on my heels or lying on my stomach watching the private lives of the creatures around me' (Durrell 1959: 36). Norman Moore, who spent thirty years working for the Nature Conservancy in England, recalled how he escaped from school work to the fields whenever he could (Moore 1987: xix). Arne Naess, who coined the term 'deep ecology' (1973), wrote: 'From when I was about four years old until puberty, I could stand for hours, days, weeks in shallow water on the coast, inspecting and marvelling at the overwhelming diversity and richness of life in the sea' (Naess 1982: 270). Lewis Mumford, one of America's most influential environmental thinkers, spent his childhood summers in Vermont where encounters with wildlife helped to shape his ecological ethic (Mumford 1982). His experience was similar to that of other prominent American environmentalists, 'from Henry Thoreau to Edward Abbey, via Muir, Leopold and Joseph Wood Krutch – whose love of nature followed directly from their engagement with the diversity and beauty of the North American wilderness' (Guha and Martinez-Alier 1997: 186).

Research seems to confirm the impression gained from these famous examples. In a study conducted in the early 1990s, Palmer asked a sample of 232 environmental educators in the UK to provide autobiographical statements indicating what had influenced their commitment to environmental concerns. Among the most important influences, cited by ninety-seven respondents (42 per cent), were childhood experiences of being '"outdoors" – in the natural world'. These included living in rural areas, spending holidays in the countryside and engaging in outdoor pastimes. A further 114 respondents (49 per cent) cited direct experiences of nature, not necessarily in childhood, as formative influences. These included activities such as walking, camping, birdwatching, practical conservation, gardening, farming and spending time in remote natural landscapes (Palmer 1998: 149–51). This study has been extended to include data from Australia, Canada, the USA, Greece, Slovenia, Sri Lanka, Uganda and Hong Kong. Analysis of these data 'suggests a reinforcement of the crucial importance of early childhood experiences in the natural world, and of experiences in the outdoor world in general' (Palmer 1998: 151).

This is supported by the findings of a small research project I conducted during the late 1980s. I interviewed twenty-eight conservationists – six paid staff members and twenty-two volunteers – working for environmental organizations in Northern Ireland.[4] When asked why nature conservation was important to them, twenty said they had been influenced by personal experiences in nature. For sixteen of the interviewees, such experiences dated from early childhood. Nine had spent time as children living in rural areas, walking or cycling through the countryside or 'poking around in hedgerows'. Four mentioned an early interest in birds – one had received his first pair of binoculars as a Christmas present at the age of 5. Two mentioned an early love of plants, particularly trees and wildflowers. In a manner that would please supporters of the biophilia hypothesis, three respondents could not recall how or when their attraction to nature had started: 'It was just something that was in me.' One told me, 'My mum said I always cried as a baby until I saw leaves move, and once I saw leaves move I stopped crying and watched the leaves.'

The message of these personal histories seems quite clear. These environ-mentalists believed that they had come to love nature at least partly through their direct experience of natural things. Implicit in their statements is that they had come to love nature in the process of learning *about* nature, by discovering what nature is like. This brings to the foreground the relationship between emotion and the development of knowledge.

Emotion, perception and memory

In Chapter 3, I used Neisser's (1976) model of perception to describe how knowledge is produced. The perceiver anticipates receiving particular information from their environment. Their anticipations guide their exploration of that environment and alert them to what it affords. The information they pick up influences their future anticipations, which guide their future exploration, and so on. The process continues as long as the perceiver is awake. As they acquire more information, reflect on it and interpret it, their perceptual skills develop; they get to know their environment better, and they get to know themselves as physical agents within an environment. Some theorists of emotion have assumed, argued or at least implied that emotion is part of this perceptual cycle.

Izard (1991), taking his lead, as others have done, from William James, argued that 'interest' is the main emotion involved in the production of knowledge. Interest, for Izard, plays the same role as anticipation in Neisser's model of perception: it prepares us to pick up particular information (cf. Plutchik 1982: 535). It thus makes possible, not only perception, but all the other mental processes (imagining, reflecting, theorizing, and so on) that depend on perception: 'Interest literally determines the content of our minds and memories, for it plays such a large part in determining what it is we actually perceive, attend to, and remember' (Izard 1991: 92–3). In fact, even though their meanings are not identical, it is probably appropriate to treat 'interest' and 'anticipation' (also referred to as 'expectancy') as alternative labels for the same emotion. In the sixteen lists of basic emotions reviewed by Kemper, interest appears five times and anticipation (or expectancy) appears twice. In the one list in which they both appear (Osgood 1966), they are explicitly treated as alternatives (Kemper 1987: 266).

Some level of interest is continually present in consciousness; 'interest is the most prevalent motivational condition for the day-to-day functioning of normal human beings' (Izard 1991: 91). But how does interest in particular parts of the environment arise? In Neisser's model, interest (or anticipation) is a product of past perceptions used in the context of active engagement with the environment. Izard suggested that interest is activated by change, animation and novelty (1991: 93–6). But of course these phenomena can only activate interest if they are perceived. So

Izard's model is cyclical in exactly the same way as Neisser's; perception both precedes and follows interest.

That emotion is involved in the perceptual cycle is also implied in Lazarus' model of the relationship between emotion and cognition. He argued that 'cognitive activity causally precedes an emotion in the flow of psychological events' (Lazarus 1991: 127), and that the emotions so produced then influence future cognitive processes. The kind of cognitive activity Lazarus was referring to is 'appraisal', which he sees as a continuing evaluation of objects and situations encountered (1991: 144). This sounds like a deliberate, conscious exercise, which it often is, but, according to Lazarus, appraisal can also be 'automatic, unreflective, and unconscious or preconscious' (1991: 128, cf. Arnold, cited by Strongman 1996: 63). This idea of unreflective appraisal seems very similar to Neisser's (and, to a lesser extent, Gibson's) model of perception. As the immediate recognition of what the environment affords, perception is clearly an evaluative process.

Significantly, when Lazarus described the role of emotion in cognition, he was not thinking of interest or anticipation, neither of which appears among the emotions discussed by him. He was thinking of other emotions – sadness, joy, anger, fear, love, guilt, and so on – that arise when situations are appraised (evaluated, perceived) as harmful or beneficial. Izard also sees these other emotions as playing a role, though a less central one than interest, in the production of knowledge; he suggested that interest often operates in combination with other emotions (1991: 91). It is easy to envisage how this happens. If something frightens or saddens us, for instance, we are likely to be particularly attentive to its presence in future, if only for the purpose of trying to avoid it. If something gives us pleasure, we attend to it more closely in the hope of prolonging or repeating the experience. In this way, the intensity of interest is influenced by the intensity of the other emotions experienced.

It has been suggested that the presence and intensity of particular emotions affect the ease with which the things we perceive are remembered (Rolls 1990, Christiansen 1992), a point alluded to in Chapter 2. This is not a simple relationship, but Izard (1991) cited evidence that both heightened interest (Renninger and Wozniak 1985) and enjoyment (Bartlett et al. 1982, Nasby and Yando 1982) during a task or event increase the chances of recall. Whitehouse (1996) has argued that surprise, an emotion which, like interest, is neither positive nor negative, and which results when our perceptions do not match our anticipations, is particularly likely to increase the memorability of events.

If emotions do, indeed, affect memory in this way, then anything that affects the emotional quality of a perceived event or situation might ultimately affect the impact of that event or situation on the perceiver's knowledge of the world. So, for instance, the presence of other individuals, the state of significant events in the perceiver's life, the aesthetic quality of the surroundings – all these things and many more can affect the emotions generated in any act of perception, and so ultimately affect the impact of the information received on memory and knowledge. And, of course, memories are, themselves, extremely effective inducers of emotion, recreating the emotions originally experienced in the perception of events in the past (Izard 1991: 97, Svašek 2000).

What all this suggests is that, whatever else they are, emotions can, indeed, be seen as learning mechanisms. They enable information to be picked up and they influence the ways in which that information is retained, interpreted and used (cf. Hochschild 1998: 6). It also implies that emotions do not necessarily give us the truth. In other words, the common western assumption that our learning is biased by the emotional state in which we learn is well founded. On the other hand, the equally common western assumption that knowledge can be emotionally neutral has no foundation. Knowledge unbiased by emotion cannot exist, for it is emotion that enables the development and use of knowledge. This argument could be seen as representing what Barbalet (1998) called the critical approach to the relationship between emotion and reason (see Introduction). It challenges the conventional opposition between emotion and rationality by suggesting that, instead of hindering rational thought, emotions make reasoning possible. It is a view supported by findings in neuroscience; individuals who, through selective brain damage, have lost a part of their emotional repertoire, also lose their ability to make rational decisions (Damasio 1999: 41).

Does all this mean that conservationists have got things the wrong way round in trying to educate people about nature in order to generate enjoyment and concern? Clearly not, for the process described above flows in both directions. Emotions are necessary for learning to take place, but the knowledge gained through learning induces emotions, which contribute to future learning, and so on. People do indeed come to love, enjoy or fear things in the process of getting to know them. They also get to know them as a result of loving, enjoying, hating or fearing them. The complexity of the process makes it extremely difficult to explain how, for any individual human being, particular emotions come to be associated with particular objects. This can only be fully understood with reference to the total past experience of that individual as a perceiver of and thinker about their environment. But there is more to it even than this, for emotions play a role in our perceptions, not only of our external environment, but also of ourselves.

Emotion and self-perception

An essential part of James' model of emotion is the understanding that bodily changes come first and induce feelings. He argued that the general understanding of emotion, in which the feeling is assumed to come before the bodily change – we feel sad, therefore we cry, we feel afraid, therefore we tremble, and so on – is incorrect. Instead, he argued, we feel sad because we cry and afraid because we tremble (James 1890: 449). Laird and Apostoleris (1996) cite a number of studies conducted to test this theory, in which participants have been asked to adopt particular facial expressions or postures and to describe their feelings. These studies appear to indicate, for instance, that smiling generates happiness, that scowling generates anger, that a slumped posture generates sadness, and so on. Laird and

Apostoleris (among others) have interpreted this to mean that our feelings are our perceptions of our own bodily changes (Laird and Apostoleris 1996: 287–9).

As indicated in Chapter 3, Gibson (1979) and Neisser (1988) saw the perception of self as emerging out of, and simultaneously with, perception of the environment. As we pick up information on our surroundings, we also pick up information on ourselves as physical bodies and agents within an environment. But clearly, this is not the only information we receive about ourselves. We continually pick up information about what is going on within our bodies. Some of this information is about what we commonsensically classify as physical states: hunger, thirst, cold, fatigue, illness, and so on. Some of it consists of what we think of as emotions – feelings of anger, fear, sadness, happiness, love, surprise, and so on.

If feelings are perceptions, then in order to understand how they come about, they need to be separated, in analysis, from the objects of perception. For this reason, Damasio (1999) maintains a strict distinction between the two components in James' model. He uses the term 'emotion' to refer only to the bodily changes, and reserves the term 'feeling' for the subjective experience of those changes. In his model emotions are empirically observable. Changes in heart rate, brain activity, glandular secretions, and so on can be monitored, and some of the effects of these changes are plainly visible, when we blush or turn pale, tremble or become agitated, for instance. This means that we can, to some extent, perceive emotions in others as well as in ourselves. Feelings, on the other hand, are never observable; they are our private experiences of our own emotions (Damasio 1999: 42).

According to Damasio, it is not until an emotion is felt (perceived) that we become aware of it. This means that emotions (in Damasio's narrower sense) must be induced outside consciousness. This in turn raises the possibility that we might not discover, even once we have felt an emotion, what induced it in the first place. Damasio assumed that this is a common occurrence (1999: 37). Of course, this does not prevent us from attributing our emotions to particular causes. We reflect on our feelings just as we reflect on the other information we pick up from the environment and from our bodies, perhaps more so, since our feelings define the quality of our lives.[5] The conclusions we come to, about why we felt happy or sad or angry at a particular moment, regardless of what might have triggered the emotions that produced those feelings, help to shape our knowledge of ourselves, and affect our future perceptions in the way described above. If emotions are unconsciously induced by things which may never be recognized as their inducers, this adds to the difficulty of trying to explain how particular individual human beings come to feel as they do about particular things (a difficulty which psycho-analysis was specifically designed to overcome). It also emphasizes the point that knowledge, including knowledge of ourselves, is inevitably biased by emotions.[6]

So far I have not said very much about what sociologists and anthropologists consider to be the most important influence on our emotions: the social context in which those emotions generally operate. This neglect has been justified, in my view, because it is important to try to understand what kind of phenomenon we are dealing with, before we can begin to assess how anything, including social context, influences it. Those theorists of emotion who see it as a cultural construct would argue that it is impossible to understand what kind of phenomenon emotion is without reference to its social context, for, in their view, it is social interaction that constitutes or 'constructs' emotion, as it does all cultural phenomena. This implies that, without social experience, we would not be capable of having emotions. It will be clear from the discussion presented above that this is no more acceptable than the implication (discussed in Chapter 3) that without social experience we could not come to know our environment. Through perception, we pick up information directly from the unconstructed environment. We could not do this unless that unconstructed environment was able to induce the emotions necessary for us to learn.[7] Having argued that emotions can usefully be understood as learning mechanisms, I shall try to show how they operate as such within the context of social interaction.

Emotions in their social setting

The general assumption that people's emotional commitments are affected by the social contexts in which they live has influenced the study of human–environment relations in western culture since the 1960s. It enabled social scientists to relate the emergence of a romantic attitude to nature to the industrial revolution (Thomas 1983, Simmons 1993), and to see the recent commoditization of nature as part of a broad postmodernist trend (see e.g. Urry 1990, 1995, Macnaghten and Urry 1998). It also generated, in the 1960s and 1970s, various studies of the social bases of environmental concern (Harry et al. 1969, Devall 1970, Cotgrove and Duff 1980, 1981, Van Liere and Dunlap 1980). But these analyses all present a very broad picture of the relationship between social experience and emotions. In order to understand how people's feelings about nature are related to the social contexts in which they develop, we need to consider those contexts in far more detail.

This is precisely what anthropologists do when creating ethnographic accounts of social and cultural life, and those who have sought to understand specific emotions (for instance, Briggs 1970, Rosaldo 1980, Abu-Lughod 1986, Lutz 1988) have done so by setting them in the context of particular interpersonal relationships, and the strategies and actions employed by people within those relationships (Lutz 1988: 5). Parkinson (1995), from a social-psychological viewpoint, also sees interpersonal relationships as the primary context in which emotions are generated. He argued that emotions are communicative mechanisms, which enable us to pick up information about what others are feeling (cf. Neisser 1976: 189). This, I suggest, enables the emotions of others to affect us in two significant ways.

First, it enables us to learn through direct perception what to fear, love, enjoy, hate, and so on. It is an indisputable fact that much of what we know and think about the world is learned from other people – not everything, as I argued in Chapter 3, but a great deal of it. If this were not the case, then cultures, as more or less distinguishable systems of ideas shared by groups of people, would not exist. As we have seen, emotions are, to some extent, observable, because they include (or, in Damasio's model, consist entirely of) bodily processes which affect appearance and behaviour. Although we cannot perceive the feelings of others directly, we can infer them from the way they look and behave. We can do this because we know how we feel when behaving in similar ways; we know what it feels like to blush, to look surprised, to smile, to cry, to sulk, and so on. Of course, we do not always read the emotions of others correctly – perceiving what others feel is as much a learned skill as perceiving anything – and, in any case, they sometimes deliberately mislead us. But, on the whole, we get a good idea of what others are feeling from their appearance and behaviour.

This enables us to learn from the emotions of others what it is appropriate to feel about particular things, to learn what Hochschild (1983) called 'feeling rules'. By seeing others cry at a funeral, we learn that sadness is an appropriate response to bereavement. By seeing others run away at the sight of a snake, we learn that snakes are considered dangerous. By seeing in others the joy and excitement of winning, we learn that happiness comes from success. By seeing others gain pleasure from investigating and discovering their surroundings, we come to understand that the process of learning can itself be enjoyable. In each instance, the effect is that of being shown, rather than told, of learning by example rather than by instruction. Like all learning, it can occur at any time, but is most effective during childhood, when we most need to learn in order to get by in a world that is relatively new and unknown. Children will tend to develop the emotional responses of those who play the most significant roles in their upbringing. This makes emotions important mechanisms for transmitting cultural values, but also for undermining them, for we can learn any emotional response by perceiving the emotions of others. We can learn that it is enjoyable to please others, or that it is enjoyable to hurt them. We can learn that it is better to give than to receive, or that greed provides the surest guarantee of happiness.

The second way in which the emotions of others affect our own is by directly inducing them. Psychologists have observed that the emotional intensity of an experience increases when that experience is shared. For instance, we laugh more at something when others are present than when we are alone (Parkinson 1995: 185). But the effect of sharing varies according to the behaviour of others and our relationship with them. For instance, Chapman and Wright (1976) showed that a child laughs more when watching humorous material with a friend than when watching with a child they do not know, and that they laugh more when the other child laughs more (cited by Parkinson 1995: 185). There could be several reasons for these effects, but I suggest that an important factor is the level of interest we have in our relationship with the others present.

When sharing an experience, we pay more attention to individuals who are particularly important to us than to those who are less important. If the relationship is particularly close, if it is with someone we care about and live with, then we have a deep personal interest in the quality of that relationship, in whether it is rewarding or distressing, turbulent or harmonious. This is why we feel happy when someone whom we love feels happy; not just because we feel 'for them', but because their happiness makes our lives more pleasant. This is why we sometimes say, 'I wish X was here to see this', because we know that their pleasure would enhance our own. Their pleasure is also a sign that the relationship is going well, which in turn means that the energy we have invested in making it go well is rewarded. Their happiness increases our own self-confidence.

Of course, how we respond emotionally to the emotions of others will depend very much on what we have already learned to feel, including what we have learned to feel about interpersonal relationships. We are unlikely to gain pleasure from someone's happiness if we have learned, through example, to enjoy others' suffering and discomfort. If, on the other hand, we have learned to enjoy pleasing others in general, then the relationship we have with them becomes less significant. Whatever the case, it is the impact of others' emotions on our own that motivates us to share pleasant experiences. This is why conservationists tell each other what they saw on their holidays, and why sports fans relive the details of a match or a race in conversation. It is why my friend who saw the otter flagged down a passing car in the hope of pleasing a total stranger.

Learning to enjoy nature

In the ways described here, other people's emotions can have a profound impact on how any particular individual comes to feel about nature and natural things. In Palmer's study, mentioned above, out of a sample of 232 environmental educators in the UK, eighty-eight (38 per cent) claimed to have been influenced, in their commitment to environmental concerns, by their parents or other close relatives, while forty-nine (21 per cent) claimed to have been influenced by close friends or other individuals (Palmer 1998: 150). In my sample of twenty-eight conservationists in Northern Ireland, there were fourteen who told me, when asked why conservation was important to them, that they had been influenced by one or more individuals, by parents or other close relatives or, in two cases, by a university teacher. One, who became interested in conservation during middle age, was attracted to it by the enthusiasm of his two sons.

The profound impact of interpersonal relationships on the development of an individual's emotional commitments complicates further the task of trying to understand how someone comes to enjoy nature in the ways described at the beginning of this chapter. It means that their past experience as a participant in social interaction needs to be considered, alongside their past experience as a perceiver of and thinker about themselves and their environment. To end this chapter, I provide the following fictional account as an attempt to suggest how enjoyment of nature might develop. The details are taken from the personal histories of myself, people I know well, and people whom I have met and interviewed in the course of my research on environmentalism.

A child is born to a well-educated couple who live in an English suburb. Their house has a small, mature garden where, on warm days, the child lies in her pram, and later plays while her mother weeds the flower beds. She feels secure – her mother is in view – so she is free of anxiety and can let her attention wander. The garden is full of things to activate her interest. Breezes move the leaves of a birch tree, making them flutter, birds sing, a squirrel occasionally runs along the fence. Her mother warns her not to touch the bees or wasps in case they sting. She suffers no pain or discomfort to mar these first experiences of nature. Her favourite toys are fluffy animals; they are more pleasing to hold than her plastic dolls. They come to life in her imagination, in the stories her parents read to her, and in the adventures pictured daily on children's television.

Her father, who has an office job, is an amateur botanist who likes to walk in the countryside. They regularly visit a local nature reserve, where he searches for rarities along the hedgerows. She shares his pleasure when he finds what he is looking for. She does not understand the reason for it, for the plants that delight him are never the big, bright ones that impress her most, but his excitement pleases her all the same. When she is about 5 years old, on one of their regular walks, she tries to impress her father by gathering as many different flowers as she can. His reaction, when she presents him with the bunch, surprises and disappoints her. He is not angry, but neither is he delighted. Later, he explains that it is wrong to pick the flowers, for if everyone picked them the plants would eventually disappear.

A few years later, the family moves to a new estate at the edge of the town, fringed by farmland. They acquire a dog, which gives her a reason for long walks with a dog-owning friend. Together they explore the nearby fields. They find wildflowers, which they never pick, and she proudly tells her friend their scientific names. They discover a small pond where frogs gather in early spring. It becomes their special place. She brings home jars of frog-spawn and watches the tadpoles hatch and grow.

For a few teenage years, other interests take over her life; music, films, soap operas, clothes and her developing sexuality become her main obsessions. Impressing her friends becomes more important than pleasing her parents. Her father, once a source of wisdom, now seems silly and eccentric. Someone else walks the dog. The pond, fields and hedgerows give way to the expanding town and she hardly notices their disappearance. Years later, when she becomes involved in a campaign to save local woodland, she will recall her childhood adventures and mourn the passing of her rural playground. Meanwhile, despite the distractions of adolescence, she does not completely lose the enjoyment of learning, and she looks forward to the independence of student life.

One day, when she is sitting in her room revising for her final school exams, her attention is caught by the birds feeding in the garden. It is a welcome distraction from her studies, and she realizes, as she watches them, that she can detect subtle differences among them. She finds that she can tell the male greenfinches from the females. She notices that some of the sparrows have larger and blacker bibs than others, that blue tits and coal tits, though the same size, are different colours, and that coal tits and great tits, though the same colour, are different sizes. Her interest is aroused and she wants to learn more.

She buys herself a pair of binoculars and joins a birdwatching group at her university. Each new species she sees enhances her interest. With new friends, she seeks out rarities and shares with them the triumph of seeing what they anticipated, and the disappointment of failing to do so. Birds become, for her, what plants were for her father. When she has children of her own, she will show them the differences between blue tits and coal tits, and hope that such details will enrich their lives as they have enriched hers.

There is no need to carry this fictional life history any further. A nature lover has emerged from a process of learning reinforced by enjoyment. Her experience could have been very different. Her nature-loving father might have been cruel and abusive, turning her against nature for life. Her early experiences might have been marred by illness or discomfort. Other priorities might, at any time, have become strong enough to distract her permanently from an interest in nature. All this is well understood by environmental educators and campaigners. Those who count themselves as nature lovers and who, not infrequently, become involved in conservation, are the survivors of this process; people whose interest in nature has been sustained or revived by enjoyable experiences and memories. Looking back, they might be able to recall the moment at which their original interest was activated. It might have come in adulthood, when, in a rare moment of relaxation, they noticed the beauty of a flower, or admired the resilience of a weed emerging from a concrete path, or when their son or daughter came home from school with their first biology project. Or they might just know that it began sometime in childhood, perhaps when moving leaves captured the attention of a baby, halting the flow of tears.

5

IDENTIFYING WITH NATURE

Human nature is such that with sufficient all-sided maturity we cannot avoid 'identifying' ourselves with all living beings, beautiful or ugly, big or small, sentient or not.

(Naess 1988: 20)

In June 1999 I visited the Findhorn Foundation in Scotland to attend a conference entitled 'For the Love of Nature?' (referred to by its organizers and participants, and henceforward in this book, as FLON?). The organizers described it in the programme as 'our unique academic *and* experiential conference' (emphasis in original). As well as presenting conventional accounts of scientific research, many of the speakers sought to engage the audience emotionally, using poetry, music and visual images, and telling their own and others' personal stories of pleasure and pain in their relationship with what one of them called the 'more-than-human-world'. For me, and I suspect for many others, the emotional climax of the conference was Jane Goodall's talk entitled 'Chimps: so like us'. I had looked forward to this with some apprehension, for I have never been able to read Jane Goodall's books or watch her films about chimpanzees without dissolving into tears. But this had always been in the privacy of my home. How would I remain composed in this very public arena? I need not have worried. I quickly realized, as she traced the tragedies and triumphs of chimpanzee life – Flint dying of grief after the loss of his mother Flo, others scarred by human cruelty and restored to health – that the men on each side of me were quietly sobbing. I gave up the struggle. A more stoic anthropologist colleague commented afterwards that at least half the audience were openly weeping. At the end of her talk, Jane Goodall was given a standing ovation.

Had I been less emotionally engaged, and more mindful of my duties as an observing anthropologist, I might have asked other participants why they were so affected, though the question would undoubtedly have struck them as superfluous and silly. I have no doubt that many would have said that they 'identified' with the chimpanzees whose stories they had heard, that they imagined sharing their experiences, suffering as they suffered, and so felt *for* them. People's ability to identify with non-human entities plays an important role in discourses about the protection of nature and natural things. In particular, it helps those engaged in campaigns for animal rights and the conservation of biodiversity to win support for their views (see Chapter 7). But the concept of identification is most explicitly articulated by deep ecologists, for whom identification with natural entities, and with nature as a whole, forms the basis of an ecologically sensitive way of living. In this chapter, I consider what it means to say that nature protectionists, and people in general, 'identify' with nature and natural things, drawing, once again, on ideas from several disciplines (anthropology, psychology, philosophy, neuroscience) to explore the character of this relationship.

Identification and deep ecology

Fox (1995) argued that the key to understanding what deep ecologists mean by identification is the way in which their attitude to nature departs from a moralistic approach. Most environmentalist perspectives encompass a set of values, which in turn generate ideas about right and wrong actions towards nature and natural things. For instance, the value of human health makes it wrong to release hazardous substances into the environment, the value of biodiversity makes it wrong, in general terms, to allow a common species to expand at the expense of a rare species, the value of natural beauty makes it wrong to scar a mountainside with a quarry, and so on. In deep ecology, particularly as it is described in the work of Arne Naess (1985, 1988, 1989), identification with nature and natural things makes moral rules redundant. We act protectively towards nature, not because, for various reasons, we think we *ought* to, but because we *feel inclined* to.

This distinction draws on Kant's (1785) observation that benevolent actions can be performed either out of duty or out of inclination. An action performed out of duty is a moral action, and a commitment to moral values is most evident when people act against their inclination, when they do what they know they should despite wishing to act otherwise. A benevolent action performed out of inclination is, in Kant's terms, a 'beautiful' action (Naess 1989: 85). Naess regards morality as a 'treacherous basis for ecology' because it requires people to act unselfishly, against their own interests, for the benefit of nature (1988: 24), a benefit which they might consider less important than their own or that of humanity in general. An alternative, and, in the long run, a much sounder basis for ecology, according to Naess, is to work on people's inclinations rather than their morals (1988: 28), so that they will feel inclined to act benevolently towards nature, rather than feeling obliged to do so. This is the alternative offered by deep ecology.

Identification with nature and natural things is the process through which this inclination towards benevolent action is thought to develop. Identification with something elicits empathy. Naess offered the following illustration:

> My standard example has to do with a nonhuman being I met forty
> years ago. I looked through an old-fashioned microscope at the

dramatic meeting of two drops of different chemicals. A flea jumped from a lemming strolling along the table and landed in the middle of the acid chemicals. To save it was impossible. It took many minutes for the flea to die. Its movements were dreadfully expressive. What I felt was, naturally, a painful compassion and empathy. But the empathy was *not* basic. What *was* basic was the process of identification, that 'I see myself in the flea'. If I was alienated from the flea, not seeing intuitively anything resembling myself, the death struggle would have left me indifferent.

(Naess 1988: 22, emphasis in original)

The key point here is that Naess saw *himself* in the flea. Identification, in his terms, entails an expansion of the self to include other beings, so that 'one's *own self* is no longer adequately delimited by the personal ego or the organism' (Naess 1989: 174, emphasis in original). 'Because of an inescapable process of identification with others, with growing maturity, the self is widened and deepened. We "see ourselves in others"' (1988: 20). Identification makes morality redundant because we care for ourselves, and whatever is a part of ourselves, by inclination, without the need for moral exhortation. Anyone who identifies with natural things, who sees them as a part of themselves, is therefore likely to feel inclined to protect them.

It would be easy to dismiss Naess' view as naive and impracticable in the context of western capitalist society. We could point out that, given the number of people who abuse their own bodies with alcohol, tobacco and other drugs, there is little reason to suppose that they might feel protective towards other beings, even if they were to identify with them. Deep ecologists might respond by arguing that self-abuse is a symptom of a pathological society, whose sense of separation from nature runs so deep that it has alienated us even from our own bodies. They might argue that a love and respect for nature goes along with a love and respect for ourselves, and that, in a truly ecologically benevolent society, self-abuse would not take place. Or we could point out that there is little hope of getting people to act benevolently towards creatures whom they regard as adversaries, even if they recognize in them something resembling themselves. A farmer might acknowledge the ingenuity of a predator that kills his livestock, but he is unlikely to feel inclined to protect that predator. Deep ecologists might answer that identification does not guarantee that nature and natural things will never be destroyed – we need to kill in order to eat, or to protect what we eat – but it does mean that destruction will be limited to what is necessary, because all destruction will be deeply regretted:

The farmer who mows down a thousand flowers in his meadow, in order to feed his cows, should be on guard, as he turns homeward, not to decapitate some flower by the roadside . . . For then he sins against life without being under the compulsion of necessity.

(Schweitzer, in Gottlieb 1996: 408)

But I am not concerned here with whether deep ecology is a realistic and practicable programme for living; rather, with what it means to identify with nature and natural things, and with how deep ecologists and other nature protectionists come to do it. This is a complex and ambiguous relationship variously expressed in at least four different ways: it (the object identified with) is *similar to* me (Naess 1988), it *is* me (Livingston 1981, Macy 1987), it is *part of* me (Naess 1989), I am part of *it* (Seed 1985). If we want to understand how human beings come to identify with other entities, we need to explore the ideas and emotions that lie behind these kinds of statements.

From his example of the dying flea, and from the quotation at the beginning of this chapter, it appears that Naess regards identification as a basic response, something that occurs 'naturally' and 'intuitively' in particular situations (just as some cognitive psychologists see certain ideas as arising naturally, whenever the appropriate stimuli are present – see Chapter 2). He also implies that identification is a recognition of similarity between ourselves and the object with which we identify – his empathy with the flea depended on his seeing in it something resembling himself. This appears to be slightly at odds with Fox's understanding of identification as 'a sense of commonality' (as distinct from similarity) with something:

> one can have a sense of certain *similarities* between oneself and another entity without necessarily identifying with that entity, that is, without necessarily experiencing a sense of *commonality* with that entity. On the other hand, the experience of commonality with another entity does imply a sense of similarity with that entity.
>
> (Fox 1995: 231, emphasis in original)

This suggests that, while some sense of similarity may be necessary before we can identify with something, this alone is not enough to induce identification. So, for Fox, identification is not a basic or intuitive response to things which we recognize as being like ourselves in some way. The sense of similarity needs to be qualified, or perhaps added to, before identification takes place.

It is worth examining Fox's ideas on identification in some detail. Although he appears to present an enlightening analysis of the concept of identification in deep ecological thought, what he says about it departs, in significant ways, from what some deep ecologists say about it. In the following sections, I present my own thoughts on how people come to identify with nature and natural things as a response to Fox's analysis. Although his ideas may be used to illuminate some of the emotional commitments that play a role in nature protection, I shall argue that he has omitted the most important basis for identification, one that makes sense of Naess' empathy for the dying flea, the response of Jane Goodall's audience at the FLON? conference to the plight of the chimpanzees and, to some extent, the deep ecologists' feelings for Gaia and for nature as a whole.

Identification and identity: Part 1

Fox distinguished identification, as a sense of commonality with something, from 'identity', as the idea that one object literally *is* another, 'that I literally *am* that tree over there' (Fox 1995: 231, emphasis in original). He assumed, perhaps because they often use the term 'identification', that deep ecologists experience a sense of commonality, rather than a sense of identity, with natural entities. And yet, some of the statements made by deep ecologists (and quoted by Fox) seem to suggest that a sense of identity is precisely what they mean: 'All that is in my universe is not merely mine; it is me' (Livingston 1981: 113); 'I am part of the rainforest protecting myself' (Seed 1985: 243); 'we *are* our world' (Macy 1987: 20, emphasis in original). How are we to understand such statements? Returning to distinctions made in Chapter 2, we can treat them as literal representations, as metaphoric representations, or as simply untrue. If they are literal representations, we have to conclude that they do, indeed, refer to a sense of identity rather than a sense of commonality. It seems more likely, however, that they are intended metaphorically. They are communicative devices rather than straightforward statements of belief. Seed claimed that 'methods for inspiring the experience of deep ecology' include prayer and poetry, wilderness vision quests, direct action and ritual (1988: 12). We should thus expect metaphor, on which prayer, poetry and ritual thrive, to be prominent in the discourse of deep ecology.

If statements of identity with nature and natural things are metaphoric, and not, therefore, simply untrue, we can ask what truths they are believed, by those who use them, to embody. It seems clear, from the work of deep ecologists, that they refer to a vision of the 'oneness' of nature, in which our past and future identity with natural things *is* taken as a literal truth. On the understanding that matter is never destroyed, only transformed, deep ecologists point out that the matter that makes up our human bodies must, at some time, have existed in other natural forms and will do so again after our deaths. I may not, at this moment, literally be that tree over there, but I may, in the past, have been other trees. The consciousness of our past in other forms has been described by Seed as 'evolutionary remembering':

> As your memory improves, as the implications of evolution and ecology are internalized . . . there is an identification with all life. Then follows the realization that 'life' and 'lifeless' is [*sic*] a human construct. Every atom in this body existed before organic life emerged 4000 million years ago. Remember our childhood as minerals, as lava, as rocks? Rocks contain the potentiality to weave themselves into such stuff as this. We are the rocks dancing.
>
> (Seed 1988: 36)

Just as we share a past with the natural things around us, so we share their future: 'the fate of the sea turtle or the tiger or the gibbon is mine' (Livingston 1981: 113). This is so, not only in the sense that we and all other life forms are 'in the same boat', on the same fragile and threatened planet, but also in the sense that our bodies will decay and so sustain other organisms, which will in turn sustain others, and so on as long as (and this is the warning) the Earth is able to support life.[1]

So I suggest that identity plays a more significant role in some deep ecologists' understanding of identification than Fox implied. Their knowledge of our past and future *identity* as other life forms (and as things not regarded, in western scientific convention, as living, such as rocks), forms a basis for their *identification* with other contemporary life forms, such as the sea turtle, the tiger, the gibbon or the flea. It is not only that deep ecologists see in them something resembling themselves, as Naess suggested – though I shall argue that this is indeed an important basis for identification. They also see in other natural objects their own material past and future; individual human beings were once something else, and will be transformed again. This sense of identity is, at least in part, what enables deep ecologists to advocate an expansion of the self to incorporate other things. And because they envisage the material universe as a continuity, in which distinctions between living and non-living are, to some extent, blurred, this sense of identity enables the expanded self to include anything and everything in nature, including rocks, mountains, ecosystems, Mother Earth and nature as a whole. I shall return later to the question of how identification with these kinds of entities comes about, suggesting that it has other bases as well as the sense of identity described here.[2]

Other bases of identification

For Fox, a sense of identity with other entities was not a basis for identification with them, but he did suggest three general bases of identification, which he referred to as personal, ontological and cosmological. Personally based identification with other entities comes about through personal involvement with those entities. In this sense we identify with, for example, our own families, our possessions, the sports clubs we support, the countries we live in. When these things are attacked we feel personally affronted, and when they are praised we feel proud (Fox 1995: 249–50). Ontologically based identification, according to Fox, is derived from the realization of common existence; my understanding that I and other entities simply exist can lead me to identify with them. This form of identification is found in Zen Buddhism and some other spiritual disciplines (ibid.: 250–2). Cosmologically based identification is generated by the realization that we and other entities belong to 'a single unfolding reality'. Fox stressed that this can come about 'through the empathic incorporation of *any* cosmology (i.e., any fairly comprehensive account of *how* the world is) that sees the world as a single unfolding process' (ibid.: 252, emphasis in original). This means that a Christian, for instance, might identify with other entities on the basis that we are all part of God's creation, and that a biologist might identify with other living organisms on the basis that we are all products of the same process of evolution. Fox argued that deep ecologists emphasize ontologically based, and especially cosmologically based identification. They argue that identifying with other entities on the grounds that we and they belong to the same unfolding reality can generate the result they desire, that people will, by inclination, seek to protect nature.

Fox's analysis of identification is illuminating but incomplete. The discussion presented in the previous sections suggests that to his three kinds of identification could be added a fourth, which might be labelled, rather clumsily, 'identity-based identification' – that which is based on a sense of identity with something else, which in deep ecology means the understanding that we and the other entity are of the same substance and can be transformed into one another.[3] But I would say that even this four-part classification omits one of the most common forms of identification found in western cultures, that based on the perception of personhood. In order to develop this argument I need to return to the idea that identification depends on (according to Naess) or implies (according to Fox) a sense of similarity with something, that in order to identify with an entity we must perceive in it something resembling ourselves. I suggest that the quality of personhood, which we perceive in ourselves, in other human beings and in non-human entities, is the similarity which most effectively, in western cultures, induces identification with other things. Thus we can speak of a fifth category, 'person-based identification', as distinct from Fox's 'personally based identification' which, as indicated above, depends on personal involvement rather than a sense of similarity.

In Chapter 3, I considered how we perceive personhood in others. I suggested that it is easy to see non-human animals as persons because they actively relate to us and to each other in ways that create 'intersubjectivity' in the sense described by Neisser (1988: 41). And I suggested that we can perceive personhood in other natural entities, such as ecosystems, Mother Earth and nature as a whole, because these things can also relate to us, and/or appear to do so, in responsive ways. If personhood is, as I suggest, a perceived similarity between these other things and ourselves, something that enables us to identify with them, we must also perceive ourselves as persons. The question of how we do this was addressed briefly in Chapter 3, and in Chapter 4 I discussed the view that feelings are perceptions of processes going on in our own bodies. Here, I shall show how a more detailed examination of self-perception can improve our understanding of how we come to identify with other natural entities. This means exploring the creation, not of *inter*subjectivity (Neisser 1988), but of *subjectivity*. I know that my human friends are persons, that my cats are persons, and that whales and chimpanzees are persons. I know this because I am a person and because they relate to me and to others in ways that indicate that they are like me. But how do I know that *I* am a person? One answer, suggested by Damasio (1999), is that it is because I know that I have feelings.

Emotions, feelings and consciousness

> . . . the mind is, when all said and done, an organ nature has created in order to perceive itself.
>
> (von Uexküll, T. 1982: 4)

In Chapter 4, I drew attention to the distinction made by Damasio between emotion and feeling. Unlike most theorists of emotion, who treat emotion as a composite process involving bodily changes and subjective feelings, Damasio used the label 'emotion' to refer only to the empirically observable bodily changes (including those that are easily observable, such as blushing and trembling, and those that can be measured using specialist equipment, such as glandular secretions and brain activity). He used the label 'feeling' to refer to the subjective experience of those changes. This distinction makes it easier to think of feelings as perceptions of emotion, as information picked up about things going on in the body.

According to Damasio (1999), feeling – the perception of emotion – is an important step in the emergence of consciousness, both in the development of an individual organism and in the history of evolution. As pointed out in Chapter 4, emotions, though they can be consciously induced (for instance, by thinking about particular things) are often unconscious or pre-conscious; they occur, in human beings and many other organisms, as automatic responses to particular stimuli. Their importance for survival is that they produce an appropriate reaction to a particular situation – to run or freeze in the presence of a predator, to fight a rival, and so on. Damasio assumes that many of the organisms which have emotions as part of their life-regulating equipment never become aware of them because they are not able to perceive them. Organisms that *are* equipped to perceive emotions, in other words, to have feelings, can use those perceptions, just as they use other kinds of information, to guide their actions. As Laird and Apostoleris pointed out, 'knowing that we are about to punch someone in the mouth is useful, because we can decide not to' (1996: 292).

But feelings still do not constitute what Damasio regards as consciousness. In order to be fully conscious, he argued, it is not sufficient merely to have feelings; we need to know that we have feelings. In other words, we need to perceive feelings in ourselves, as distinct from, and in addition to, perceiving the emotions that generate those feelings. This implies that it is possible for an organism to feel afraid, or happy, or sad, without knowing that they do. He acknowledged that this is a difficult point to grasp, specifically because we *are* conscious beings and, therefore, tend to be aware of our feelings. But he pointed out that we often become aware, quite suddenly, 'that we feel anxious or uncomfortable, pleased or relaxed, and it is apparent that the particular state of feeling we know then has not begun on the moment of knowing but rather sometime before' (Damasio 1999: 36). Organisms equipped with consciousness, those that know they have feelings, are able to regulate their actions more efficiently than those that merely have feelings. In this way, consciousness, like its precursors feeling and emotion, increases the survival chances of an organism. With consciousness comes the ability to plan, to seek pleasure and satisfaction, to avoid fear or anger by avoiding the conditions that induce these feelings (Damasio 1999: 285). It enables us to enter situations knowing that we are likely to feel angry, happy, sad or afraid, already having decided how we shall respond.

In Damasio's account, consciousness is equated with a sense of self (1999: 8). It would be wrong to assume that 'self' can be equated unproblematically with 'personhood' (see below), but in this instance I think a sense of one's own personhood is exactly what Damasio is referring to. Knowing that I am having a particular feeling is, essentially, the knowledge that it is *I*, a thinking and intentionally acting being, who am having this feeling. Awareness of feelings contributes to a sense of personhood in the same way as awareness of other perceptions does so. Just as my awareness of the flow of information continually entering my mind as I move through my environment gives me a sense of myself as a physical being and agent, so a continual flow of information about my inner world of feelings gives me a sense of myself as an emotional being.

Emotions, personhood and identification

The role of emotions and feelings in the perception of ourselves as persons adds another dimension to the perception of personhood in others. As well as perceiving personhood in the things that appear to relate to us in responsive ways and/or appear to act intentionally, we also perceive personhood in things that appear to have emotions. If Damasio is correct in arguing that feelings, as perceptions of emotion, are central to our own sense of personhood, then the perception of emotions in others could, in fact, be the most powerful indication of their personhood. Of course, not having Damasio's specialist perspective, we do not normally distinguish between emotions and feelings. Most of us operate with a commonsense understanding of emotion in which, as William James observed, the feeling is assumed to provoke the bodily response. So when we perceive signs of emotion in any entity, we assume that they indicate an inner world of feeling which, in others as in ourselves, means personhood.

If emotions and feelings are central to our perception of personhood, we can also expect them to be important in the process through which we identify with others as persons, the process I refer to as 'person-based identification'. We can expect it to be easiest to identify, on this basis, with things that clearly display emotions, especially if their ways of doing so are similar to our own. In these terms, the emotional effect on her audience at the FLON? conference, of Jane Goodall's account of the suffering of chimpanzees, is very easy to understand; they are, as she said, 'so like us':

> all those who have worked long and closely with chimpanzees have no hesitation in asserting that chimps experience emotions similar to those which in ourselves we label pleasure, joy, sorrow, anger, boredom and so on . . . We make these judgements because the similarity of so much of a chimpanzee's behaviour to our own permits us to empathize.
>
> (Goodall 1990: 13–14)

Even when the behaviour is less like our own, we have little difficulty in understanding it. The pleasure of a purring cat is unmistakable. So is the distress of a bird whose agitated calls tell us that we have strayed too close to its nest. And the movements of the flea trapped in a bath of acid in Naess' laboratory were 'dreadfully expressive'; its suffering was as plain to him as if it had cried out in pain. Of course, if Damasio is right in saying that emotions are often pre-conscious and that even feelings are not necessarily known to those who have them, we cannot know the extent to which any non-human animal is conscious of feeling what it appears, to us, to feel. It is this uncertainty, generated by science, but perhaps, as Wolpert might argue, running against common sense, that sustains debates about the acceptable limits of our treatment of non-human animals.

I am not suggesting, here, that emotions and feelings are the sole basis for the perception of personhood and, therefore, for person-based identification – to do so would be to deny the arguments presented in previous chapters. I am suggesting only that they make a significant contribution to these processes. Person-based identification also uses the other signs of personhood already described in this book, such as responsive relatedness and the appearance of acting intentionally. I am suggesting that, through various combinations of these perceived similarities between ourselves and others, we identify with a range of entities. Person-based identification is easiest with those things that are most like us, things that possess a wide range of person-like qualities. Many non-human animals, for instance, appear to act intentionally, to relate to each other, and often to us, in responsive ways, and seem to express emotions (they can appear frightened, angry or contented). But person-based identification is also possible with other entities, for instance, with ecosystems, with Gaia and Mother Nature. As suggested in Chapter 3, we perceive person-like qualities in these entities insofar as they can appear to relate actively to ourselves; nature does things to *us* – it makes our crops grow and it destroys them, it provides what we need and it frustrates our efforts to survive. It also responds to what we do to it; ecosystems are changed, the climate becomes more violent and unpredictable, nature behaves differently as a result of human activities. In view of the discussion presented above, it is worth pointing out that natural events have often been interpreted as expressions of emotion, as the anger or pleasure of the gods or the ancestors.

I suggest that person-based identification plays a significant role in many people's commitment to nature protection. It is particularly important in generating empathy for non-human animals, and therefore in motivating concern for animal rights and welfare. It also helps to generate support for nature conservation. I shall consider some of the practical aspects of this role in Chapter 7. But what about the process of identification described and advocated by deep ecologists? Fox suggested that deep ecologists emphasize ontologically based and, in particular, cosmo-logically based identification. This is not to say that they exclude other bases for identifying with entities, only that they consider ontology and especially cosmology to be the most important (Fox 1995: 266). In other words, he suggests that deep ecologists identify with other entities primarily on the basis that they, like us, exist as part of the same unfolding reality, the same cosmos. I would argue that person-based identification is just as important in deep ecological thought as these other forms. It describes perfectly Naess' empathy with the dying flea and with other single organisms, and it can make sense of identification with any entity in which person-like qualities are perceived; these, as we have seen, can include ecosystems, the planet and nature as a whole.[4] This point can be substantiated by considering one of the central doctrines of deep ecology: that of self-realization.

Identification and self-realization

I mentioned in Chapter 2 that deep ecologists believe in the right of all entities to self-realization, their right to unfold in their own way (Fox 1989, 1995). Human beings, of course, are no exception. Naess presents a very specific understanding of what self-realization entails for a human being; it is achieved through the widest and deepest possible identification with other entities. As mentioned earlier, this is seen as bringing about an expansion of the self. It creates what Naess refers to as a 'Self' (with a capital 'S'); 'Self-realization' is seen by Naess as the natural destiny of every maturing human being (Naess 1988).

This description of self-realization is clearly very different from the way in which the process is widely understood in western society. Conventionally, self-realization is more likely to be thought of in terms of personal fulfilment, the development of a person to their fullest potential. This might be achieved in any number of ways: through the successful pursuit of a career, a satisfying family life, the accumulation of wealth, the broadening of experience through travel, the deepening of spiritual awareness through meditation or prayer, or, indeed, through the very path advocated by deep ecologists, namely a deep sense of oneness with everything in the cosmos. The point is that individuals are generally expected to decide or discover for themselves which path will lead to the fulfilment of their own potential. The idea that self-realization can only be achieved by following a *particular* path, while not unfamiliar (it is, after all, central to many religious traditions, including Christianity), does not sit easily with the western liberal ideal of personal freedom of choice.

Deep ecologists would argue that this form of self-realization, in the sense of personal fulfilment, depends on a 'narrow, atomistic or particle-like' concept of the self (Fox 1995: 216), an ego or 'empirical self' (Naess 1989: 172), delimited by a physical body. The 'Self', on the other hand, which Naess described as 'the deep, comprehensive and ecological self' (1989: 175), is not delimited by the organism; it is a 'wide, expansive or field-like conception' (Fox 1995: 217). Fox coined the term 'transpersonal ecology' to describe the philosophical orientation of deep ecology, implying that, in the process of Self-realization through the widest and deepest possible identification with other beings, the narrow, atomistic self or 'person' is transcended (cf. Rolston 1999: 415).[5]

By describing the orientation of deep ecology as 'transpersonal', Fox seems to be suggesting that personhood, at least one's own personhood, is subordinate to other valued qualities. If so, then it might indeed make sense to argue that deep ecologists identify with other entities primarily on the basis of their common membership of a single unfolding reality, rather than on the basis of their similarities as persons.

However, I think Fox underestimates the importance of personhood in deep ecological thought in at least three senses. First, in Naess' description of identification, the self is not transcended but expanded – widened and deepened, 'starting with narrow ego gratification as the crudest, but inescapable starting point' (Naess 1988: 27). Thus our 'egos develop into selves of greater and greater dimension, proportional to the extent and depth of our processes of identification' (Naess 1989: 174). The expanded Self (or ecological self) is continuous with the narrow self (or person), and totally dependent upon it. The Self is created by an identifying subject – 'The ecological self of a *person* is that with which this *person* identifies' (Naess 1988: 22, emphasis added) – brought into existence through a process of personal development and, presumably, ceasing to exist when the person dies.

Second, in deep ecology the process of identification with other beings is understood, at least partly, in emotional terms, or at least in terms of *feeling*. Self-realization, in the deep ecological sense, is assumed to generate a much greater and more satisfying sense of joy than is possible through mere ego-gratification. It is also said to generate a deeper sense of sadness or despair, when the beings with whom one identifies are harmed or destroyed (Naess 1989). And, as we have seen, a consequence of identification with other entities is assumed to be that people will *feel* inclined to act benevolently towards them (Naess 1988). Who or what are the subjects of all this feeling? Who or what could they be other than individual human persons, selves (with a small 's') delimited by physical bodies? Or are deep ecologists suggesting that emotion and feeling can somehow transcend the boundaries of the organism? If so, they must conceive of these phenomena in ways that few theorists of emotion would recognize.

Third, and most important for my argument, the belief that all entities have the right to self-realization must be based on the assumption that all entities have or are 'selves'. In other words, they share, with human beings, the quality of selfhood. Mathews (1991) has explored in detail the question of what makes something a 'self'. She identified a category of 'self-realizing systems', of which organisms are the archetypal examples. Self-realizing systems have interests in their own maintenance, indeed they actively maintain themselves; they possess what Spinoza and other philosophers called 'conatus', an impulse to persist in their own being (Mathews 1991: 109). While this quality is not easily observable in all things other than organisms, it is observable in some, and the support for such observations often comes from science. Dawkins (1976) suggested that genes are self-maintaining systems, and biologists have often appeared to assume that species, as collections of organisms sharing a gene pool, seek to maintain themselves. Scientists have often described ecosystems as self-regulating, and Lovelock's Gaia theory (1979) described the whole planet in these terms. Mathews argued that the very action of maintaining itself gives an entity value for itself (1991: 104), gives it an interest in its own continuation. She also pointed out that self-realizing systems have to draw on their environment in order to keep themselves going, so the quality of self-realization or self-maintenance actually ties an entity into its environment, emphasizing its interconnectedness with other parts of the cosmos. According to

Mathews, the deep ecologists' doctrine of 'Self-realization', which is most fully expressed through identification with the universe as a whole, only makes sense if the universe is seen as a self-realizing system (ibid.: 151–4).

This argument clearly indicates that self-realizing systems, the entities seen by deep ecologists as having some kind of right to self-realization, appear to act with a purpose – the very purpose of realizing or maintaining themselves, of persisting in their own being, of unfolding in their own way, or however else it might be expressed. Mathews described this quality of purposiveness quite explicitly:

> A self-realizing system . . . actively determines and preserves its own perimeters, thereby creating an objective unity. Such self-affirming activity marks off the self-realizing being as an *agent*, as opposed to a mere link in a causal chain, with no interests or purposes of its own to dictate its action.
>
> (Mathews 1991: 104, emphasis in original)

As we saw in earlier chapters (particularly Chapters 1 and 3), the appearance of acting with a purpose is one of the bases on which personhood is perceived. For this reason, it is appropriate to suggest that, when deep ecologists identify with (apparently) self-realizing systems, which include not only other individual organisms, but also species, ecosystems, the Earth and the universe, they do so on the basis of the perceived personhood of these entities. In other words, their identification with these things is at least partly person-based, as well as, or rather than, ontologically or cosmologically based.

It is worth noting that Mathews' analysis of selfhood does not lead to the suggestion that all things in the cosmos can be identified with on the basis of our perceived common personhood, because not all things, in her analysis, are self-realizing systems. Rocks, for instance, do not qualify:

> A rock is in no way self-affirming, demarcating and preserving its own identity; a rock is just a lump of matter, arbitrarily hewn out, waiting to be worn away by wind and rain. It is only an individual by chance, and its individuality does not 'matter' to itself.
>
> (Mathews 1991: 104)

Some deep ecologists might take issue with this. They might argue that it is by crumbling away to soil and dust that a rock realizes itself, that self-realization, for a rock, is an act of self-transformation. But there is no need to resort to such an argument, or to explore its implications, for, as we have seen, deep ecologists have other reasons for identifying with rocks. They use what I have called 'identity-based identification', the understanding that all things in the universe are ultimately of the same substance, that all things are transformable into other things, that the atoms in our bodies might once have belonged to rocks, and might do so again.

Personhood and the enjoyment of nature

Before leaving the subject of person-based identification, it is worth discussing briefly how it affects people's enjoyment of nature and natural things. In the analysis presented in Chapter 4, I tried to emphasize that all encounters with the external world involve emotion (a point to be developed further in Chapter 6); they must do so if we are to learn from such encounters. This view differs from the conventional perspectives in sociology, anthropology and social psychology, in which emotion is assumed to operate primarily, if not exclusively, in interpersonal contexts (for instance, Lutz 1988). Parkinson pointed out that love, hate and anger, which, according to Fehr and Russell (1984), people consider to be the 'best' examples of emotion, 'are all intrinsically relational states: they are inconceivable without the real or imagined presence of another person' (Parkinson 1995: 21). I assume that Parkinson was thinking only of human relationships, that other persons, for him, are other *people*. Following the discussion in Chapter 3, we know that personhood is perceived in many things other than human beings. In terms of the kind of relational epistemology described by Bird-David (1999), we can perceive personhood in anything that appears actively to relate to us, that engages our attention in ways that suggest the possibility of interaction. And, following the discussion in this chapter, I would add that we can perceive personhood in anything that appears to experience emotions.

However, although I am suggesting a broader meaning of the term 'person' than that employed by Parkinson, Lutz and others, I would accept the implication of their arguments, that persons, of all the objects in our environment, are particularly good at inducing emotions. This is why we find interpersonal relationships particularly rewarding or upsetting, and why they are such an effective context in which to learn about the world. It is why, as reported in Chapter 4, the emotional intensity of an experience increases when that experience is shared, so that we laugh more at something when other people are present.

I suggest that this is also the case when experiences are shared with non-human persons, with entities other than human beings in which personhood is perceived. The perception of personhood in non-human others, as in other human beings, offers the possibility of an intersubjective relationship, and so adds a dimension which is not present, for instance, in a purely aesthetic experience. This is most obviously the case, for reasons already discussed, when the entity is an individual non-human animal. We can enjoy a game with a dog because the dog relates responsively to us in ways which suggest that it too is enjoying the game. I suggest that, for those who enjoy watching wild animals, the enjoyment comes at least partly from identification with them as persons, from a sense of commonality which induces empathy and enhances understanding. This is also the case in less benign encounters with animals, such as sport hunting and fishing. Fox-hunters describe their enjoyment of a hunt in terms of the fox's 'performance', 'what the fox did; the challenges it posed; what it made the hounds do' (Marvin 2000: 194). The fox is regarded as an 'artful rogue', and praised for its cunning, its courage and its spirit (ibid.: 192), qualities which clearly imply an inner world of thought, purpose, feeling; in other words, personhood.

If these suggestions are reasonable, then it also seems reasonable to suggest that our emotional experience of the more abstract natural entities, like ecosystems, forests, the planet as a whole, Mother Nature, etc., is enhanced if we see them as persons, or as governed by persons. This helps to make sense of the view, discussed in Chapter 1, that religious experiences are particularly emotional. Religion, as discussed in that chapter, is characterized by personal understandings of nature. It thus offers the possibility of meaningful relationships with natural things and processes, which impersonal views of nature do not. Religion offers the possibility of interaction, of mutual communication, enabling us to look at a beautiful sunset, for instance, and appreciating it not only for its beauty, but also as the creation of a being whose actions might be influenced by our own. Of course, it is not only the positive emotional experiences that are enhanced by the perception of personhood. We may enjoy nature more if we perceive persons in it, but we may also get more angry with it; if the fox is an intentional agent, it meant to kill our chickens and so deserves to be punished. And we feel more sad when nature and natural things appear to suffer. As a result of person-based identification, living in a personalized universe carries more emotional reward, and more emotional punishment, than living in an impersonal one.

Identification and identity: Part 2

Thus far, in this chapter, the term 'identity' has been used in the sense described by Fox, to mean a kind of relationship in which matter or substance is literally shared. An understanding of identity in this sense, as we have seen, can form a basis for identification with nature and natural things, giving metaphoric meaning to statements such as 'I am part of the rainforest', and 'we are the rocks'. However, this is not the sense in which 'identity' is most commonly understood in social science nor, I suggest, in western public discourse. It is more often seen as something that things, persons and groups 'possess', something that defines what or who they are in a way that is not reducible to physical substance. A person's identity is a complex of social roles, physical characteristics and other elements which combine to create a continuous sense of who or what that person is. In this final section of this chapter, I show how this understanding of identity reverses the relationship between identity and identification discussed earlier. Instead of a process of identification based on a sense of identity with other things, we have a sense of identity which is constituted through identification with other things. The particular form of identification involved is that which Fox called 'personally based identification' (1995: 249).

It is a common observation in anthropology and related disciplines that our sense of who or what we are is constituted through relationships. Opinions differ on whether these relationships are most crucially, or, indeed, solely, with other human beings. The view that our understanding of reality is socially constructed implies that they are. But the emotions and feelings, the perception of which, in

Damasio's (1999) model, creates self-consciousness, are induced by an infinite range of stimuli, human and non-human. And, as we have seen, Gibson (1979) and Neisser (1988) described our self-knowledge as emerging out of perceptual engagement with our total environment. This view, which is pursued in this book, has been developed within anthropology by Ingold (2000a), Bird-David (1999), Richards (1993) and others. But whether one advocates the more orthodox constructionist perspective or this broader understanding of relational epistemology, the underlying theme is that the self is formed in relation to the other.

Not surprisingly, given their emphasis on identification as the route to self-realization, this theme is echoed in the work of deep ecologists. Naess wrote, 'The identity of the individual, "that I am something", is developed through interaction with a broad manifold, organic and inorganic. There is no completely isolatable I, no isolatable social unit' (1989: 164). DiZerega made the same point through a poetic simile: 'Our individuality is real but no more separable from the world than a whirlpool is from water' (diZerega 1997: 64). This understanding is often said to be at odds with the typical western concept of self or personhood. As pointed out in Chapter 2, Strathern (1988) described the western concept of a person as an irreducible or indivisible entity. Morris (1994: 16) wrote, 'The Western conception of the person is . . . that of an "individuated" being, separate from both the social and the natural world', and Bateson (1991: 190) wrote, 'We . . . boggle at the proposition that our own character is only real in relationship. We abstract from the experiences of interaction and difference to create a "self", which shall continue (shall be "real" or thingish) even without relationship.' I would tend to agree with Morris (1994: 17) that this is a misleading view of western thought. Not only is there a long-standing critique of this way of thinking in western discourse, to which anthropology has contributed, but also the fact that we often describe ourselves in terms of social roles (I am a wife, a daughter, an anthropologist, a home-owner) shows that we recognize the composite and divisible nature of our identity. This view is further borne out by the role of identification in the constitution of identity, described below.

Identity has been a recurring object of interest among anthropologists. As analysts of social life, they have focused primarily on those components of identity that are most obviously expressed and, to varying degrees, contested, negotiated and manipulated in social interaction. These include ethnicity, gender, sexuality, religious and political affiliation, and social roles. Fox is more concerned with subjective experience, with how a sense of self emerges out of experience of the other, and this he links explicitly with what he called 'personally based identification'. This concept was described briefly earlier in this chapter; here I quote Fox's description in more detail, recalling that, for him, identification is 'a sense of commonality' with something.

> Personally based identification refers to experiences of commonality with other entities that are brought about through personal involvement with these entities . . . We generally tend to identify most with those entities with which we are often in contact (assuming our

experiences of these entities are of a generally positive kind). This applies not only to concrete entities (e.g., the members of our family, our friends and more distant relations, our pets, our homes, our teddy bear and doll) but also to those more abstract kinds of entities with which we have considerable personal involvement (our football or basketball club . . . our country). We experience these entities as part of 'us', as part of our identity.

(Fox 1995: 249–50)

Anthropologists often encounter the institutionalized consequences of the experiential process described here. Expressions of group or individual identity, of varying degrees of formality, often make reference to things with which people are personally involved. For instance, throughout the world we find people who are known by the name of the place where they live or originate from, or the land which they own or work on. In many cultures, clans are associated through totemism with species of plants and animals with which their ancestors had special relationships. Individuals are often named after objects in their environment which have some significance for their family or are associated with their birth in some way. In a series of statements by indigenous people about the role of biodiversity in their lives, Henrietta Fourmile, who is from the Cairns area of Australia, described how she was given a 'language name' of part of a vine, which connects her with the land and country where her grandfather was born. Both her father and her son have the name of 'bush turkey' and, 'just to show the connection', she described how a bush turkey visited their garden only around the time of her son's birth (Posey 1999: 125). Ruth Lilongula, from the Solomon Islands, described her own and her people's identity as follows:[6]

Let me start with my identity to describe how we think of our place in nature and biodiversity. I am Ruth and I identify with my father and mother, my sisters and brothers, my extended family, my clan, and my tribe. On top of this, I identify with the land that is given to me, with the trees that grow on it, the animals that live on it, the medicinal plants that grow on it, the streams and rivers that run through it, the birds and the snakes that live on it, the spirits that are in the trees, and the land, and the rivers. I also identify with the sea and the fishes and the creatures that live there. My tribe identifies with the eagle and the bird. At sea we identify with the shark and the crocodile, and on land, the lizard. The rivers mark the boundaries where we live. The spirits, both good and bad, live in the trees and on the land and take a part in our everyday existence.

. . . We don't see our land and everything else in terms of money. Rather, we value our surroundings as our identity, as who we are and our inheritance that is given to us.

(Posey 1999: 162)

This statement describes very clearly how people's sense of who and what they are can emerge, at least partly, from their identification with familiar things with which they experience a degree of personal involvement. But is this the same process that Fox described as 'personally based identification'? Identification with close family and more distant relations is common to both, but are dolls, teddy bears and football clubs comparable with trees, rivers and birds as objects of identification? I suggest that they are. The process described by both Fox and Ruth Lilongula is identification with significant objects in a person's or group's environment. It varies according to what that environment has to offer in terms of opportunities for personal involvement. Some environments offer trees and rivers, others offer dolls and football clubs. In both cases, a sense of identity emerges out of personally based identification with these things.

It might appear that personally based identification with natural objects is more typically found in non-industrial than in industrial cultures, an impression which almost certainly contributes to the western environmentalist myth that non-industrial peoples are necessarily ecologically benign (Ellen 1986, Milton 1996), or have a special 'oneness' with nature (Milton 1998). But if the process is one of identification, not with natural objects as such, but with whatever a person is most familiar with, then the crucial difference is not between industrial and non-industrial societies, but between different environments, environments which vary in the amount of 'nature' they contain. So, in a modern industrial society, with a diverse economy and an elaborate division of labour, an inner-city dweller might identify most closely with their place of work, their local sports club, the streets and buildings close to their home, while a suburban dweller might identify with all or none of these things, plus the birds that feed in their garden and the trees in the park across the road. A rural dweller in the same country might have less experience of city streets or suburban parks, but would identify instead with the fields and hedgerows around their home and the plants and animals that live there. Thus, personally based identification with nature and natural things can help to shape the identities of groups and individuals in western societies, just as it can and does in non-western societies.

In this chapter, and in Chapter 4, I have examined the emotional content of responses to nature and natural things. As a result of countless personal experiences, which include both direct and socially mediated encounters, natural things – plants, animals, rivers, mountains, storms, sunsets – induce emotions in us. These bodily changes, which, according to Damasio and others, arise outside our consciousness, are then perceived by us as feelings of fear, anger, disgust, interest, enjoyment or, in the case of identification, feelings of commonality which I have taken to be a kind of loving. In turn, we become aware of these feelings – we perceive ourselves perceiving – and so gain an understanding of ourselves as emotional beings. In this way, our engagement with nature and natural things, and with all the things in our environment which, according to our particular cultural inclinations, we may not classify as natural, contributes to our sense of who and what we are, to our identity. For deep ecologists, the constitutive effect of nature on ourselves is essential for well-being:

> To distance oneself from nature and the 'natural' is to distance oneself from a part of that which the 'I' is built up of. Its 'identity', 'what the individual I is', and thereby sense of self and self-respect, are broken down.
>
> (Naess 1989: 164)

I suggest that this emotional and constitutive role of nature and natural things has been underplayed in western environmental debates, which have been dominated by a rationalist scientific discourse in which emotion is suppressed and emotionalism denigrated. I shall explore this point further in the remaining chapters.

6

VALUING NATURE

Meaning, emotion and the sacred

We live adoring nature and then it becomes sacred.
(Johan Mathis Turi, quoted in Posey 1999: 152)

In the late 1980s, at the beginning of my research on environmental issues in Northern Ireland, I became involved in efforts to protect some lagoons in Belfast Harbour from industrial development. The lagoons were the result of land claim operations that had begun in the 1930s, and although they were not 'natural', they had become important roosting and feeding areas for birds, important enough, in fact, for the government to designate them an Area of Special Scientific Interest (ASSI) in 1987. In June 1988, I was one of several representatives of environmental NGOs putting the case for nature conservation at a Public Inquiry into a proposed development plan for the Belfast urban area. At this Inquiry it was revealed that, two months earlier, the government had granted the landowners permission to fill in the lagoons. The conservationists were incensed. Statements were issued to the press and letters were exchanged with government officials. In this correspondence and later discussions it became clear that the conservationists and the officials were guided by very different concerns. The conservationists wanted only to protect the lagoons, while the officials were more concerned that the correct legal procedures be followed. This was quite a revelation to me. Until then I had naively assumed that the officials who had designated the ASSI were simply the official face of the conservation movement, dedicated, within the constraints permitted by their position in government, to the same ideals as the NGOs. It was an important lesson in cultural diversity.[1]

Why are some people in western societies actively concerned to protect nature and natural things while others are not? What motivates people to become involved in nature protection? It might appear that this question has already been answered in Chapters 4 and 5, where I discussed how some people come to love, or specifically to enjoy and to identify with, nature and natural things, for is not that love of nature the motivation for its protection? I would agree that it is, and in this chapter I shall consider how motivation operates through emotion and feeling. Although it might seem self-evident that emotion is central to motivation, the point still needs to be argued, rather than merely stated or assumed, because the emotional character of motivation has been largely neglected in recent decades by those scholars who have sought to understand it.

Studies of motivation are often centred around the concept of value. Another way of asking the above question would be: Why do some people value nature and natural things more than do others? A great deal has been written by anthropologists, psychologists, economists and philosophers about value, but in much of the recent literature value has been presented as a cognitive phenomenon. This is because the emphasis has been on 'values' as guides to decision making rather than on 'valuing' as part of the process of living in and engaging with the world. This chapter is about valuing things in the world rather than values held in the mind.[2] As in previous chapters, a particular process is presented as an instance of a general one. In seeking to understand how and why some people value nature and natural things, I find myself addressing how and why people value things in general. What emerges is, I believe, a model for understanding all values, not just those espoused by nature protectionists. Before describing this model, I present a brief summary of some of the conventional approaches to value, in order to show how the perspective presented here differs from those already in use.

Value in anthropology, psychology and philosophy

Nuckolls described value as 'a concept whose time has come back' (1998: 3) after a long period of neglect. Like most anthropologists who have written about value, he treated it as a noun rather than a verb, asking what 'a value' is, rather than what the process of valuing involves. This raises the question of how values are constituted, to which Nuckolls' response was that they combine both cognitive and emotional elements, that they relate 'knowledge and desire'. Nuckolls was by no means the first anthropologist to think of values in this way. Recalling an earlier phase in the study of values, he described the work of Clyde Kluckhohn (1951), who in turn drew on Parsons' understanding of value. Nuckolls paraphrased Kluckhohn's concept of values as 'ideas for the formulation of action commitments, but . . . not just ideas, because their motivation depends on psychological processes that may be unconscious' (Nuckolls 1998: 20). These processes, which, one presumes, also may be conscious, give values their emotional force. Kluckhohn followed Parsons (1951) in describing values as 'cathected', that is, 'endowed with emotional significance' (Nuckolls 1998: 25). But in a project that was intended to demonstrate the comparative study of values (Vogt and Albert 1966), the concept of value became so ambiguous that it was difficult to distinguish from other cultural phenomena such as beliefs and preferences. Consequently, the quality which, according to Parsons and Kluckhohn, made values distinctive, namely their emotional significance, was lost, and their motivating power was left unexplained (Nuckolls 1998: 25–6).

Thereafter, in social and cultural anthropology, the word 'value' survived, but the distinctively emotional quality of what it conveyed did not. Values have been treated, alongside norms, goals and preferences, as cultural phenomena that some-how guide or govern action (and, at the same time, are products of action), but in the absence of an understanding of their emotional component, the question of how they do this has remained unanswered.[3] Like emotions themselves (see Chapter 4), from the 1970s onwards values fell victim to a cognitivist approach which effectively placed all cultural phenomena within the realm of knowledge and ideas. Strang's analysis of environmental values in North Queensland illustrates this point. She posed the question, as I do in this and the previous chapters, of what makes people care about the environment, and specifically about the land (Strang 1997: 5). She acknowledged that '"values" effectively integrate conceptual cognitive structures and subjective emotional responses' (ibid.: 176). But her description of how values are learned focused on how particular knowledge and styles of discourse are acquired rather than on how emotions and feelings are induced. She suggested that particular cultural forms encourage certain kinds of values and, therefore, presumably, certain kinds of emotions, but how this happens was left unspecified.

According to Munro (1997), the study of values and motivation underwent a similar history in psychology. In the late 1960s and 1970s, approaches which treated emotion as central to an understanding of motivation were swept away in the 'cognitivist revolution' which replaced biological and psychoanalytic models (as well as 'naive' behaviourism). As a result, 'the affective in human experience tended to be neglected or to be seen through the filter of cognitive and linguistic interpretation, and with affect theory goes much of motivation theory' (Munro 1997: ix). Despite acknowledging that values are 'important sources of motivation', Schwartz still defined them primarily in cognitive rather than emotional terms: 'When we wish to characterize a culture in terms of values, we describe the *ideas* about what is good, right, and desirable that the members of a society . . . share' (Schwartz 1997: 70, emphasis added). He conceded that 'when values are activated, they become infused with feeling' (ibid.: 71), but this view seems to offer little advance on that of Kluckhohn over forty years earlier (values are ideas with emotional significance) and it is difficult to see how it can bring us any closer to an understanding of motivation.

Given their concern with the nature of knowledge, wisdom and reasoned argument, it is not surprising that philosophers have also been drawn to study the cognitive rather than the emotional aspects of values. Nowhere is this clearer than in the literature on animal rights. Philosophers have explored the reasons why the rights of non-human animals should or should not be considered important. Their arguments have focused on whether non-human animals can suffer, whether they are sentient beings (Singer 1976), whether they are self-conscious (Clark 1981, Regan 1983), and whether they can be said to act morally (Clark 1985). The principles of similarity and kinship have been invoked to argue that human beings should extend their moral considerations at least to their closest non-human relatives (Cavalieri and Singer 1993). Although there are many different philo-sophical positions on the human treatment of non-human animals, they are united in the assumption that such treatment should have a sound basis in reason, that it should be capable of being argued. The title of one of Stephen Clark's papers – 'How to *calculate* the greater good' (1978, emphasis added) – seems to typify this approach.[4]

In similar ways, environmental philosophers have explored the logical bases on which the wider non-human world is valued. Some of the arguments focus on human welfare (O'Neill 1993). Non-human nature matters because we depend on it for our own survival and well-being. This kind of argument places our treatment of nature within the context of moral obligations to other human beings, and particularly to future generations (de-Shalit 1995). Other arguments rest on the assertion that nature and natural things are valuable in and of themselves, independently of their use to human beings (for instance, Eckersley 1992). This assertion generates ecocentric perspectives on nature protection such as those discussed in Chapter 5 – for instance, the view that natural things and processes are or have 'selves'. Whatever the arguments under discussion, what concerns philosophers is whether and in what way it makes sense to say that nature and natural things have value. Arguments for the protection of nature and natural things are assessed by philosophers in terms of whether they allocate value in logically coherent ways.

The approach developed in this chapter focuses instead on emotion and feeling as central to the process through which we value things. I am not suggesting that reasoned arguments are unimportant, or that people are not persuaded by them. If they were not effective, campaigners for nature protection and other causes would not spend so much effort on them. But to be *effective*, they have to be *affective*. The motivating force of an argument (and of anything else) lies in its emotional impact, and we need to recognize this, as well as its logic, if we are to understand how it moves people to action. Arguments occupy a very small proportion of the things we encounter in the world, and there is no reason to suppose that they are inherently more motivating than other things. One particular approach in environmental philosophy, Goodin's green theory of value, forms an appropriate starting point from which to move from a cognitive model of value to an emotion-centred one.

Value and meaning

In formulating his green theory of value, Goodin addressed a question very similar to that posed at the beginning of this chapter: Why do environmentalists value nature and natural things? He presented his answer in two stages. First, he argued that natural things are valued, not because of their physical attributes, but for the 'history and process of their creation' (Goodin 1992: 26). He pointed out that value is often allocated on this basis. Decisions may be valued more for the processes through which they are reached (for instance, if they are reached democratically or through correct legal procedures), than for their potential consequences (an example was given at the beginning of this chapter). Genuine works of art are valued more highly than copies, however accurate those copies might be. Natural things, he argued, are valued because they were created by natural processes rather than by human agency. This clearly assumes the distinction between nature and humanity which, it has been suggested many times, is central to a western understanding of the world.

But why should things produced specifically by natural processes, as distinct from human agency, be valued? The answer to this question forms the second part of Goodin's green theory of value, which he summarized in the following three points:

> (1) People want to see some sense and pattern to their lives. (2) That requires, in turn, that their lives be set in some larger context. (3) The products of natural processes, untouched as they are by human hands, provides [sic] precisely that desired context.
>
> (Goodin 1992: 37)

The first point, Goodin assumed, is indisputable; 'What makes people's lives seem valuable to those who are living them is the unity and coherence of the projects comprising them' (ibid.: 38). Like most anthropologists, I am wary of accepting such broad generalizations but would have to acknowledge that most, if not all, anthropological analysis is based on the assumption that people need order in their lives, that chaos is intolerable. The second point is also difficult to dispute. People consistently seek to understand things by setting them in context, by identifying their relations with other things. The reason why natural (or non-human) processes form an appropriate context is that 'People cannot set their lives in the context of something larger than themselves if that context is merely one which they have themselves created' (ibid.: 50). Insofar as people are seeking a context for their own individual lives, there are many products of human agency which perform this role: families and wider social groups, nations and other social institutions – I shall return to this point at the end of the chapter. But natural processes, as the only things that appear to be beyond human control and influence, form the only context in which human life in general can be set, and therefore constitute the widest possible context for the understanding of individual lives (see Milton 1999). 'They serve to fix our place in the external world. They help to "locate the self" in a deep psychological sense that matters enormously to people' (Goodin 1992: 39).

I am interested in the words Goodin used to describe this human need. We need to see 'sense and pattern', 'unity and coherence' in our lives. A word which might appear appropriate, but which Goodin specifically tried to avoid, is 'meaning'. He thought that to say that natural processes '"give meaning to our lives" would be to skate dangerously near thin theological ice' (Goodin 1992: 39). The implication that natural processes themselves have 'meaning' would, he feared, give environmentalist arguments spiritual connotations which he did not wish to give them. His reluctance to use the term 'meaning' is interesting for two reasons. First, though this was presumably not his intention, his green theory of value is an appropriate model for a general theory of religion (see Milton 1999: 446). The reasons he suggests for why some people value nature are the very reasons, according to some anthropologists, why people hold religious beliefs. People believe in the divine because it provides a context in which their own lives, and human life in general, can be seen as having sense and pattern, or, if you like, meaning.

Second, in order to see pattern in natural processes, it is not necessary to assume that they are products of spiritual forces or divine will. Scientists seek patterns in nature, which they refer to as 'laws', without needing to assume the existence of a divine lawmaker. As we have seen in Chapter 1, such an assumption would be regarded by some (for instance, Wolpert 1992) as incompatible with scientific principles. I assume that Goodin is reluctant to describe such patterns or laws as 'meaning' because he wishes to avoid any suggestion that divine will might be involved. But this belies an assumption that meaning is necessarily a property of mind, that, without thought and intention, meaning cannot exist. Some ecologists and anthropologists use a broader concept of meaning which, I shall suggest in the next section, is more appropriate to an understanding of how and why people value nature.

Goodin's perspective on the value of nature is very similar to those presented by McKibben (1990) and Evernden (1992). For Evernden, 'wildness' is nature's most important feature, because it cannot be encompassed by human horizons: 'Wildness . . . is the one thing that can never be ours. It is self-willed, independent, and indifferent to our dictates and judgements' (Evernden 1992: 120). McKibben also saw the perceived separateness or independence of nature from human agency as its most important feature. In modern western culture, nature is 'the separate and wild province, the world apart from man to which he adapted, under whose rules he was born and died' (McKibben 1990: 43–4). McKibben argued that we need to believe in wild, separate nature, to know that there are 'pristine places . . . substantially *unaltered* by man' (ibid.: 51, emphasis in original). For him, one of the major consequences of our understanding of the effects of human agency on the non-human world is the death of this belief in wild, independent nature. Because we now know that we are changing the Earth's climate through our actions, we can no longer believe there is anywhere on the planet that is beyond human influence. Consequently, 'We can no longer imagine that we are part of something larger than ourselves' (ibid.: 77).

McKibben described this as a change, not in nature itself, but in what nature and natural things mean to us. He thus placed at the centre of his own argument the concept that Goodin seemed anxious to avoid. The following quotations make the point most effectively:

> it isn't natural *beauty* that has ended; in fact . . . there may be new, unimagined beauties. What will change is the meaning that beauty carries.
>
> (McKibben 1990: 58, emphasis in original)

Yes, the wind still blows – but no longer from some other sphere, some
inhuman place . . . the *meaning* of the wind, the sun, the rain – of nature
– has already changed.

(Ibid.: 44, emphasis in original)

By changing the weather, we make every spot on earth man-made and
artificial. We have deprived nature of its independence, and that is
fatal to its meaning. Nature's independence *is* its meaning; without it
there is nothing but us.

(Ibid.: 54: emphasis in original)

Goodin fully acknowledged the similarities between his own and McKibben's
perspectives (Goodin 1992: 38–9). Indeed, I do not think he would object if we
were to replace McKibben's word 'meaning' with his own, 'value': 'We have
deprived nature of its independence, and that is fatal to its value. Nature's
independence *is* its value.' The difference in terminology appears to depend on the
fact that, while McKibben acknowledged a religious component in his own
understanding of nature (1990: 66ff.), Goodin explicitly sought to avoid such
connotations. I suggest that this difference is related to another more subtle, but
still detectable, divergence in the two perspectives. While Goodin favours the
language of mind and reason, McKibben appears more willing to refer to emotion
and feeling. For instance, Goodin presented a carefully reasoned argument to show
how his theory stands up to the view that humanity is a part of nature and not
separate from it (1992: 45ff.). McKibben's response to the same point was 'one can
argue this forever and still not really feel it. It is a debater's point, a semantic
argument' (1990: 60). I take this as a cue for the next stage in my argument, which
is that meaning can usefully be seen as operating through emotion.

Meaning and emotion

So far in this chapter I have suggested, following other authors (Munro 1997,
Nuckolls 1998), that to understand how value motivates people to action, we need
to examine its emotional power. I have also suggested that some of the work on
how environmentalists in western societies relate to nature and natural things
(McKibben 1990, Goodin 1992) seems to suggest a convergence between value and
meaning, that we can describe what nature means to us, and how we value it, in very
similar terms. But this latter point does not advance our understanding of the
emotional power of value as long as meaning is understood to depend solely on mind
and reason. The suggestion that meaning can operate independently of mental
processes is implied by Hornborg's argument, based in turn on the work of von
Uexküll, that ecological relations in general, the relations between organisms and
the various parts of their environment, are based on meaning (Hornborg 1996).

Hornborg criticized Rappaport's distinction between ecosystems and cultural
systems. Rappaport argued that, while ecosystems work through the transfer of

energy and materials, cultural systems depend on the communication of meaning through symbols (Rappaport 1979: 57–8). A different understanding of ecological relations was suggested by Jakob von Uexküll who, in his 'theory of meaning' (1982), argued that all organisms respond to signs in their environment. For instance, the metabolism of foliage plants responds to changes in the levels of sunlight falling on their leaves. Diurnal animals respond to increasing darkness by preparing to sleep, a predator responds to the sight or sound of its prey by preparing to attack, and potential prey respond to the signs that a predator is near by preparing to flee, or freeze, or otherwise defend themselves. In other words, an organism lives by picking up meanings from its environment. These meanings and the things that convey them constitute what von Uexküll called the *Umwelt* or 'subjective universe' of an organism (von Uexküll, J. 1982, see also Ingold 1992). Von Uexküll's theory thus leads us to see ecological systems, as well as cultural systems, as dependent on the communication of meaning.[5]

Von Uexküll's theory of meaning might appear superficially similar to Neisser's understanding of perception, discussed in Chapter 3. According to Neisser (1976), the perceiving individual picks up whatever information their anticipations have prepared them to receive; in other words, they pick up *meaningful* information, that which is significant in terms of what they expect. Von Uexküll used the term 'perception' (*Merken*) to describe how organisms respond to signs. But since he argued that all organisms live by perceiving meaning in their surroundings, it is clear that, for him, this is not necessarily a mental process (though it involves mental processes in those animals equipped with them). Neisser argued that perception is, at least partly, a mental activity (see Chapter 3), and because he was concerned with *human* perception, its dependence on mind was not problematic.

Von Uexküll's model places meaning at the centre of the relationship between an organism and its environment, and, therefore, at the centre of the process through which organisms and environments evolve in relation to each other. Damasio, whose work has been discussed in Chapters 4 and 5, suggested that emotions have played an important role in biological evolution. Remember that, according to Damasio, emotions are not feelings, but changes that take place in the body in response to some stimulus. All emotions, he stated, 'have some kind of regulatory role to play, leading in one way or another to the creation of circumstances advantageous to the organism exhibiting the phenomenon . . . their role is to assist the organism in maintaining life' (1999: 51). The most obvious example is fear, or rather the bodily changes which (in some animals) precede a feeling of fear, which prepare an organism to respond to danger. Placing Damasio's ideas about emotion alongside von Uexküll's theory of meaning leads to the suggestion that emotions are responses to meanings in the environment; they prepare an organism to act appropriately (for its own survival) on the meanings it perceives.

According to Damasio, we cannot say that emotions play this role for all organisms, for emotions have evolved only in some organisms; others regulate their lives through simpler responses, such as reflexes (1999: 55). It is also an important part of his argument, as we have already seen (in Chapter 5), that emotions are often induced unconsciously. In those animals equipped to perceive their emotions, they generate feelings, and in those animals like ourselves, which are equipped to perceive their feelings, they generate consciousness. None of this depends on reasoned thought (though reasoned thought can be involved in inducing emotions – see below). It is a perceptual process, the picking up of information, or meaning, from our surroundings and from our own bodies. It involves mental activity, insofar as we anticipate what we perceive (Neisser 1976), but it does not depend on reason.

A more or less complete argument may now be outlined. As we engage with our environment we perceive meanings in it; this is how it becomes known to us. It is the meanings which give things their value. In other words, we value things by perceiving meanings in them. These meanings become known to us through the emotions they induce, which we then experience as feelings. In other words, meanings literally 'make themselves felt', and in doing so they make themselves known. Thus the process of valuing things in the world is inseparable from the emotions and feelings they induce in us; without these emotions and feelings there would be no value.

As an example, take the case of a beautiful landscape, a landscape which, we would say, is valued for its beauty (regardless of what else it might be valued for). The only way in which we become aware of its beauty is through its emotional impact on us, because it gives us pleasure to see it. If it ceases to have this effect on us, we cease to value it in this way. The process is the same whether we are talking about things that seem to have a direct emotional appeal (like beauty) or about things presented in the form of reasoned arguments. As McKibben implied (see above), arguments will only have force if we feel them. An argument only motivates when it induces feelings – satisfaction, pleasure, excitement, interest, anger, distress. If it generates no feelings at all, it will not persuade. It is important to stress this, in case it is assumed that I see reasoned arguments as irrelevant to motivation. Clearly they must be relevant; otherwise, as I pointed out above, campaigners for various causes, including nature protection, would not use them. But arguments motivate in the same way as other things motivate. Like the sight of a beautiful landscape, or a child or animal in distress, they motivate by inducing emotions which generate feelings. Without grasping this, we cannot understand how or why arguments persuade or fail to do so.

One further point needs to be clarified here. It might be thought that, in setting emotions in an evolutionary context, I am using a crude, biologically deterministic approach to understand what anthropologists think of as cultural phenomena – how we feel about, and therefore value, particular things in our environment. This is, emphatically, not what I intend, and I hope that my views on this kind of approach have been conveyed clearly enough in earlier chapters. But I am assuming that some consideration of how our minds/bodies work can help us to understand how we experience our relationships with our surroundings. If, as Damasio argued, emotions can be induced unconsciously, this must have a bearing on how I, as an anthropologist, understand their role in human lives. I have no problem with the idea of 'biological machinery' for processing emotions, just as I have no problem with the idea that there are 'basic emotions' common to all normal human beings (see Chapter 4). But I assume no evolutionary 'fixing' of the things that induce emotions, or of the ways in which emotions are understood by those who experience them. All this, I assume, emerges out of personal experience in the way I have tried to describe in Chapter 4.

Emotion and the sacred

The question of why some people value nature and natural things more highly than do others often leads, in environmental discourse, to observations about sacredness. In particular, the difference between the way in which modern western societies treat nature, and its treatment by indigenous and traditional societies, is often said to hinge on the quality of sacredness. In western societies, natural things, like land and trees, it is suggested, are seen primarily as resources for human use. They can be bought and sold, and so are subject to control by particular owners. In indigenous and traditional cultures, it is often observed, natural things are rarely the property of any individual, but are available to the whole community and are sustained through conventions which accord them respect. Among these conventions is the understanding that nature is sacred (Posey 1998). But what is this quality of sacredness and where does it come from? If sacredness gives things value then, according to the argument presented above, it must have an emotional basis which needs to be fully acknowledged if it is to be a useful tool in helping us to understand how and why people value nature and other things. In this section I examine several understandings of sacredness, and suggest one which makes its emotional basis explicit.

Sacredness has been understood by anthropologists in many ways.[6] Posey appears to equate it, more or less, with spirituality. Indigenous and traditional peoples, he suggested, generally view knowledge about the environment as 'emanating from a spiritual base':

> In indigenous and local cultures, experts exist who are peculiarly aware of nature's organizing principles, sometimes described as entities, spirits or natural laws. Thus, knowledge of the environment depends on the relationship not only between humans and nature, but also between the visible world and the spirit world.
>
> (Posey 1998: 93)

A sacred landscape is thus an enspirited landscape, one that is inhabited by spirits or bears the imprint of their activities. There are many descriptions of such landscapes in the ethnographic literature. Australian Aborigines read the 'story lines' left on the land by the creative journeys of ancestral beings (see Munn 1973, Strang 1997). In some indigenous cultures of North America, everything that has power was assumed to have spirit, and power was perceived in anything that moves or changes – the sun and moon that cross the sky, the water that flows, the rocks that decompose into soil, the animals and plants that move and grow (Callicott 1982). An enspirited environment is, in effect, one occupied by 'persons' or intentional beings (as discussed in previous chapters), with which ecological relationships take place within a 'subject–subject' frame (Bird-David 1993: 121). So, for instance, hunted animals are persuaded to give themselves as food, or sometimes tricked into doing so, and are thanked with ritual offerings to ensure that their generosity will continue (Tanner 1979).

The difficulty with tying sacredness to the spiritual is that it depends on a distinction that often appears to sit very uneasily on the cultures being described: that between the spiritual and the physical or mundane worlds. There has always been some confusion over whether vernacular labels for natural forces can be translated as 'spirit' (see Abram 1997: 13). As Strang pointed out in her analysis of environmental values in North Queensland, 'Aboriginal cosmology is both practical and spiritual – there is no division between sacred and secular or between spiritual beliefs and the laws governing everyday life' (Strang 1997: 238). If there truly is no division in the understanding of those who hold such cosmologies, then the suggestion that they somehow combine or integrate the spiritual and the physical is a distortion imposed by a language which happens to have difficulty describing an undifferentiated world. Some anthropologists have tried to avoid this difficulty by referring to the visible and invisible worlds rather than the spiritual and physical worlds (for instance, Dwyer 1996). But this simply imposes another distinction which, though valid in some cultures, is unlikely to stand the test of generalization, and raises the question of why vision should be privileged above the other senses (see Ingold 2000a: 243ff.).

A particularly rich source of ideas about sacredness is provided by the work of Gregory Bateson, which contains more of a commentary on the sacred than a clear formulation. His primary understanding of sacredness, and one which reflects how the concept is used in several religious traditions, is in terms of 'wholeness' or 'unity', which is recognized by perceiving the relationships among things (Bateson 1991: 267). He used the example of the hand to illustrate this point, suggesting that a hand is not composed of five digits, but of four relationships between digits. The sacredness or beauty of the hand – these two concepts are closely related in Bateson's work – is only recognized when it is seen as a totality of relationships (ibid.: 302, 310).

This description of sacredness appears to fit quite neatly the observed contrasts between indigenous views of nature and the prevailing western view. As we have seen in Chapter 3, 'personalized' understandings of nature, which have been identified many times by anthropologists, particularly in hunter-gatherer cultures, are linked to a focus on the relationships among natural things and people (Bird-David 1999). In her study of environmental values in North Queensland, Strang characterized Aboriginal interaction with the land as (among other things), 'Unboundaried, Connected/immediate, Holistic/integrated . . . Collective/ relational'. In contrast, interaction between white Australians and the land was 'Boundaried, Alienated/distanced, Specialized/fragmented . . . Individuated/

independent' (Strang 1997: 285). But this way of describing the sacred does not highlight its emotional basis. Bateson was offering a kind of epistemology (1991: 310), effectively a 'relational epistemology' (see Chapter 3), which implies a way of knowing rather than feeling, and, although I am confident that he would have seen the sacred as a unity between knowing and feeling, the language he used tends to perpetuate the distinction between them, and fails to make the emotional basis of sacredness explicit.

Bateson indicated a more promising path when he suggested that sacredness depends on non-communication, on things remaining hidden (Bateson and Bateson 1987: 80). He cited the example of a religious ceremony which, its participants agreed, would have been desacralized had they allowed it to be filmed (ibid.: 72–3). What the sacred needs to be hidden from, according to Bateson, is the rational, calculating, purpose-oriented mode of thought associated with the left hemisphere of the brain:

> one of the very curious things about the sacred is that it usually does not make sense to the left-hemisphere, prose type of thinking . . . Because it doesn't make any prose sense, the material of dream and poetry has to be more or less secret from the prose part of the mind.
>
> (Bateson 1991: 267)

Non-communication is important, he suggested, because 'communication would somehow alter the nature of the ideas' (Bateson and Bateson 1987: 80).[7] Although Bateson was still using words that suggested cognition rather than emotion, he clearly implied that the sacred is experienced through that part of the mind which is assumed to process emotional or affective responses. One of his illustrative examples is particularly helpful in developing this point.

To support his argument that the sacred depends on non-communication, Bateson used Coleridge's epic poem, *The Rime of the Ancient Mariner*. He focused on those lines that describe the turning point in the story. The Ancient Mariner, the sole survivor of the disasters which began with his killing of an albatross, is watching water snakes in the shadow of the ship. Unknowingly, he blesses them, and thus sets off a train of events that lead to his salvation. Bateson pointed out that it is essential, to the meaning of the story, that the Ancient Mariner did not know he was blessing the water snakes. Had he blessed them knowingly, purposefully, in order to save himself, his act would not have been sacred, and he would have remained in a state of despair. But how is it possible to bless something without knowing it? What Bateson did not draw attention to was the emotional quality of the Ancient Mariner's response to the water snakes, which is best illustrated by quoting the relevant verse (lines 282–7):[8]

> O happy living things! no tongue
> Their beauty might declare:
> A spring of love gush'd from my heart,

And I blessed them unaware:
Sure my kind saint took pity on me,
And I blessed them unaware.

The Ancient Mariner was able to bless the water snakes unknowingly because, in conventional dualist language, he blessed them with his heart and not with his head. He did not think the blessing, but felt it, as 'a spring of love'. In many non-western cultures, emotions and feelings are assumed to have direct effects in the world beyond the body/mind in which they are experienced. Many anthropologists who have conducted fieldwork in Africa, including myself, are familiar with the idea that, through feelings of anger or jealousy, one person can unknowingly cause harm to others (see, for instance, Evans-Pritchard 1936, Harris 1978). The Ancient Mariner blessed the water snakes in the same way; in poetry, as in traditional African cultures, emotions make things happen.

It is also the central tenet of this book that emotions make things happen, but in conventional western terms we do not expect this to take place without the conscious intervention of the bodies/minds experiencing those emotions. Bateson's description of the sacred as dependent on non-communication is a useful starting point from which to highlight its basis in emotion, but it cannot help us to understand how sacredness motivates people to do things like protect nature. For this, I suggest, we need a much simpler concept of sacredness which, as it happens, is also present in Bateson's work. At the end of one of his lectures, Bateson described what it meant to him to be a scientist. 'If you're seriously dedicated to anything,' he said, 'be it art, science, or whatever, that which you are dedicated to is going to be a pretty big component in what is sacred to you.' He went on to point out that 'What is not immediately knowable [most people] throw into the supernatural, or into guesswork, or into folklore'. But the scientist, he said, 'cannot allow himself to do this. We really believe that someday we shall know what all these things are about, and that they *can* be known. This is our sacred' (Bateson 1991: 270).

The meaning of sacredness implied here is simply that it describes what matters most to people. In everyday discourse we are very familiar with this use of the word. What is sacred to someone is simply what they value most highly, be it their mother's memory, their religious traditions, the mountain scenery near their home, or the football team they support. Sacredness in this sense does not depend on a holistic vision, on whether something is seen as a unified whole. Nor does it depend on the absence of communication between different kinds of experience. Quite the opposite, in fact, since if the things we hold sacred are to influence what we do, our experience of them must be translatable into purposive action. What this understanding of sacredness depends on very heavily is emotion and feeling. A scientist's commitment to the pursuit of knowledge, a fan's commitment to supporting their team – these are emotional responses, as are all commitments. It is also important to recognize that this understanding of sacredness encompasses all others rather than excluding them. An enspirited landscape will still be a sacred landscape as long as spirit is what makes things most meaningful to people, what induces their strongest emotional responses. Similarly, wholeness, beauty and mystery will form the basis of sacredness wherever these are the most valued, the most emotionally powerful qualities.

Defining the sacred in terms of what matters most to people brings us back to Goodin's point that, to be valuable to those living them, individual lives need sense and pattern, or, as I would prefer to say, meaning. It makes sense to expect that what matters most to people, in other words, what they hold sacred, will be precisely those things that give their lives sense, pattern and meaning. What I hope I have established is that people's responses to these things are emotional. If they were not, we could not say that such things are valued.

Sacredness, identity and self-realization

At the end of Chapter 5, I discussed how identification with nature and natural things contributes to a sense of personal identity, a sense of who and what we are. In so doing, it contributes to our 'self-realization', whatever cultural form that might take. Here I want to relate that discussion to the more general question of how we define ourselves through the perception of meaning in our relationships with our surroundings; in other words, as Goodin suggested, by setting our lives in context. By doing this I hope to show how the valuation, through emotional engagement, of nature and natural things, is related to the valuation of things in general. The work of Hornborg, who has considered the relations among meaning, identity and context in some detail, is particularly useful for this purpose. Hornborg explicitly linked a sense of personal identity to the perception of meaning which, in turn, 'has to do with a perception of order, intelligibility, and familiarity based on a relationship of compatibility between past and present experience'. Meaning, he argued, depends on 'experiences of recognition and reassurance'. The opposite of meaning is 'an experience of chaos or arbitrariness variously referred to as anomie, alienation, or anxiety' (Hornborg 1993: 133).

Like other theorists, Hornborg assumed that meaning emerges out of our engagement with the world around us, and he suggested that the quality of meaning, and therefore its ability to provide a secure sense of personal identity, depends on the kinds of reference points we use. He distinguished two kinds of reference points which guide the construction of personal identity in the contemporary world. One, which he referred to as 'local', consists of everyday personal relationships and immediate surroundings. 'Local' constructions of identity are grounded in 'tangible reference points (specific places, people, artefacts) from which they cannot be extricated' (Hornborg 1993: 131). A good example of locally grounded identity is described in the words of Ruth Lilongula, quoted at the end of Chapter 5 (Posey 1999: 162). Strang provides another example in her description of Aboriginal ties to the land of their ancestors in North Queensland:

> The attachment of specific groups to specific places is an immensely powerful basis for identity, because it is both immortal and unique,

based on reproducing an ancestral past. The communal nature of this identification with land creates an unparalleled collective sense of belonging. Thus, for Aboriginal people, who they are and where they are 'from' are not divisible.

(Strang 1997: 159–60)

Personal identity can also be constructed, Hornborg suggested, in relation to 'global' reference points. Whereas local identity is grounded in tangible things that are tied to particular places, global identity depends on movable things (like money and material commodities) and 'conceptual abstractions' like occupation (Hornborg 1993: 131). He sees this polarity not as an 'either or dichotomy but as a divergence of inclination' (ibid.: 133), which some might recognize as 'running down the middle of their existence' (Hornborg 1994: 258). While some people undoubtedly define their identity primarily in relation to either local or global reference points (see Hannerz 1990), many depend on both – I am both a wife and an anthropologist, a neighbour and an academic – and can experience a conflict between the two, for instance, when the possibility of moving within a global job market threatens to sever local connections.

Hornborg argued that a movement from local to global identity involves a movement from 'concrete' to 'abstract' (1993: 131). It is thus symptomatic of the 'decontextualizing' process which, it has often been observed, characterizes the condition of modernity (cf. Giddens 1990). What is meant by this is not always clear, so it is worth trying to clarify it here. Science and general-purpose money are taken to be the main decontextualizing influences in modernization. Science decontextualizes by producing knowledge that is assumed to be valid everywhere. In traditional or 'pre-modern' cultures, knowledge is gained by living in a local community and learning from others and through direct engagement with the local non-human environment. The knowledge gained is appropriate for living in that particular place. Scientific knowledge is learned outside the local community, in purpose-built institutions (schools and colleges), and is deemed to be universally valid. As more scientific knowledge is generated, it encourages greater specialization, so that, 'as we come to know more and more about ever more limited domains, the domains themselves become ever more isolated, and ever less meaningful to whatever lies outside of them' (Rappaport 1979: 130), including, of course, the everyday local contexts in which people live. Rappaport pointed out, as others have done (for instance, Shiva 1993), that the supposed universal validity of scientific knowledge degrades local knowledge, turning it into belief or superstition (Rappaport 1979: 130).

General-purpose money decontextualizes by making anything exchangeable for anything else: 'If it weren't for general-purpose money, nobody would be able to trade tracts of rainforest for Coca-Cola' (Hornborg 1998: 5). General-purpose money has been assumed to enable an accurate comparison of values, thus making it easy to bring all kinds of 'goods' into the process of economic planning; hence the move, in the late 1980s and early 1990s, to attribute monetary values to all kinds of environmental benefits, such as clean air, attractive scenery and wildlife habitats (see Pearce *et al.* 1989, Pearce 1991, 1994). Rappaport pointed out that this assumption is illusory. Instead of making all valued things comparable, all-purpose money 'renders the distinctions among them irrelevant, which is to say meaningless, from the beginning. The application of a common monetary metric to dissimilar things reduces their *qualitative distinctiveness* to the status of mere *quantitative difference*' (Rappaport 1979: 130, emphasis in original). In other words, money removes 'value' from the process of valuing, from the emotional encounters in which meanings make themselves felt.

Hornborg's summary of the polarity between local and global points of reference for personal identity is shown in Figure 6.1. If meaning depends on context, then it makes sense to suggest, as Rappaport and Hornborg have done, that decontextualization diminishes or destroys meaning. This leads to the judgement that the local provides a secure sense of personal identity, while the global provides alienation and anxiety. Interestingly, Hornborg expressed this judgement with reference to sacredness. He acknowledged that 'the Sacred, the ultimate, the irreducible' is, like money, an abstraction, but one that is 'rooted or embedded in local resonance', whereas money, which, like science, is 'disembedded abstraction', destroys sacredness by making everything reducible (Hornborg 1998: 5). This implies that it is possible to experience sacredness only in local contexts, where personal identity is defined in terms of local associations, and not in a global arena, where it depends on mobile and abstract criteria.

I am going to suggest that this polarization is misleading, and so is not a sound interpretation of how and why people value things as they do. I accept that meaning depends on context, and that people can only develop a sense of personal identity through an experience of context, so it is extremely important, if we want to understand this process, how we identify that context. I do not believe this is something on which an observing anthropologist should arbitrate. It is up to the people whose lives we are intent on understanding to define for themselves, and therefore for us, the context in which their lives are meaningful. It is not a question of whether *we* think that global reference points are an impoverished source of

	'Local'/Irreplaceable	*'Global'/Abstract*
Space	Specific community Natural landscape	Mobility Urbanism
Relationships	Kin Neighbours	Colleagues Peers
Objects	Handicrafts Heirlooms	Consumption goods

Figure 6.1 Local and global reference points for identity
Source: From Hornborg (1993: 133)

meaning, but whether the people we are studying find them so. Hornborg clearly thought that they do:

> The contemporary pursuit of historical, genealogical, and ethnic 'roots', 'primitivism' . . . and the nostalgia for 'nameable places' . . . are only the most explicit of the myriad indications that the exchange of a 'local' for a 'global' identity leaves many people unsatisfied.
>
> (Hornborg 1993: 131)

But there are also indications that many find the global more attractive than the local. Throughout the world, rural communities have declined and urban areas have expanded as people have sought to exchange local subsistence for paid employment. Many people actively pursue careers that enable them to develop associations with distant people and places (see Hannerz 1990), and which give them status in global arenas such as business and academia. Interaction through the internet, currently the most extreme expression of disembedded sociality, continues to grow at a phenomenal rate. My point is not that Hornborg is wrong to suggest that many people find global identity less satisfying than local identity, but that it is not a realistic generalization about western society. The markers of global identity – mobility, consumption goods and relationships with peers and colleagues (and, one could add, the pursuit of knowledge through science) – are precisely what makes many lives meaningful, they are what matters most, what is most sacred, most emotionally compelling, to many people in the contemporary world. Modernity has not 'selected for money and science, at the expense of the Sacred' (Hornborg 1998: 5), it has made money and science sacred (cf. Rappaport 1979: 167).

Another way of making this point is to ask whether it really makes sense to argue, as Hornborg, Rappaport and others have done, that modernizing processes 'decontextualize'. I suggest that it makes more sense to say that modernizing processes have created new contexts in which meaning is perceived, new inducers of emotion and feeling, new paths to self-realization. For those participants in environmental discourse who, like Hornborg, Rappaport, Shiva and, indeed, myself (see Milton 1996), believe that 'localism' offers a better chance of ecologically sustainable living than 'globalism', the attractiveness of the global arena is the major obstacle. It is precisely because the global arena is so enticing, so emotionally compelling to many people, as a context for self-realization, that the prospects of a return to local points of reference look so bleak. And, of course, the liberal, democratic cultures in which many westerners live encourage a globalist perspective.

In this chapter, I have tried to answer the question of why some people value nature and natural things by considering why people value things in general. To summarize, anything has the potential to be valued, to induce emotions which generate feelings which motivate action. And anything has the potential to become sacred, to become what matters most. What each individual comes to value most will depend on the context in which they learn about the world, the kinds of personal experiences they have, the ways in which they engage with their fellow human beings and with their non-human surroundings. The process of living, and learning to live, in particular contexts provides each individual with the reference points for defining their own personal identity; it provides them with a mode of self-realization. Rather than dividing these reference points into 'local' and 'global', I see them as infinitely varied. Some individuals find self-realization in wealth or international recognition; some find it in their relationships with colleagues or peers; some find it in a particular style of music or dress, and some find it in encounters with nature. The things that matter most to people are, self-evidently, the things that make their lives most meaningful. What I have tried to argue in this chapter is that these are also, and inevitably, the things that induce their strongest emotions and feelings. A recognition of the fundamentally emotional character of all personal commitments is essential if we are to understand any public discourse, including that on nature protection. Only if we start from the understanding that people are all and always emotional beings can we make sense of the debates that develop around matters of personal and public interest.

In this and the previous two chapters, I have sought to describe how people's emotional attachments to nature and natural things (and, in passing, to things in general) arise and develop. In the final two chapters I shall describe how these emotional attachments find expression in debates and discourses about nature protection. This means a change in emphasis from theoretical discussion to ethnographic description. I shall consider how people seek to protect what they value most about nature and natural things, and describe how they are both constrained and enabled in their attempts by the social and cultural contexts in which they operate.

7

PROTECTING NATURE

Wildness, diversity and personhood

> Which is more important, her life or her skin? Look into her eyes and then decide.
>
> (Campaign leaflet opposing the trade in wildlife products)

At the FLON? conference, hosted by the Findhorn Foundation in Scotland in 1999 (see Chapter 5), some of the most memorable moments were provided by sequences of photographs which opened three of the plenary sessions. Projected on to a large screen and accompanied by haunting music, these photos portrayed, on three separate mornings, the conventionally recognized kingdoms of the natural world: minerals, plants and animals. On the first morning there were delicate rock strata, pristine sand-dunes, towering stacks of impossible shapes; on the second morning, tiny sculptural fungi, brilliant flowers, magnificent trees, and on the third, velvet-winged butterflies, a jewel-backed lizard, an elegant flamingo, a majestic lion.

These displays celebrated what western nature lovers appear to love most about nature and natural things, their most highly valued, most sacred qualities – their beauty, their diversity, their wildness or independence and, in the case of the animal sequence at least, their personhood. Undoubtedly, the audience's appreciation of these qualities was selected for by the photographer/compiler. There was no death or destruction, little sign of the pain and violence of nature. A very broad range of natural things was represented. Each image metonymically suggested the wider class to which its subject belonged; a single frond said 'ferns', and a single dolphin said 'cetaceans'. There was no sign of human activity, save the photographer's own framing influence. All these things were 'wild', had become what they were without human intervention. They were evidence of a world beyond our margins, something bigger than ourselves. Collectively they constituted a context in which our own lives, and the whole of human life, could find meaning.

The animal sequence invoked a tension between the sense of otherness, which was preserved by stopping short of a human representative, and feelings of closeness induced by person-based identification. The majority of images showed single animals, their individuality reflecting our own. In those that showed two or more – a young elephant and its mother, penguins greeting, butterflies mating – the intersubjectivity created by their interaction was self-evident. Some, in a semblance of responsive relatedness, seemed to look straight at us. In the final slide, we looked deep into the eyes, into the soul, of a mountain gorilla.

So far, in this book, I have focused on how and why nature protectionists in western society come to think and, in particular, to feel as they do about nature and natural things. In this chapter and the next I consider how they seek to protect nature, particularly its qualities of beauty, diversity, wildness and personhood. In the next chapter I shall also discuss attempts to protect the sacredness of nature. From a constructionist perspective these qualities are shared values, produced and continually reproduced in the very process of their protection. It is through the social practice of protecting, for instance, the diversity of nature, that this quality comes to be valued and its value is reinforced. I have no quarrel with this as an interpretation of part of what goes on, but the arguments presented in previous chapters have been intended to show that it is not the whole story. The ways in which nature and natural things are valued depend on their emotional impacts, on what they make people feel. And these impacts arise out of a complex developmental process which is unique to every individual and which is constituted partly through social experiences, but also through diverse other experiences of perceptual engagement with nature and natural things. In these two final chapters I extend this theme by describing the role of emotion, and of common western understandings of emotion, in the practice of nature protection.[1]

I shall consider, in particular, two conventional western ideas about emotion. One, to be addressed in Chapter 8, is the understanding that emotion is opposed to reason, that it hinders rational thought and decision making. The other is the more or less taken-for-granted assumption that emotions motivate. People are expected to act on their feelings, even if doing so is not always wise (given that feelings are thought to hinder reason). From this assumption follows another: that if you can influence what people feel you can also influence what they do. This is why, as mentioned in Chapter 4, nature conservationists want people to feel as they do about nature. In western liberal democracies, people expect to participate in political processes in various ways – by electing their representatives in government, by lobbying politicians, by exerting pressure through NGOs, by registering formal objections to proposed developments and by direct action. In such circumstances, when public power is perceived as a reality, campaigners put considerable effort into trying to shape people's emotional attachments. Later in this chapter I shall discuss some of the ways in which nature protectionists seek to influence how people feel about nature.

It is important to explain why I have chosen to focus on the four qualities identified above – the beauty, wildness/independence, diversity and personhood of nature and natural things. Nature protection is a complex endeavour, and this focus might seem to simplify and misrepresent it. The dilemma I face is one of moving from people's emotional attachments to their practical activities. Emotional attachments can remain unarticulated, but activities need to be targeted; purposes need to be identified, along with words for describing them and actions for bringing them about. In this process – the process through which feelings are acted upon – there is no way of telling how far what is said and done reflects people's emotional experiences. I can say that western nature lovers *appear* to value nature's beauty, wildness, diversity and personhood. But what this means is that the discourse about nature protection has tended to crystallize around these qualities, that these qualities are often and explicitly objectified in the efforts of nature protectionists. They are what emerges when feelings about nature are given a voice in public discourse; they are the moulds into which western culture pushes the expression of feelings about nature. But it is important to acknowledge, as well as recognizing the emotional basis of all action, that there may be a gap between people's emotional experience and the forms in which that experience is expressed, between what they feel and what they are constrained to say and do in particular contexts. This will be discussed more fully in Chapter 8, where I shall consider the constraints imposed by cultural convention and attempts to break out of those constraints.

Of the four qualities identified above, the protection of natural beauty will be discussed in Chapter 8. In this chapter, I shall focus mainly on the protection of diversity and personhood in nature. The discussion draws primarily on my experience, over the past fifteen years or so, of research on environmental issues in the UK. I make no claim that what I say is general to nature protection in western societies, though I expect, without having done systematic research, that some of it is. The relationship between diversity and personhood in the practice of nature protection is particularly interesting. It is often harmonious, in the sense that the efforts to protect nature's diversity support the protection of personhood, and vice versa. When this is so, nature protection organizations with different orientations can co-exist peacefully. But in some instances it is difficult to protect nature's diversity without violating personhood, or to protect the personhood of natural things without threatening nature's diversity. In such cases, quite bitter divisions can develop between nature protectionists. There is also a close relationship between the personhood of natural things and their independence, in the sense that the capacity to act as an autonomous agent is, as we have seen, one of the criteria of personhood. I shall begin by describing how nature protectionists seek to protect the wildness or independence of nature, since this is the most fundamentally problematic of the four qualities.

Protecting nature's independence

As we saw in Chapter 6, environmentalist writers such as McKibben (1990) and Evernden (1992) assert the importance of nature's independence or wildness, while theorists such as Goodin (1992) have sought to explain it. Perhaps more importantly, the everyday discourse of nature protection continually asserts the value of nature's wildness. In what is often described as its most common western understanding (see Chapter 1), the very concept of nature implies wildness; it is what distinguishes it from the human world (Soper 1995, Ellen 1996), and sets nature conservation apart from the conservation of human products, such as historic buildings or rare breeds of domestic animals (see Milton 1997). The essential wildness of natural things is embodied in the terms used to describe them (wildlife, wildfowl, wild birds, wildlands), and in the names of organizations dedicated to their protection (World Wildlife Fund, National Wildlife Federation, Wildfowl and Wetlands Trust, Irish Wildbird Conservancy, The Wildlands Project).

Not surprisingly, 'naturalness', in the sense of freedom from human influence, has often been an important criterion in the selection of nature reserves. Primary habitats, such as old-growth forests and uncut peatlands, tend to be valued more highly than habitats that have recovered after human interference (see Ratcliffe 1997). In addition, species that are indigenous to an area, or which colonize it without human assistance, are generally considered more important than those that have been deliberately or accidentally introduced by people. As Goodin observed (see Chapter 6), 'real' natural phenomena have authenticity in the same way that real works of art have authenticity, because of the history and process of their creation. In a discussion with nature conservationists, I suggested (rather mischievously) that the rare white-headed duck (see below) might be conserved by cloning rather than by eradicating the introduced species that threatened it. I was told that this would be like building a replica of a cathedral while allowing the original to be destroyed (see Milton 2000).

And yet the effort to protect nature's wildness is inherently contradictory, for if nature's independence of human activity has to be protected *through* human activity, it is immediately and unavoidably compromised. Conservationists, of course, have always been aware of this contradiction, and have sometimes tried to minimize the degree to which nature's wildness is compromised by their efforts. Two recent examples are the Wildlands Project in North America, and the Future Nature Project in the UK.

The Wildlands Project is a group of conservationists and biologists who aim to develop and implement a 'North American wilderness recovery strategy'. Working with local conservation groups, they help to develop proposals for each region, providing funding and expertise, encouraging research and generally promoting the kinds of activities that can help to realize their vision. This vision is expansive in two senses. First, they seek to establish a network of conservationists and other like-minded people across the whole continent, 'from Panama and the Caribbean to Alaska and Greenland, from the high peaks to the continental shelves'. Second, they envisage the restoration of wilderness on an enormous scale:

> we live for the day when Grizzlies in Chihuahua have an unbroken connection to Grizzlies in Alaska; when Gray Wolf populations are restored from Durango to Labrador; when vast unbroken forests and flowing plains again thrive and support pre-Colombian populations of plants and animals.[2]

One of the project's key concepts is 'rewilding', which 'emphasizes the restoration and protection of big wilderness and wide-ranging, large animals – particularly carnivores' (Soulé and Noss, n.d.). This is based on the understanding that large carnivores are often 'keystone species', whose removal seriously damages the operation of an ecosystem. By seeking to restore vast tracts of wilderness, they hope to create areas where natural processes can thrive without the need for management; 'we see wilderness as the home for unfettered life, free from human technological and industrial intervention'. Although none of this can be achieved without enormous initial human effort, the ultimate aim is to create enough space for nature to be itself.

The Future Nature Project, initiated by the British Association of Nature Conservationists (BANC) and funded by both statutory and non-governmental organizations, was set up to produce a new vision for nature conservation in the UK. Bill Adams, a geographer and writer on environmental and development issues, was commissioned to write a book describing this vision (Adams 1996), and an advisory committee, on which I served as a Northern Ireland representative, was established to steer the project and comment on drafts of the manuscript. The book's strongest message, and the one which seemed to strike readers who were knowledgeable about conservation as genuinely new in a UK context, lay in its recommendations for conserving nature's wildness.[3] Adams argued, along similar lines to Goodin (1992), Evernden (1992) and McKibben (1990), that people need the wildness or 'otherness' of nature, its 'capacity to stand outside human action and thought' (Adams 1996: 8), and established, early in the book, that 'the most important task for conservation is to address the wildness of nature' (Adams 1996: 9). The managerial approach of conservation agencies since the 1940s had failed to do this. Nature's wildness had been 'drained away through "wise management"' (Evernden, quoted in Adams 1996: 99). So much emphasis had been placed on preventing the extinction of species, and on designating and managing particular sites, that the capacity of nature to operate independently of human intervention had been stifled. A different approach was needed:

> For the wildness of nature we must have regard to natural processes and not simply the static notion of natural places. We need . . . not only to recreate nature in specific forms and places but also to conserve the capacity of nature to recreate itself.
>
> (Adams 1996: 163)

Examples of what Adams had in mind include allowing a coastal dune system to be eroded by the action of waves and wind, and protecting it only from large-scale human damage rather than trying to hold it static. Or restoring a river in such a way that it is permitted to erode its banks and transform its surroundings in ways that rivers always did before people tried to control them (Adams 1996: 166–7). The essential point is that what is being protected is not a particular place or a species or even a habitat, but a natural process.

Protecting diversity and personhood in nature

Of the four qualities identified above, it is nature's diversity that currently receives more attention, more funding and more official recognition than any other, not only in western countries but worldwide. Diversity in nature is usually taken to mean diversity in living nature,[4] and, since the late 1980s, has been commonly referred to as 'biodiversity' (Wilson 1988) or 'the variety of life' (HMSO 1995). Animals, plants and ecosystems thus become 'components' of biodiversity (as noted in Chapter 2). The protection of biodiversity is enshrined in national laws and in international agreements whose principal aim is to conserve particular species and their habitats.[5] In such official documents, biodiversity is described as a resource. The preamble to the UN Biodiversity Convention, for instance, establishes the responsibility of its signatory states for 'conserving their biological diversity and for using their biological resources in a sustainable manner'. It also lists the values of biodiversity as 'ecological, genetic, social, economic, scientific, educational, cultural, recreational and aesthetic' (Grubb et al. 1993: 76). All but the first of these seem to refer, unambiguously, to human interests – nature's diversity is a resource for us to use in our production of food and other essentials, in our creation of material wealth and our pursuit of health, knowledge and enjoyment. When natural things are valued as resources for human use, what matters most are their numbers, their distribution and their capacity to sustain themselves or to be sustained through human activity.

As we saw in Chapter 2, a different set of concerns arises when nature and natural things are understood as persons. To perceive something as a person, and to identify with it as such, is to see in it the qualities we associate with our own personhood: individuality, a capacity for autonomous action and emotional experience (feeling), a capacity for self-realization (see Chapter 5). There is no reason to suppose that person-based identification with non-human entities will necessarily generate sympathy for them, especially when they are assumed to cause harm (like foxes who steal chickens and spirits who cause damaging storms). But where there is concern for natural entities as persons, rather than as resources, it is for their individual well-being and their freedom to 'unfold in their own way' (Fox 1995). Thus the difference between thinking of nature and natural things as resources and thinking of them as non-human persons has tended to create a divergence of priorities within nature protection.

Before discussing this further, however, I want to highlight one context in which this divergence is not present, a sense in which the diversity, personhood and, indeed, the independence of nature can be said to converge in a single, coherent perspective. The UN Biodiversity Convention states that, as well as being a resource for human use, biodiversity also has ecological value (see above). This seems to suggest that biodiversity is a resource for nature itself, and reflects a view expressed by many of the nature protectionists whom I have met during my research. It is understood that biodiversity worldwide is decreasing as a result of human activities, and that by reducing biodiversity we are damaging nature's potential to recover from the effects of ecological change. The more diversity there is, the greater the chance that some life forms will be able to adapt to changing conditions, and that life itself will continue. In this way, the protection of biodiversity can be seen as safeguarding nature's long-term independence, which is also its autonomy, its capacity for self-realization; in other words, its personhood. As we have seen, Adams and others have argued that the way to protect nature's wildness or independence is to allow natural processes to flourish. Biodiversity is essential for the process of evolution to flourish, and, for some nature protectionists, not just deep ecologists but also those whose love of nature is linked to a passion for science, this is the most important reason for protecting it.

Many nature protectionists think of nature in general and natural processes as objects of concern, but for both conceptual and practical reasons their activities are focused on lower-order entities, such as habitats, species and individual organisms. It is the perceived personhood of non-human animals which I have found most often juxtaposed with the protection of biodiversity, and here the divergence of priorities noted above becomes relevant. Alongside laws and institutions which provide for the conservation of biodiversity, there are laws and institutions which provide for the protection of individual non-human animals. There is no clear division of labour, however; the relationship, in practice, between the protection of biodiversity and the protection of personhood is highly complex.

One reason for this is that personhood is, as we have seen, a complex phenomenon. At any one time it might be assumed to consist in a capacity for autonomous action (including a capacity to relate responsively to others), or in a capacity for emotional experience (feeling), or in a combination of these qualities. A concern for personhood might be expressed through defence of an individual's right to autonomy or through defence of their welfare. Of course, these converge insofar as a denial of autonomy can cause suffering and so threaten welfare, but they can also be distinct. There are many circumstances in which the welfare of an individual is protected by bringing them under control, and so denying their rights as an autonomous agent. This separation of rights and welfare as objects of concern has generated countless dilemmas in human society, from the treatment of mental illness to the management of international relations. It also complicates our relationships with non-human animals. Ingold (1994) argued that domestication marked an end to the understanding of animals as autonomous persons, typical of hunter-gatherer cultures, and turned them into objects of domination. But it could also be argued that domestication, by making non-human animals a continuous part of people's lives, made us more sensitive to their emotions and more concerned about their suffering; made them, perhaps, more like children (Feit 1991), also persons whose autonomy is curtailed.

In general, the practical measures involved in the protection of biodiversity tend to inhibit the autonomy of non-human animals, as well as of other natural things (plants, ecosystems, natural processes). There is no doubt that some animals benefit individually through such measures. If they belong to a rare species their welfare is paramount. Their breeding sites and wider habitats are protected, and they might be allowed to live their lives with no human interference except for occasional monitoring of their progress. But if they are particularly rare their autonomy might be severely curtailed; they might be captured and moved to a more secure location, or even taken permanently into captivity where their young can be reared in safety. Individuals unfortunate enough to have rare or endangered species among their prey, particularly if their own species is common, may have their autonomy and welfare threatened in the most draconian ways, by being excluded from parts of their habitat or by being killed.

What this means is that concern for biodiversity and concern for non-human animals as persons sometimes can, but often cannot, sit easily together in practice. This divergence of priorities produces, in many western countries and in the international arena, an approximate division of labour among nature-protection NGOs. For example, those operating within the UK fall into the following broad categories:

- Organizations concerned primarily with the protection of biodiversity. These include the World Wide Fund for Nature (WWF), the Royal Society for the Protection of Birds (RSPB), the Wildlife Trusts and the Wildfowl and Wetlands Trust (WWT).
- Organizations concerned with both the conservation of species (biodiversity) and the protection of individuals. These include the Born Free Foundation (BFF), and several organizations covering particular categories of animals, such as the Whale and Dolphin Conservation Society (WDCS), bat groups, badger groups, and so on.
- Organizations concerned primarily with the protection of non-human animals as persons (their rights and welfare). Of these, Care for the Wild aims to protect wild animals, while most others concern themselves with domestic and captive as well as wild animals. For this reason, only some of their activities fall into the category of nature protection. They include the International Fund for Animal Welfare (IFAW), the World Society for the Protection of Animals (WSPA), the Royal Society for the Prevention of Cruelty to Animals (RSPCA), Animal Aid and the Animal Liberation Front (ALF).

In the remainder of this chapter I consider how the relationship between biodiversity and the perceived personhood of non-human animals is played out in the practice of nature protection. As elsewhere in this book, I use the term 'conservation organizations' or simply 'conservationists' to refer to those engaged primarily in the protection of biodiversity. Those groups concerned with personhood I refer to as rights and/or welfare organizations. I use the term 'nature protectionists' for the broader category which includes both. I begin by showing how the perception of non-human animals as persons, and specifically people's tendency to identify with them, can support efforts to protect biodiversity. In this context there is a degree of continuity between the activities of conservation organizations and those of rights and welfare organizations. I then discuss cases in which there is a degree of conflict between the personhood of non-human animals and the protection of biodiversity. I show how, in both contexts, the organizations involved seek to mobilize public support by influencing how people feel.

Diversity and personhood in harmony

The fact that animals can and often do benefit individually from measures to protect biodiversity gives conservation organizations an important tool for eliciting public support. It means that they can draw on people's capacity to identify and sympathize with animals. I have often heard conservationists observe that, although bio-diversity encompasses all living things, certain flagship species bear the burden of public sympathy. This is partly a result of particular animal images being used as logos by the organizations that promote biodiversity conservation – a panda for WWF, a badger for the Wildlife Trusts, a lion for BFF. But the choice of such icons is, in any case, based on certain assumptions about identification with animals.

First, it is assumed that we identify more easily with animals closely related to ourselves – with chimpanzees, say, more easily than with other mammals, and with other mammals more easily than with birds, fish or insects. Second, it is assumed that we identify more easily with animals familiar to us, those which are part of our lives and part of our personal identity. This is what Fox (1995) referred to as 'personally based identification' (see Chapter 5). So most people in the UK will identify with a robin or a blackbird more easily than with a white-necked picathartes.[6] Third, it is assumed that we identify more easily with animals that have faces similar to our own, especially forward-facing eyes into which we can look directly, and childlike or 'neotenic' faces, such as that of an owl or a cat (Winter 1996: 198). The NGO Friends of the Earth made good use of this assumption in a 1999 campaign leaflet. On the front cover were four photographs arranged in a vertical sequence and showing, from the top, the eyes of an owl, of a tree frog, of a human child and of a tiger. The caption above read, 'Look forward to a better future'. Finally, a face which appears to express emotion, like the dolphin's smile, is assumed to be more easily identified with because it suggests an inner world of feeling. WWF's panda logo is particularly effective since the black patches around its eyes make it look sad, an appropriate way for an animal on the brink of extinction to feel. This is an example of what I have called 'person-based iden-tification' (see Chapter 5). Because we experience and express feelings, we assume that animals who appear to express feelings also experience them. And because feelings give us a sense of our own personhood, evidence of them induces the perception of personhood in others.

None of these assumptions makes allowances for personal tastes and experiences, for the kind of developmental process described in Chapter 4 which might lead people with similar backgrounds to identify with entirely different things. Nevertheless, they are the kinds of assumptions which, in my experience, underlie nature protectionists' decisions about the images they use to elicit public support. I have observed several discussions on this theme during my research. One in which

I participated in the 1980s, when I first began studying environmental issues in Northern Ireland, provides a good illustration of how decisions are reached.

An Irish stoat

The Ulster Wildlife Trust (UWT) was running a campaign to raise public aware-ness of the need to conserve local wildlife. An appropriate image was needed and it was quickly decided that a mammal would be the most effective icon for the reasons outlined above. But which mammal? The discussion was informed by the knowledge that Northern Ireland's economy is heavily rural, and that animals with which urban and suburban dwellers might identify, such as foxes, rabbits and squirrels, are regarded as pests by much of the rural population. Hedgehogs, though fairly popular, were not considered cuddly enough, and badgers and hares were already in use; an Irish hare was depicted on the UWT's own logo, and a badger was used by the Wildlife Trusts (then the Royal Society for Nature Conservation), the umbrella organization to which the UWT belongs. The campaign committee eventually settled on a stoat, which, with its forward-facing eyes, could be depicted looking appealingly straight out from the page. It was also a distinctively local animal, Irish stoats being different from those found in Great Britain.[7] The only problem was that it was unfamiliar. Stoats are not often seen, and at campaign events we were repeatedly asked what it was.

In this instance, any one of several species could have been selected. But what if nature protectionists need to generate public support for a particular kind of animal which is not easily identified with? One example was referred to in Chapter 2 (p. 29).

Transforming whales

When strict controls were imposed on commercial whaling in the 1970s, it was to conserve whale populations for future exploitation. But the opposition to whaling is now driven primarily by moral arguments (Payne 1995). In the meantime, many people in western countries have come to identify with whales as intelligent, sensitive beings, and to perceive them as non-human persons. But on the criteria suggested above (closeness, familiarity, expressive faces), both person-based and personally based identification with whales seems unlikely. In appearance they are more like huge fish than mammals, they live in an environment which many people fear, and, even today, relatively few westerners have seen a whale. The change in people's perceptions was brought about by groups such as Greenpeace and WDCS, who drew attention to their plight, and by biologists like Roger Payne, who studied whales and made them known to a non-specialist public. What turned whales from relatively unknown animals into persons were revelations about their complex family relationships, their intelligence and their systems of communication. In particular, the song of the humpback whale, known to science since the early 1970s (Payne and McVay 1971), caught the public imagination and its haunting sounds were incorporated into popular music and films. The transformation of whales exemplifies what nature protectionists generally hope will be achieved by educating people about nature, that knowledge and understanding will generate love.

Bats need friends

A second example comes from the UK in the late 1980s. Legislation introduced in 1981 had given bats stronger legal protection than most other animals, but their numbers continued to decline. This was partly because they often roost in the roofs of buildings, and so are vulnerable to deliberate eviction and to poisoning by chemicals used in timber treatment. Bats had a bad reputation. Their presence in the margins of people's homes gave them, like rats and mice, the status of vermin. They were also feared as creatures of the night, associated in folk-tales and classical literature with witches and vampires. Persuading people to identify and sympathize with bats would mean overturning these traditional views. A national campaign was launched in 1987 (designated 'National Bat Year') with the slogan 'Bats need friends'. This was an ingenious device, since it did not try to do what seemed impossible; it did not try to persuade people directly that bats are lovable. It used a less direct approach by invoking the desolate condition of friendlessness. In British culture, friendship is valued at least as highly as kinship. To be without friends is to be emotionally destitute, without hope, a condition which even those who have not experienced it can at least imagine and sympathize with. It is difficult to say how successful this campaign was, but since the late 1980s local bat groups have emerged throughout the UK, and bat conservation is now a well-established and popular part of the nature-protection scene.

What is missing from this analysis so far is any explicit reference to the individuality of personhood. As suggested at the beginning of this chapter, an image of a single animal is particularly effective in inducing person-based identification because the animal's individuality reflects our own. Identification with an object, like any act of perception, requires attention, and if there is more than one object our attention, and the emotional response induced by what we perceive, is divided. This is not usually acknowledged explicitly, but it is noticeable that most of the animal images used to promote nature protection depict single animals. The following examples show how the individuality of animals is used to induce particular emotional responses. The aim in some instances is to encourage personally based as well as person-based identification. Ways are found, not only of highlighting the personhood of the animals depicted, but also of drawing attention to or creating connections between these animals and their potential supporters and sympathizers.

'Look into her eyes . . .'

The quotation that opens this chapter comes from campaign literature, delivered to my house a few years ago, opposing the international trade in wildlife products such as skins, rhino horn, elephants' tusks and tiger bones. I do not know how widely it was distributed, but such campaigns are usually directed at members and known supporters of conservation NGOs. The words were superimposed on a photo of a lioness, whose face filled the page and whose eyes looked directly into the camera. The image was totally unambiguous. This particular lioness was appealing for help. In case there was any doubt, the words confirmed the message. 'Look into her eyes', then decide whether she should live or die, and whether you are willing, by supporting the campaign, to help her to live. It used the emotional power of eye contact, mentioned above, a power well documented in the literature on both western and non-western cultures. Eye contact is not always friendly, indeed it is often hostile, but it is always interpersonal. How many hunters have spared the life of an animal after it has looked directly into their eyes? And how much more likely is such an appeal to motivate people predisposed to feel sympathy for wildlife?

'A friend for life . . .'

For some years the RSPB has used a particular image to recruit new members during the winter months: photographs of a robin in the snow, feathers fluffed out against the cold. The accompanying words are: 'This winter make a friend for life . . . *by joining the RSPB*' (RSPB 1994, italics in original), and '*Help* save a life this winter . . .' (RSPB 2001a, italics in original). The pictures and the words reinforce each other in personalizing the message: make *a* friend, help save *a* life, *this* life, the one depicted here. The contract, should you choose to accept it, is not between you and an impersonal organization, but between you and this robin, and, by implication, the many other individual birds who need your help.

The idea of a robin as a friend resonates with the personal experience of many British suburban dwellers, the sector of the population from which conservation organizations expect to draw much of their support. Robins are not just familiar garden birds, they are particularly confiding birds who make the most of human contact, sometimes feeding from a hand, often watching from nearby as a gardener turns the soil and exposes morsels of food. Robins thus play a role in human personal histories and in the construction of British cultural identity. We identify with them, not only on the basis of a perceived common personhood (person-based identification), but also because they 'belong' to us (personally based identification), they have helped to make us what we are, a so-called nation of nature lovers. It is an additional advantage, for those who seek to draw on their emotional power, that they have become symbols of Christmas, a time for giving.

'Give him a home'

A new nature conservation organization, the Waterways Trust, was launched in the UK in 1999 with the objective of protecting and restoring the wildlife habitats along canals and rivers. The front of their recruitment leaflet shows a photograph of a water vole, facing the camera and nibbling a leaf, accompanied by the words,

'Your gift helps give him a home'. Three devices are used here to induce person-based identification. First, as in the examples given above, the photograph is of an individual animal. Had there been two, our sympathy would have been divided, more and it would have been dissipated; a single individual concentrates feeling. Second, the use of the gendered pronoun further personalizes the animal. This is not just any water vole, it is a male water vole, whose personal life is shaped by the demands of maleness. Third, there is the use of the word 'gift'. Donations are given to organizations, but gifts are given to persons, often on culturally defined occasions such as Christmas and birthdays, but also out of sheer love.

Personally based identification also plays a role in this message. Unlike robins, living water voles are unfamiliar to most people in the UK, but like robins they hold a special place in British culture, having been immortalized in Kenneth Grahame's book, *The wind in the willows* (Grahame 1936 [1908]). Many who are now middle-aged and affluent probably think of this book as a formative influence, something that helped shape their feelings about nature. For such people, the second page of the Waterways Trust leaflet contains a particularly violent tug on the heart strings: 'Imagine telling our grandchildren that the loveable Ratty from *The Wind in the Willows* is extinct.'

Adopt a duck, sponsor a swan

One of the main ways in which nature protection organizations seek to personalize the relationship between potential supporters and the objects of their concern is through adoption schemes. For many years, the Wildfowl and Wetlands Trust (WWT) in the UK has offered sponsorship of ducks, barnacle geese and whooper and Bewick's swans as a way of supporting the work of the Trust. As part of the organization's population monitoring activities, wild birds are caught and given leg rings (bands), each with a personal code which can be read from a distance, enabling them to be identified in the field. Each sponsor, in return for an annual subscription, is allocated an individual bird and kept informed of its whereabouts, family history, and so on. An enthusiastic sponsor can build up quite a detailed picture of their bird's life, its migratory journeys, its mates, its offspring, and its eventual death or disappearance. When my swan died some years ago, the Trust sent me a brief letter of condolence.

There are now many similar schemes run by conservation groups, wildlife welfare organizations and those operating in both of these fields. They vary in detail but follow the same general pattern. Individual animals, some living in the wild and some in sanctuaries or animal orphanages, are offered for adoption, sponsorship or fostering (various terms are used). In most cases, the animals are individually named and sponsors receive information about their animal, sometimes with a photograph and an adoption certificate. The rise in popularity of adoption schemes in the UK can be monitored by dating the appearance of advertisements in *BBC Wildlife Magazine*, one of the country's most popular monthly publications for nature lovers. WDCS' orca adoption scheme was the first to appear in 1992. In the following year they offered dolphins as well as orcas, the International Wildlife Coalition offered adoption of humpback whales, and Care for the Wild offered fostering of mountain gorillas, elephants and rhinos. In 1997, the November issue carried adoption advertisements from eight organizations, and the animals offered included whales, dolphins, tigers, gorillas, otters, rhinos, wolves and ducks. Since then, the number of adoption advertisements has declined, with only one appearing in the November 2000 issue, probably because nature-protection organizations are choosing the cheaper option of advertising through the internet. In March 2001, at least five of the eight NGOs that had offered adoption schemes through BBC Wildlife Magazine in November 1997 were still offering them through their own websites.[8]

The personalizing impact of these schemes is all the more striking when we compare them with child sponsorship, offered by organizations (such as World Vision) seeking to alleviate poverty in developing countries. In both, concern is channelled and intensified by person-based and personally based identification. In the case of child sponsorship, the personal connection created can be actively maintained on both sides; the publicity material for such schemes often describes the satisfaction of receiving a letter from a sponsored child. In an attempted simulation of this effect, 'adoptive parents' who join the scheme operated by Bat Conservation International, based in Texas, are sent 'an endearing letter' from their bat.

Diversity and personhood in conflict

Biodiversity conservation is, as we know, about sustaining the widest possible variety of living things – protecting rare and vulnerable organisms and their habitats, trying to prevent extinction. Although conservation organizations can use the personhood of non-human animals to win public support for their work, they must, to be true to their objectives, give priority to the numbers and distribution of species and subspecies of animals rather than to their personhood. This means that the divergence between concern for diversity and concern for personhood can emerge as a conflict between what conservation organizations appear to do in their campaigns – that is, care about individuals – and what they actually do in practice – try to maintain numbers and distribution. Managing this conflict is a delicate public relations exercise.

For example, people who find injured birds or abandoned fledglings often call the RSPB for advice on how to care for them. Each time, the RSPB staff have to explain that they are not a welfare organization and direct the caller to their local branch of the RSPCA or, if there is one, a wildlife hospital in their area. However sensitively this is done, it exposes a gap between the organization's real concerns and some people's expectations of them, expectations which are created or reinforced every time they see the photo of the robin in the snow and are asked to 'Help save a life . . .' or 'Make a friend . . .'. This gap can generate criticism and turn people away. I have occasionally heard the RSPB criticized for not helping with the care of oiled birds, when it is the pictures of those birds, broadcast on national news bulletins after every major oil spill, that help to win them public support.

Tension between concerns about diversity and concerns about personhood are potentially most acute in debates over the conflicting interests of non-human animals. Self-evidently, non-human animals (like human ones) routinely impinge on the interests of others. Predators cannot survive without denying life to others, and there is constant competition for food, mates and living space. An essential difference between the conservation (biodiversity) perspective and the rights and welfare (personhood) perspective is that, while those concerned about rights and welfare generally consider all lives to be equally valuable (since it is the value of an animal's life to itself that matters), conservationists are obliged to value some individual animals (those belonging to rare or endangered species) more than others. This means that conservationists often have to take sides; they have to protect the interests of some animals against the interests of others. This can generate some awkward situations in which decisions about how to solve particular conservation problems are governed partly by the wish not to generate public anger. The RSPB has had to deal with the following issues which illustrate this point.

Peregrines and terns

In Wales, from the late 1970s, roseate terns, a very rare breeding bird in the UK, were being hunted from above by peregrines. Although, by this time, peregrines were much more numerous than roseate terns, their numbers had only recently recovered from the serious effects of pesticide poisoning in the 1950s and early 1960s. In addition, birds of prey in general are vulnerable to persecution and some are seriously endangered. The RSPB has put a lot of effort into persuading the public to value them. The problem in Wales was one of how to protect a rare species without seeming to persecute another highly valued species; how to protect the terns without seeming to turn against peregrines and undermining their own efforts to improve the popularity of birds of prey. Several possible solutions, including artificially feeding the peregrines, moving their nest sites and scaring them away from the tern colony, either failed or were ruled out. Eventually, from 1988, the terns were provided with artificial nest sites which hide them from the peregrines' view (Batten et al. 1990: 211).

Hedgehogs in the Hebrides

The Outer Hebrides off the west coast of Scotland are important breeding areas for wading birds, partly because there are few native species which prey on them. In the 1970s, however, hedgehogs, which are native to mainland Britain but not to the Scottish islands, were introduced. Seven animals were originally released on the island of South Uist, and, by the late 1990s, they had spread across causeways to neighbouring islands and their numbers had increased to an estimated 5000. Their impact on the numbers of wading birds, particularly dunlin, redshank and snipe, has been considerable. The population of dunlin, for example, declined by 63 per cent from the mid-1980s to the mid-1990s. A Wader Recovery Project has been set up by the RSPB and the statutory conservation authorities in Scotland to address the problem.

Hedgehogs are relatively common in much of the UK and are popular with suburban gardeners, some of whom put out food for them, because they eat animals regarded as pests. They also have a place in British culture as characters in children's stories, the most well known being Beatrix Potter's Mrs Tiggywinkle. Hedgehogs have also been the object of campaigns by animal welfare organizations, mainly because they are often killed or injured on the roads. It is assumed that lethal control of hedgehog numbers in the Hebrides would be highly unpopular if not publicly unacceptable; as one conservationist put it, 'We are not about to start killing Mrs Tiggywinkle.' The RSPB are conducting research to test other ways of protecting the birds. They reported in a recent issue of *Birds* magazine (RSPB 2001b) that possible solutions include fencing and moving hedgehogs to the mainland.

These two cases are relatively straightforward clashes of interest between members of different species. The following is a much more complex case which has aroused a lot of public attention in the UK over the past decade.

Ruddy ducks and white-headed ducks

Since the early 1990s, several conservation organizations have been engaged in a campaign to reduce significantly, and possibly eradicate, the ruddy duck population in the UK. Ruddy ducks are native to North America, where they are relatively common (see UK Ruddy Duck Working Group 1995: 2), and were introduced into wildfowl collections in Britain in the late 1940s. Some escaped and bred, and the wild population in the UK is now thought to be around 4000. From Britain, ruddy ducks spread across Europe into Spain, where they bred with native white-headed ducks; the first hybrid was seen in 1991 (Stiles 1993). Hybridization is considered a problem by conservationists because it can cause one or other of the parent species to lose its genetic distinctiveness and become, effectively, extinct in its original form. The number of white-headed ducks in Spain had been reduced, by hunting and habitat destruction, to just twenty-two birds by 1977, but the efforts of Spanish conservationists had restored the population to 800 by 1993 and to over 1000 by 1997 (Hughes 1993, Hughes and Williams 1997). Because Britain was assumed to be the source of ruddy ducks in Europe, pressure was exerted on the UK government to address the problem. A working group was set up in 1992, with representation from both statutory and non-governmental conservation organizations. Research was conducted on methods of controlling the ruddy duck population, and shooting during the breeding season was found to be the most effective method. Trial culls were planned, but, ostensibly for financial reasons, only started in 1999, following further pressure from other European countries (Birdlife International 1997).

Conflicts between members of different species often involve death, or at least severe disadvantage, for individuals; the members of one species kill and eat members of another or compete with them for food or habitat. In such cases, arguments about rights and welfare are more or less equally applicable to both sides, making it difficult for people concerned about such issues to protest without appearing inconsistent. If anyone suggests that the rights and welfare of hedgehogs in the Hebrides are violated by the campaign to remove them, it can be argued that the hedgehogs are themselves violating the rights and welfare of the birds whose eggs they eat. Hybridization is a very different kind of inter-species relationship, one which does not involve the destruction of individuals. So when it is suggested that members of one species be killed in order to prevent hybridization, the arguments against this, from a rights and welfare perspective, are relatively clear. The conservationists' campaign against ruddy ducks generated considerable opposition from organizations and individuals concerned about the personal rights and welfare of animals.

Those NGOs supporting a cull of ruddy ducks include the RSPB and the Wildfowl and Wetlands Trust (WWT), both of which are membership-based organizations sensitive to public opinion. They also, as we have seen, routinely use campaigning mechanisms which personalize birds. The WWT has, for many years, been encouraging members of the public to support their work by adopting ducks. The ruddy duck debate has given both them and the RSPB the uncomfortable task of asking people to accept that ducks should be killed in the interests of what is, for them, a greater good, the conservation of biodiversity. Opposition to the cull has come mainly from Animal Aid and, to a lesser extent, from the League Against Cruel Sports (LACS), with prominent individual writers occasionally taking a critical stance (for instance, Vidal 1993, Lawson 1996, 1999). Elsewhere (Milton 2000) I have discussed what the ruddy duck debate can teach us about how conservationists think about nature. Here I am concerned with how the protagonists tried to influence the feelings of the British public. Information on the conservationists' approach comes from published comments and articles (Hughes 1993, Stiles 1993, Hughes and Williams 1997), media interviews and personal conversations and correspondence. Information on the opposition to the cull comes mainly from published articles (Lawson (1996) and press reports) and from Animal Aid's website (www.animalaid.org.uk), which gives details of their press releases and other statements from May 1997 to August 1999.

Conservationists sought to forestall public anger at their support of the ruddy duck cull in the following ways:

- They stressed the vulnerability of the white-headed duck, as a globally threatened species with a total population which could be as low as 5000 (Hughes and Williams 1997: 15).
- They stressed that conservation of the white-headed duck is an international obligation under various agreements to which the UK is a party, and that control of the ruddy duck population is necessary for this purpose.
- They stressed that the decision to cull ruddy ducks was based on sound science. This included an understanding of the consequences of hybridization and the

systematic testing of methods of population control (UK Ruddy Duck Working Group 1995: 7–8).

- While supporting the cull, they expressed regret that it was necessary (*Daily Telegraph*, 29 June 1995).
- They drew attention to the enormous effort that had been made to save the white-headed duck in Spain, and to the human distress that would result if this effort were wasted. Thus they invoked feelings, not for ducks, but for fellow human beings: 'Imagine how we would feel . . . if a species we had saved from extinction in Britain became threatened by the arrival of a species from another country which was not even native to that country' (Stiles and Delany 1993).
- Sales items depicting ruddy ducks were removed from shops run by the conservation NGOs, in order to avoid actively encouraging their popularity.

The opposition to the cull, led by Animal Aid, sought to induce public sympathy for ruddy ducks, and public anger at the conservation organizations, in the following ways:

- They engaged in acts of 'eco-drama' (Harries-Jones 1993) to draw attention to their case, using banners, duck whistles and costumes. These included demonstrations at the RSPB's reserves and annual general meetings, and at the WWT's visitor centres. During a 'Week of Action' in the spring of 1999, they extended these activities to the headquarters of English Nature, the statutory conservation agency for England.
- They publicly held the conservation NGOs responsible for the cull. On a protest banner, the RSPB was presented as standing for 'Royal Society for the Persecution of Birds' (Lawson 1996: 31). During the week of action in 1999, demonstrators dressed as an 'RSPB bird killer' and a 'WWT bird killer'.
- They presented the conservationists' support for the cull as a betrayal of trust:

> Those of us concerned with the rights and welfare of animals thought we could trust conservation bodies, such as the RSPB, to make all the necessary arguments in defence of wildlife, while we concentrated on issues such as factory farming, vivisection and hunting. That's obviously not the case.
>
> (Animal Aid statement, October 1998)

- They stressed the qualities of ruddy ducks as persons: their capacity for suffering and for emotional experience, and their right to autonomy. One protest banner read 'Ruddy Ducks love life too!' (Lawson 1996). Animal Aid press releases (2 March 1999, 6 July 1998) reported that the trial shootings had caused great suffering to some birds, and expressed the view that the ducks' mating preferences should not be a matter for human concern.
- They attacked the 'logic' behind the cull, suggesting that it is driven by the

racist concerns of a small number of purists who are 'deeply offended' by the mixing of blood (Animal Aid press releases, 2 March and 1 April 1999).

The fundamental difference between the biodiversity (conservation) perspective and the personhood (rights and welfare) perspective is clear from this example. Conservationists emphasized obligations to other people (Spanish conservationists) and to a broader human community through the agreements signed by the UK government, thereby implying that wildlife is a resource for human use. Their opponents emphasized obligations to the animals, not to cause them suffering and not to impede their autonomy, thereby implying that their lives have value for themselves.

A further observation follows from this point. A striking difference between the two approaches is that opponents of the cull openly criticize the conservation organizations, but conservationists do not openly criticize the opposition. The conservation case gives the impression of 'talking past' the opposition (cf. Satterfield forthcoming). This is understandable given that conservation organizations do not wish to appear insensitive to the rights and welfare of animals. As we have seen, they benefit from public sympathy for animals as persons, and encourage it in ways outlined above. The rights and welfare case, on the other hand, can afford a direct clash with conservation interests. Rights and welfare groups do not explicitly seek to tap public concern for biodiversity conservation. They can afford to draw attention to conservation's basic insensitivity to personhood, and to do so knowing, for the reasons given above, that their criticisms will not be directly countered.

This case also draws attention to the second common western assumption about emotion identified at the beginning of this chapter: that it is opposed to rational thought. The conservationists present the cull as a rational decision based on scientific knowledge, and contrast this approach with the emotional and, by implication, irrational opposition: 'It is . . . a question of controlling the emotional response which we all have to a situation like this and trying to think logically and calmly' (Stiles and Delany 1993). Thus the difference between the conservationists and their opponents is presented as one of control. We all have feelings, but conservation requires us to overcome those feelings in the interests of rational action. In a move which turns the conservationists' own values against them, their opponents present the cull as an emotional reaction, the racist intolerance of a minority who are 'offended by the idea of genetic impurity' (Animal Aid press release, 1 February 1999). Thus they imply that the conservationists are failing to act according to their own standards of rationality. The assumed opposition between emotion and rationality has played a major role in shaping the discourse of nature protection (and other public discourses) in western society, and will be addressed in detail in Chapter 8.

8

PROTECTING NATURE

Science and the sacred

A lot of people, I mean we can go to these meetings and make lists of 50 odd stipulations and objections and environmental impact and problems that might occur in the environment, but deep down in everybody's hearts that I know of, that's really fighting this thing – figures the mountain is so damn beautiful, it's such a really beautiful place. It's a pristine, unspoiled day, it's – you know, everyone that feels anything about beautiful, natural places knows there's something there that has nothing to do with environmental impact or judgements or documents or scientific studies or anything like that.

(From *Kikwtoqiaknutmátimk – The Mi'kmaq Dialogues*, a series of group discussions sponsored by Mi'kmaq Studies at the University College of Cape Breton, January 1993, http://mrc.uccb.ns.ca/dialogues.html)

In the late 1980s, near the beginning of my research on local environmental issues, I attended a Public Inquiry in the village of Killyleagh in Northern Ireland. Killyleagh is on the shore of Strangford Lough, a sea inlet which is one of Northern Ireland's most important areas for nature conservation. The purpose of the Inquiry was to hear objections to a proposal to construct a yachting marina in Killyleagh Harbour. Although the harbour was not, in itself, seen as particularly important for wildlife, its mud-flats, exposed at low tide, provided food for wading birds. Public inquiries in the UK tend to have an adversarial character. It is common practice for parties on both sides to employ lawyers to present their case and cross-examine their opponents' witnesses. Not surprisingly, some of the techniques employed in cross-examination are designed to undermine the credibility of the witnesses in order to weaken their case. One of the peculiarities of Northern Ireland's political system at the time was that the government department which took decisions on development proposals was also responsible for environmental protection. On this occasion, an official of that department was being cross-examined by the developer's legal representative on the importance of the mud-flats in Killyleagh Harbour. In the midst of his questioning, without pause and immediately before moving on to his next question, the legal representative made what might have appeared to be a casual remark: 'You seem to be in love with mud-flats.' In fact, it was a very clever comment which invoked the tacit understanding that feelings are

129

not a sound basis for making decisions about development proposals. What he implicitly said was:

> As a government official charged with making such decisions, you should not be swayed by your feelings. Since you clearly are swayed by your feelings, you must be an incompetent government official and therefore an unreliable witness in this case.

His remark was all the more forceful because the government official was a woman. Indeed, having lived with Northern Irish gender stereotypes for many years, I believe he would not have made such a comment to a man. The accusation of emotionality therefore invoked an assumed feminine weakness and susceptibility to feelings (Lutz 1988: 73–6). Ironically, the only remark that had displayed any clear trace of strong feeling was his own, laden as it was with cynicism and sarcasm.

This incident invokes what has repeatedly been described as a conventional belief in western culture, the view that emotion and rationality are opposed (see Lutz 1988, Barbalet 1998, Williams 2001). What those present at the Public Inquiry knew was that government decisions about development proposals must be seen to be 'rational' in a conventional, commonsense understanding of that term. They should be based on discernible facts, should adhere to the legal strictures of the planning process and should not be biased by personal considerations. Feelings are assumed to be internal and subjective, so an accusation of emotionality carries the implication of personal bias. Could someone 'in love' with mud-flats be trusted not to favour unduly the case for conservation? In this chapter, I consider how the assumed opposition between emotion and rationality shapes the discourse of nature protection. I shall suggest that it is used not only, as in the above instance, to score points in public debates about protecting nature, but also to set the parameters of those debates, to determine what is and is not admissible. I shall also show how nature protectionists are seeking to expand those parameters.

Emotion and rationality

> One of the most pervasive cultural assumptions about the emotional is that it is antithetical to reason or rationality. An evaluative concept, rationality is generally used to talk about actions and ideas that are 'sensible', that seem sane or reasonable, and that are based on socially accepted ways of reasoning about problems . . .
>
> To be emotional is to fail to process information rationally and hence to undermine the possibilities for sensible or intelligent action.
>
> (Lutz 1988: 59–60)

Evidence of the assumed opposition between emotion and rationality is common in everyday discourse. It was present in a US senator's advice to an environmental activist to replace his brain with a pocket calculator, and never to be emotional or he would lose credibility (Satterfield forthcoming, Chapter 8).[1] In the UK, in the spring of 2001, we have experienced an epidemic of foot and mouth disease among farm animals. There have been repeated appeals from government to act rationally and not to get emotionally carried away by the sight of thousands of slaughtered cows on our television screens. A slight relaxation of the slaughter policy coincided with the rescue of a 12-day-old calf found beside her dead mother. The government were reported to be embarrassed that they might be seen to have responded to the wave of public sympathy that followed this rescue, instead of making a rational decision based on scientific advice.

These instances, and the one that opened this chapter, create the impression that emotionality is always valued negatively, but Lutz and others have pointed to the ambivalence in western attitudes towards emotion: 'To say that someone is "unemotional" is either to praise that person as calm, rational and deliberate or to accuse them of being withdrawn or uninvolved, alienated, or even catatonic' (Lutz 1988: 56). This ambivalence makes it possible also to argue that an absence of emotion in public decision making is harmful, because it implies a lack of sensitivity to public concerns, a lack of interest in what matters most to people, in what they hold sacred. Terry Tempest Williams appealed to the US Congress against the logging of Pacific yew-trees by asking them to visit the forest and the adjacent clear-cut areas:

> and then, my dear lawmakers, I ask you to make your decision with your heart . . . And if you cannot make a decision from this place of heart, from this place of compassionate intelligence, we may have to face as a people the horror of this nation, that our government and its leaders are heartless.
>
> (Williams 1994: 130–1, quoted in Winter 1996: 265)

So although in some contexts it is thought appropriate and effective to be seen as unemotional, in others it is considered appropriate and effective to display emotion. Satterfield (forthcoming) has shown how the value of emotionality has risen and fallen in the conflict over the logging of old-growth forest in Oregon. Both sides, loggers and environmentalists, claimed that the situation warranted emotion, that emotionality was, in a sense, reasonable in the circumstances, because forests and jobs matter, they are worth caring about and defending. Both sides also recognized the damage that could be done by accusations of excessive emotion, fuelled by media reports of their activities. Satterfield points out that this generated 'a heightened awareness and consideration of how to conduct oneself emotionally vis-à-vis the forest dispute'. Loggers, for instance, would often control their anger in public, but in interviews might contemplate the wisdom of doing so: 'maybe we should get more emotional . . . I wonder if our lack of emotion sometimes makes it seem like we're not hurt that bad' (Satterfield forthcoming, Chapter 8).

Satterfield also shows that, in accordance with the widely held assumption (noted above) that emotionality is more a feminine than a masculine trait (see

Lutz 1988: 73ff.), expressions of emotion are partly dependent on gender. Women on both sides of the old-growth forest dispute were more willing than men to express their concerns in emotional terms, more ready to take the responsibility of making an emotional case. Although men would sometimes talk about their feelings and about the need for passion as motivation, emotion was, for them, balanced by the need to apply rationality (cf. Berglund 1998: 101). Male environmentalists invoked a partnership between emotion and rationality, suggesting that either might operate in support of the other (Satterfield forthcoming, Chapter 8).

This seems to suggest that, in public discourse as well as in academic scholarship (Barbalet 1998), a critical approach to the opposition between emotion and rationality is sometimes adopted. But this impression would be misleading, for the criticism is of a very different kind. The academic debate, as outlined in the Introduction to this book, considers whether emotion necessarily supports rational thought, whether rational thought is possible without emotion. In contrast, the kinds of statement made in public discourse about the need to strike a balance between rationality and emotion are not attempts to deny the opposition between them. Instead, they depend on that opposition for their effectiveness. Because rationality and emotion are widely seen as incompatible, and because emotion is sometimes valued positively, politicians and activists can often gain credence by suggesting that the 'best' way forward is to use them in partnership. Debates which are plagued by accusations of too much or too little emotionality on either side can sometimes be advanced by suggesting that emotion should support and guide rational decision making. Such suggestions can be dropped strategically as pearls of wisdom into a seemingly deadlocked dispute.

The instances described above seem to suggest at least a partial answer to a question posed by Barbalet (1998). Why has the opposition between emotion and rationality proved to be such a durable feature of western culture, in the face of repeated attempts by scholars, over many years, to deconstruct it? What seems clear is that the opposition can be a very useful device in public discourse. It can be used to discredit the arguments of opponents by exposing them, depending on the context and the issues involved, as too emotional (and therefore irrational), or not emotional enough (and therefore insensitive), or as failing to strike an appropriate balance between emotion and rationality. Satterfield (forthcoming) cites the arguments of feminist scholars, that accusations of emotionality have been used to deny legitimacy to marginal sectors of society (such as women). Those whose actions are seen as being driven by emotion are denied a role in the supposedly rational process of public decision making. The stigma is self-perpetuating. Activists who cannot get their views heard through official channels resort to direct action – protests, demonstrations, acts of sabotage. Such actions immediately brand them as over-emotional, irrational, and therefore unfit to participate in official politics and, as a consequence, their views become even harder to express through official channels. Supporters of the most prominent social movements – socialism, the women's movement, the peace movement, environmentalism and animal rights – have, over the years, found themselves marginalized in this way.

But the stigmatization of some activists as irrational and emotional is not necessarily bad for the movement as a whole, since it can increase the legitimacy of those who act in more conventionally 'reasonable' ways. Nature protectionists and other environmentalists often acknowledge that, in this way, the publicly recognized incompatibility between rationality and emotion can work to their advantage. Some nature-protection organizations operate primarily through the formal and informal systems established in western liberal democracies.[2] They seek to influence policy by talking to elected politicians and government officials, either through official channels of communication or informally through personal contact. They use national and international law to oppose questionable decisions. They base their statements on respected scientific knowledge. Other nature protectionists use direct action to draw attention to and, if possible, physically prevent, the destruction of nature. Greenpeace is the most formally organized group to have adopted this approach; others include Paul Watson's Sea Shepherd and the many groups of activists operating under the name of Earth First!. Most direct action is probably instigated, not by named or constituted organizations, but by loosely connected individuals who gather to oppose specific developments or to call for broader social and cultural changes. In recent years, nature protectionists have been among those demonstrating, in Seattle, London and other cities, against the damaging effects of global capitalism. And throughout the 1980s and 1990s, protesters have gathered at the sites of proposed road developments, logging operations, dam constructions, airport extensions, and so on, to occupy threatened trees and to place themselves in the path of machinery.

Accusations of those who take direct action as irrational and over-emotional are used to justify the refusal of governments to listen to or negotiate with them. But this does not mean that direct action has no impact on nature protection. It is widely recognized, by nature protectionists and other environmentalists, that direct action increases the chances that NGOs operating within the formal and informal systems of western democracies will be listened to by decision makers. Views of this kind were expressed to me many times during my research. Direct activists, through their apparently irrational and over-emotional actions, make those who are willing to talk calmly to decision makers and work within legal and official parameters look rational and reasonable. In doing so, they increase their legitimacy. Direct action thus extends the parameters of nature-protection discourse. By doing what they know will be officially condemned as irrational and emotional, and by holding their ground and refusing to compromise, direct activists create cultural spaces in which the more officially respected (because more rational and apparently less emotional) nature protectionists can negotiate change. Nature protection (like broader environmentalism and other social movements) thus progresses through an informal alliance between contrasting styles of activism, an alliance which plays on the assumed opposition between rationality and emotion.[3]

Emotion, rationality and capitalism

The fact that the opposition between emotion and rationality helps some participants in public discourse, especially the more powerful, to achieve their goals, clearly helps to sustain it as a western cultural convention. But Barbalet presented a more general (though not incompatible) explanation which suggests how the opposition arose as well as why it persists. Drawing on the work of Simmel (1971 [1903]), Weber (1978 [1921]) and Heller (1979), he linked the emotion–rationality opposition to the emergence of the market as a dominant or pervasive institution, one which colours the operations of all others (Barbalet 1998: 58). In subsistence economies households generally produce what they need for themselves, so there is no separation between economic activity and the domestic sphere. When labour becomes a commodity to be sold outside the household, as it is in capitalist economies, a split between work and home is established (Barbalet 1998: 56). This split is experienced as a divergence of attachments. The demands imposed by paid employment are determined by the interests of the market, which are different from and external to those of the household.

This divergence of attachments came to be thought of in terms of an opposition between rationality and emotion. Actions which serve market interests came to be understood as motivated by instrumental rationality rather than by emotion. Emotion came to be excluded, in the developing capitalist cultural perspective, from the sphere of activity which promotes and sustains the market. This argument is present, with varying degrees of clarity, in the work of both Simmel and Weber, but Barbalet pointed to a crucial addition in Simmel's interpretation. Simmel argued that participation in the market, with its fluctuations and uncertainties, is an intensely emotional experience, so intense that human minds need some kind of protection against the psychological disturbance which it would otherwise cause. This protection is provided by a focus on 'rational calculability' and the simultaneous development of what Simmel called a 'blasé outlook' or 'blasé attitude' (1971 [1903]: 329) in which emotional attachment is suppressed and denied (Barbalet 1998: 55). If this interpretation is sound, we should think of western cultural expressions of cold, commercial rationality as smoke-screens which hide the emotional nature of attachment to market interests. And even if the analysis presented by Barbalet, following Simmel, does not reflect a general pattern in capitalist cultures, I would still wish to argue that attachments to market interests are emotional, for, if they were not, they could not motivate. I shall return to this point in the Conclusion.

With the development of the market as a dominant institution, emotion became a residual category in capitalist culture, applied to attachments which do not serve market interests. So attachments to family and friends, to places and objects of beauty, to anything valued in terms other than its market utility – for instance, for its role in constituting personal identity or providing spiritual fulfilment – could remain unashamedly and explicitly emotional. Their exclusion from the rationality of the market made them, at the same time, non-rational or, when they conflict with the pursuit of market interests, irrational. The rise of the market thus brought about a cultural shift in the meaning or scope of emotion, confining it to attachments which lie outside market rationality (Barbalet 1998: 57–8). The assumed opposition between emotion and rationality remains strong wherever the market is dominant.

The effects of this process can be seen in many areas of public life, and particularly in the mechanisms established, in western liberal democracies, for public decision making. The mechanisms of most relevance to nature protection are those used to determine how nature and natural things are used. These include land use planning systems, ways of regulating the use of water and controls on the pollution of land and water by industry. Such mechanisms vary enormously among western countries and it makes more sense to cite instances from my own experience than to attempt to generalize. In Northern Ireland, the land use planning system operates in favour of market interests in several ways. A developer who has a planning application turned down may appeal against that decision, but objectors to planning applications have no right of appeal when decisions go against them. There is a broad commitment to process planning applications within a certain time, say ten weeks from initial submission. This takes into account the needs of developers not to delay their commercial operations, but ignores the fact that it can take much longer to assess the environmental impact of a proposed development. When an environmental impact statement is required, it is the responsibility of the developer to provide it, giving them a greater influence than anyone else over the parameters and content of the statement.

Perhaps the clearest indication of the pervasiveness of the market is the way in which many nature protectionists pragmatically, though often reluctantly, welcome the commoditization of the things they value. Rainforests are valued as places of beauty, as sacred sources of personal identity for those who live in them, as habitat for countless non-human persons, and as reservoirs of biodiversity. It is unfortunate that their destruction has commercial value for the timber industry, but fortuitous that their protection might also have commercial value, as a source of new medicines for the pharmaceutical industry. It is fortuitous, too, that people are willing to pay for encounters with whales and other animals in their natural habitats; the individual personhood of these animals is protected as long as they are worth more alive and free than dead or captive (Peace forthcoming). It is also fortuitous that tourists generate income for local and national economies when they visit places of natural beauty, since, in a market-dominated world, economic benefits offer the best chance of protecting such places. In the next section I discuss one particular attempt to protect natural beauty, but, in order to understand its form and content, it is important to consider the role of science.

Science and scenery

The view that the opposition between emotion and rationality is sustained, in western culture, by the dominance of the market seems to make sense. But I suggest

135

that it is complicated by the presence of science as an authoritative arbiter of truth. Science, like the market, wears a mantle of rationality, but in a different way. While attachments to market values are simply taken for granted as rational, attachments to science can be openly acknowledged as emotional (Wolpert and Richards 1988, 1997) and can include a passion for the mysteries of nature. On the other hand, the practice of science, the creation of knowledge through rigorous, systematic testing of observations and hypotheses, is expected to be free of emotional bias. Anyone armed with the necessary scientific tools should arrive at the same set of incontrovertible facts (Berglund 1998: 193). Given their assumed independence from emotional bias, science and the market might be expected, in public discourse, to form an alliance against the emotional attachments that threaten to disrupt the smooth operation of the market. But the supposed impartiality of science saves it from this fate and gives it an extremely important role in public decision making.

Debates about nature protection may indeed be contests between market and non-market interests (for instance, forests as timber versus forests as sacred places), or between different market interests (for instance, forests as timber versus forests as tourist attractions), but they are also, in practice, contests between particular individuals and organizations – developers and environmental NGOs, timber merchants and nature lovers. In western liberal democracies it is entirely expected that governments will follow particular political ideologies, including market ideologies; this is part of what electorates vote for. But it is a different matter entirely for governments to favour particular individuals and organizations, since this attracts suspicions of corruption which undermine the democratic process. Science provides a supposedly impartial body of knowledge which can be used to legitimize public decisions.

In Chapter 3, I argued that science has served capitalism very well by depersonalizing nature and thus removing the sense of moral responsibility which might have hindered its exploitation. This argument is part of an ongoing critique of science which has repeatedly highlighted its culturally constructed character. But this is not how science is understood by those who use it. They might acknowledge the existence of biased science, but this is always bad science, not science as it should be. Ideally, science gives access to indisputable facts about the world. It is valued because, despite its many imperfections, it 'posits the possibility of knowledge without prejudice' (Berglund 1998: 193). The supposed impartiality of science and the extent to which decision makers depend on it make it a useful tool for protagonists on both sides of debates about nature protection. Both Berglund (1998) and Satterfield (forthcoming) have described how participants in particular environmental disputes are ambivalent towards science, taking it up when it suits their needs and dropping it when it does not. In this way, science remains subordinate to the emotional attachments that drive activists. What matters most, what is most sacred to nature protectionists may be wilderness and its rejuvenating effects on the human spirit, but if descriptions of the role of mychorrhizal fungi in maintaining a suitable habitat for the northern spotted owl can win the debate, then so be it (Satterfield forthcoming, Chapter 5).

But science sometimes becomes much more than a tool. Such is the respect in which it is held, or assumed to be held, by decision makers, that it can dominate a debate, colouring the terms in which arguments are made, as protagonists compete with each other to present the most scientifically convincing case. The following example shows how arguments about natural beauty can be forced into a scientific mould.

The Harris superquarry

In 1991 Redland Aggregates Ltd submitted an application to create a 'superquarry' on the island of Harris in the Outer Hebrides off western Scotland. The proposed site was the mountain of Roineabhal in the south-east corner of the island. The quarry, which would carve away much of the eastern side of the mountain, was predicted to operate for over sixty years and create about a hundred local jobs, producing rock for road construction mainly in the south-east of England and also overseas. Local responses were mixed, and the degree of local opposition has changed over the years, but initially at least a significant proportion of the population expressed support for the economic regeneration which it was hoped the quarry would bring. Reflecting this view, the local authority eventually declared (after two and a half years) that it was 'minded to grant permission'.

Meanwhile, opposition to the quarry on environmental grounds had grown. A number of environmental NGOs had objected, and local opinion close to the site had turned against it. An important factor was that the quarry would be within a designated National Scenic Area (NSA). This gave the views of the statutory conservation body, Scottish Natural Heritage (SNH), considerable weight. They eventually came out against the quarry, and opposition both locally and elsewhere in the UK continued to grow. A Public Inquiry was held from October 1994 to June 1995. There followed several years of waiting, while opinions on both sides of the argument continued to be aired, particularly in the local press. In April 1999, the report of the Public Inquiry was completed. Its recommendation, which was not made public at the time, was that permission for the quarry be granted. The report expressed the view that, despite the significant (though far from unanimous) local opposition and the environmental damage that would result, it was in the overriding national interest that the quarry be allowed to go ahead. The report was considered by the Scottish Executive, and in November 2000 they announced their decision to refuse permission, citing their duty to protect the integrity of a designated National Scenic Area. The quarry company has appealed against this decision, ensuring that the debate will continue well into 2002 and possibly beyond.

There are many issues involved in this debate, as we shall see, but in this section I shall focus only on what emerged as one of the key points in the official presentation of the decision: the impact on the landscape within the NSA. Information is drawn from the official report on the Public Inquiry (Pain 1999), which describes in some detail the case presented by the company (Redland) and SNH. It is important to recognize the legal nature of the planning process, which means that only certain factors may be taken officially into account when making a decision. These include statutory designations such as Sites of Special Scientific Interests (SSSIs), National Parks and, as in this case, National Scenic Areas.

Although some scientists have argued that perceptions of beauty and attractiveness have a biological basis, I suggest that such things are generally and popularly assumed to be a matter of personal taste; beauty is proverbially 'in the eye of the beholder'. At the same time, there is a degree of conventional agreement on what is beautiful or attractive, such that statutory authorities have felt able to designate particular landscapes in order to conserve their scenic quality for public enjoyment. As a result we have 'Areas of Outstanding Natural Beauty' (AONBs) in much of the UK, National Scenic Areas (NSAs) in Scotland and similar designations in many western countries. But the process of designation itself, and the process of defending the designated areas against developments that might damage their scenic quality, impose a burden of 'rational calculability' on judgements about natural beauty. Activists on both sides of a debate face the problem of how to demonstrate, in terms admissible into formal decision-making procedures – which, for reasons suggested above, often means scientific terms – that a particular development either would or would not have a significant impact on scenic beauty. This does not necessarily result in claims that the scenic beauty of a site can be scientifically measured, but it does result in the presentation of arguments in ways that aspire to scientific standards.

This is demonstrated by two particular features of the evidence presented at the Harris Inquiry. First, there is the extent to which techniques generally thought of as scientific, such as quantification and computer models, were used by both sides in the debate. The developer (Redland) used a computer-based Zone of Visual Influence (ZVI) technique, combined with Ordnance Survey (OS) map data, to determine how much of the quarry site would be seen from where (Pain 1999: 298). SNH used a computer-generated Digital Terrain Model (DTM), also based on OS map data, to demonstrate the potential visual effect of the quarry at selected viewpoints (ibid.: 335–6). Redland argued that, after the quarry had ceased to operate, the site would resemble a corrie (a cauldron-shaped hollow created by glaciation), and that its 'geometric parameters' would lie within the range of other corries in north-west Scotland, 'mostly being within one standard deviation of the appropriate mean value' (ibid.: 307). Both Redland and SNH were concerned to show how much of the NSA would be affected by the sight of the quarry. Redland produced calculations to show that the quarry would not be seen from about 97–8 per cent of the NSA (ibid.: 314), while SNH argued that 3–4 per cent of the NSA would afford very significant views of the quarry (ibid.: 364).

Second, each side sought to legitimize its own case and to criticize that of their opponents in terms of broadly scientific standards such as completeness and accuracy. For instance, Redland had used a visual appraisal of the site to check the accuracy of the OS map data, and found that the ten-metre contour intervals used by the OS were not sensitive enough to pick up small local variations in topography which could affect visibility. They argued that, since SNH had not done this but had taken the OS data to be accurate, their own evidence was the more reliable (Pain 1999: 298). SNH countered this by providing additional information on the accuracy of their model and suggesting that the reliability of Redland's data could be questioned because no statement of their accuracy had been given (ibid.: 336). Redland also argued that their own appraisal of the site was more complete than that of SNH, since their consultants had carried out both a visual assessment and a landscape assessment, while SNH's consultants had made only a visual assessment (ibid.: 287). A landscape assessment is an analysis of the physical features of the site (their type, extent, diversity), while a visual assessment is an appraisal of how these features appear, and can include a judgement on their attractiveness. Significantly, SNH were alleged to have neglected the more objective of these two techniques, the implication being that Redland's appraisal of the site was both the more objective (and therefore the more scientific) and also, because of its combination of objective and subjective techniques, the more complete (and therefore the more valid).

From the points referred to above, and from additional factors that were taken to be significant (such as weather conditions and the number of people potentially affected by views of the quarry), it would appear that natural beauty has been replaced by visibility as the contested issue in this particular debate. The reasons are quite clear. The appreciation of natural beauty depends on the essentially subjective experience of emotional impact, while visibility can be measured. In the legalistic arena of the planning inquiry, the most respected arguments are those that most closely conform to the standards of 'rational calculability' employed in science. Awareness of this makes it necessary for protagonists to forgo expressions of feeling in favour of reasoned arguments and statistics in order to get their case heard. This is not to say that natural beauty becomes unimportant – it was the fear that such beauty would be lost that motivated many of the objections to the quarry. But the defence of natural beauty, and the defence of the market interests that threaten it, have to be presented in an idiom that enables decision makers to appear independent. In western cultures, that idiom is scientific.

A tale of two mountains

Scenic beauty has to be seen to be appreciated, so it is relatively easy to defend it through the measurable medium of visibility. But what about those sacred qualities that are less easily translated into measurable properties? What about those qualities of natural things which are less tangible than beauty, diversity, personhood or wildness, such as their contribution to our sense of identity, and their role in the scheme of things that gives our lives their meaning? What about that quality of nature which is often described, itself, as 'sacredness'? The debate about the Harris superquarry provides an illustration of what happens when attempts are made, through the planning process, to protect the sacredness of nature. It is particularly enlightening to compare this case with a very similar debate which took place on the other side of the Atlantic at about the same time. The dispute over plans to create a superquarry on Cape Breton Island in Nova Scotia has been analysed by anthropologist Alf Hornborg (1994). In the account that follows I draw mainly on his work but also from websites connected with the case. For my information on the Harris debate I draw, once again, on the official report of the Public Inquiry (Pain 1999), but also on written statements presented by witnesses in advance of the Inquiry, and on personal conversations and correspondence with some of the people involved. I begin by describing what happened in Nova Scotia.

Kluscap's Mountain

On Cape Breton Island the proposed quarry site was Kluscap's Mountain, also known as Kelly's Mountain. In 1989, a local company (Kelly Rock) proposed a quarry on the west slope of the mountain to produce rock for road building, mainly in eastern USA. It was claimed that the quarry would be operational for up to forty years, and that it would provide over a hundred local jobs. Local residents formed the Save Kelly's Mountain Society (SKMS), and objected to the proposal on the grounds that the quarry would cause immense damage to the environment, to health and to local economic operations. Members of the indigenous Mi'kmaq population also protested, claiming that the mountain was a sacred site. The Mi'kmaq prophet Kluscap once lived in a cave on the mountain and would return there some day. There were public demonstrations by Mi'kmaq activists who became known as the Mi'kmaq Warrior Society, and later the Sacred Mountain Society (SMS).

Kelly Rock had submitted an environmental impact assessment, but the opposition to the quarry challenged this and requested a federal environmental review. In 1991, the federal and provincial governments decided to hold a joint Environmental Assessment Review, but this does not appear ever to have been completed. The quarry company pulled out, ostensibly for economic reasons (Hornborg 1994: 249). Since then the threat of the quarry seems to have subsided, but efforts to protect Kluscap's Mountain have continued. These have focused on getting it officially designated as a Wilderness Area, which would give it a degree of legal protection against potentially damaging development proposals.

Given the similarity of the proposed developments on Cape Breton Island and Harris, it is not surprising that the objectors to them raised similar issues. On Cape Breton Island, the main environmental concerns were siltation, the impact of a huge increase in shipping operations, pollution from ballast water, noise, vibrations, the effect on the local water supply, the effect on wildlife, and the question of what would eventually be done with the site once quarrying had stopped. Economic concerns included the possible impact on the local fishery and on tourism. On Harris, the main environmental concerns were, as we have seen, the impact on the landscape (including the eventual restoration of the site once quarrying had ceased), marine issues (including the proposed huge shipping operations and pollution from ballast water), noise and dust and the effect on wildlife. The main economic concerns, as on Cape Breton Island, were for the future of the local fishing industry and for tourism. One major difference between the two cases was the prominent involvement of the Mi'kmaq activists in the Cape Breton Island debate, and the impact they had on the legitimacy of particular concerns. I shall examine this in more detail below.

As a result of the Mi'kmaq involvement, one of the central issues on Cape Breton Island was the sacredness of Kluscap's Mountain and its importance as a reference point for Mi'kmaq cultural identity. This was not a marginal issue. The two prongs of organized opposition, represented by the SKMS and the SMS, pooled their information and promoted each other's arguments. So the SMS information pack included the kinds of environmental arguments put forward by the SKMS alongside the Mi'kmaq concerns,[4] and the SKMS stressed the sacredness of the mountain alongside its own concerns (Hornborg 1994: 248). A captain of the Mi'kmaq Grand Council was appointed to the Environmental Assessment Review panel, which also employed a Mi'kmaq adviser. There were, of course, attempts by supporters of the quarry to discredit the Mi'kmaq case, but what is of interest here is its impact on the opposition to the quarry. Hornborg's analysis makes clear that Mi'kmaq involvement brought into the debate arguments about the sanctity of the land which would otherwise have been inadmissible. He commented, 'It is as if native people are allowed to say things which non-native people cannot' (ibid.: 250). The reason for this is the widely assumed authenticity of indigenous peoples' connection with the land. The recognition of native peoples' right to defend the land has led to their increasing involvement in environmental activism (see Conklin 1997), both on their own initiative and at the invitation and encouragement of non-indigenous activists.

The suggestion that native people are allowed to say things which non-native people cannot implies that non-native people might also hold the mountain sacred, but that they feel unable to say so, at least on their own behalf, because they know that arguments about sacredness would not be accepted coming from them. Why not? Why should not a white Canadian citizen feel able to state publicly that this mountain, which has been part of his world as long as he can remember, is sacred to him, part of his identity, part of what gives his life meaning? Barbalet's understanding of the opposition between emotion and rationality, described above, suggests an answer. Sacred links with the land are not part of western capitalist rationality. The emotions that embody such links may be a thoroughly familiar experience to many westerners, just as familiar as a love of scenic beauty, for instance. But there is no place in the legal process of public decision making where expressions of such feelings can legitimately be taken into account. This is because, as well as lying outside capitalist rationality, and unlike scenic beauty and some of nature's other valued qualities, sacredness cannot easily be translated into terms which are treated, in the decision-making process, as the most respected arbiter of truth; it cannot easily be expressed in a scientific idiom.

In contrast to non-indigenous Canadian citizens, native people have no obligation to subscribe to capitalist or scientific rationality. The Mi'kmaq activists on Cape Breton Island come from a different tradition, one in which the sacredness of the land is fundamental. They can legitimately live by different rules, and their right to do so is enshrined in law. This makes them a vehicle through which the sacredness of the land can be defended. Although sacredness is not directly admissible into the formal decision-making process, it is indirectly admissible through the legally sanctioned rights of those who, by virtue of their membership of a different, non-capitalist tradition, are 'permitted' to hold the land sacred.

Return to Roineabhal

Returning to Harris and the debate over the proposed quarry at Roineabhal, here, as mentioned above, the arguments that were ostensibly the most persuasive were those relating to the government's obligation to protect the integrity of a 'National Scenic Area', an area which they themselves had designated for its scenic beauty. It is also clear from the report of the Public Inquiry (Pain 1999) that local concerns were listened to. These included the economic and environmental concerns mentioned above (for the future of tourism and fishing, and about noise, dust, marine pollution and wildlife). They also included fears that local cultural traditions, including the Gaelic language, might be diluted by an influx of workers from elsewhere and, perhaps most important to local residents, that observance of the Sabbath might be disrupted. In a sense, these were the Harris equivalent of Mi'kmaq concerns for their sacred mountain. They constituted what mattered most, what was held most sacred by the indigenous population of Harris, what helped shape their sense of personal and cultural identity.

But concerns about the sacredness of the land itself, though not voiced (and perhaps not felt) by residents of Harris, were also raised at the Public Inquiry. The theological case against the quarry was made principally by one witness, Alastair McIntosh,[5] a human ecologist who was brought up on the adjoining Isle of Lewis. He was supported by two other witnesses, Reverend Professor Donald MacLeod, a professor of systematic theology in Edinburgh, and Chief Sulian Stone Eagle Herney, a Mi'kmaq activist from Cape Breton Island who had been invited specifically because of his experience in that case.

Alastair McIntosh, Reverend MacLeod and Chief Sulian Herney all made written submissions to the Public Inquiry and spoke in person at the Inquiry. I shall outline briefly the main points of their case. For McIntosh, the important question was whether the quarry would 'inexcusably violate the integrity of creation'. Citing the Westminster Shorter Catechism, he asked, 'Will it further the glorification and enjoyment of God? Will it do so not just today, not even for the next sixty years, but "for ever"?' (McIntosh et al. 1995: 776). The answer, he argued, depends on whether nature is considered irredeemably fallen. If it is, then it probably does not matter how we treat it, but if nature is essentially blessed or only temporarily fallen, then we should treat it with reverence. McIntosh acknowledged that the Presbyterian tradition of the Scottish Highlands and Islands, which is the dominant religious perspective on Harris, has often portrayed nature as 'profoundly fallen', but, he argued, this was related to rather specific ideas that developed in response to the hardships of the nineteenth century, such as famine and the Highland Clearances.[6] The broader and unambiguous message of Christian theology is that God is concerned with the ongoing well-being of nature, following His covenant with Noah that, after the flood, He would never again lay waste to the Earth (ibid.: 778). McIntosh cited a number of biblical references to support this view, and argued that the quarry proposal needs to be judged on whether or not it treats nature with reverence. He gave several reasons for concluding that it does not (ibid.: 780–3).

In support of McIntosh's statement, Reverend Professor MacLeod presented the general Christian position that, 'Theologically, the primary function of the creation is to serve as a revelation of God' (McIntosh *et al.* 1995: 784). The responsibility of humanity is therefore to protect nature. He presented the capitalist interests that promoted the quarry as threatening the fulfilment of this responsibility by tempting people with much needed economic improvements:

> Torn between their love for the land and their need for jobs they face a cruel dilemma. Capitalism offers to help them in characteristic fashion: it will relieve unemployment provided the people surrender guardianship of the land (thus violating their own deepest instincts).
>
> (McIntosh *et al.* 1995: 784)

Chief Sulian Herney offered a statement of support in which he briefly described the Mi'kmaq philosophy of a spiritual connection with the Earth handed down by the Creator. He made reference to the historical connection between Scotland and his own homeland of Nova Scotia. He wrote of his duty to become involved in helping the people of Harris to save their mountain, and of a collective responsibility to protect Mother Earth against further damage:

> The destruction of any mountain, river or forest is horrifying to all of us whether it be the Hebrides in Scotland, the Shetland Islands or an oil spill in Alaska or the destruction of the Sacred Mountain in Nova Scotia. It is no longer tolerable to pretend or ignore these assaults. Your mountain, your shorelines, your rivers and your air are just as much mine and my grandchildren's as ours is yours.
>
> (McIntosh *et al.* 1995: 786)

How was the case presented by these witnesses treated in the official decision-making process? In the official report on the Public Inquiry (Pain 1999), the major areas of contention were summarized in four main sections, dealing in turn with 'Policy and economic issues', 'Environmental issues', 'Marine issues' and 'Other issues'. Each of these sections is divided into several chapters. At the end of each chapter the Reporter, the official charged with hearing the evidence, writing the report and making a recommendation to the Scottish Executive, presented her 'Findings of Fact'. These are the considerations which, in her view, should be taken into account in making the final decision on the quarry proposal. The written and verbal statements made by Mr McIntosh and his colleagues are summarized, along with evidence presented by various other witnesses, in two of the chapters in the section dealing with 'Other issues'. These chapters are unusual in having no findings of fact presented at the end. Instead they have statements indicating that the findings arising from them are incorporated into the relevant chapters of the report. In other words, any findings arising out the case for the sacredness of the land are supposedly dealt with elsewhere.

Sure enough, towards the end of a chapter on 'Economic and social impacts', in the section on 'Policy and economic issues', Mr McIntosh, Reverend MacLeod and Chief Sulian Herney are listed among others whose evidence has been taken into account under this broad heading. But the findings of fact at the end of the chapter make no reference at all to the case presented by these three witnesses. The only religious issue mentioned in the findings of fact is that of Sabbath observance. Similarly, in her 'Conclusions and recommendations', the Reporter made no reference to the case presented by Mr McIntosh and his colleagues. Again, the only religious issue mentioned is that of Sabbath observance; it is noted that the quarry company have accepted the need not to operate on Sundays.

Of course, the absence of any explicit reference to the sacredness of the land does not mean that it had no impact, either on the Reporter's conclusions and recommendations, or on the decision of the Scottish Executive to reject the proposal.[7] The point is that, even if the decision makers had thought it the most important factor, they could not have said so, because such views have no legitimacy in an arena constrained by the conventions of economic and scientific rationality. Unlike Cape Breton Island, neither Harris, nor Scotland, nor the UK as a whole, has a resident group that can legitimately express such views, a group with legally sanctioned 'permission' to speak from outside the capitalist tradition. Those who do so, who challenge the capitalist and scientific hegemony by invoking emotional attachments which neither serve market interests nor meet the demand for rational calculability, immediately find their views marginalized by being branded 'irrational'.

Nevertheless, there are signs that the stance taken by Alastair McIntosh and his colleagues has broadened the discourse on nature protection in Scotland. McIntosh himself has expressed the view that 'it shifted media interest from a low gear to a high gear', which 'impacted on the politics of environmental concern both locally and nationally . . . It helped local people to find a deeper voice, to form a deeper opinion of the matter.' He is aware of this effect because local people have told him about it. He also told me of a Public Inquiry about another quarry proposal (which was rejected) which took place some months after the Harris one. An observer had been struck by the way in which the Reporter listened to arguments about the psychological effect the quarry would have on people, and had expressed the view that this would not have happened had McIntosh not paved the way by putting such issues on the agenda in the Harris debate (Alastair McIntosh, personal communication).

Observations made by Hornborg (1994), Satterfield (forthcoming) and Brydon (n.d.), in an account of environmental protest in Iceland, indicate that this broadening of the discourse is taking place more widely. In North America it is assisted by the presence of an alternative, indigenous, non-capitalist tradition, and the active involvement of the inheritors of that tradition in cases like the Cape Breton Island debate. Hornborg implied that this case reflects a wider trend:

> the struggle to stop the quarry on Kelly's Mountain suggests a shift in
> the range of credible, public discourse . . . The framework is no longer
> restricted to the 'jobs-versus-the-environment' or 'jobs-versus-health'
> debate. Nor is it even constrained by the rational-scientific 'environ-
> mental assessment' approach. The pivotal contribution of indigenous
> activists to environmental discourse is to have redefined its framework
> so that it is becoming increasingly legitimate to evoke concepts of
> 'sanctity'.
>
> (Hornborg 1994: 250)

Satterfield suggests that the authenticity granted to indigenous peoples' connections with the land is affecting the strategies of other activists. In relation to the
conflict over the logging of old-growth forest in Oregon, she comments:

> Activists recognize that the authenticity either group can claim about
> past and future land use depends on the ease with which either activist
> group can play into notions about native people as authentic due to
> their attachment to physical territories. Practically speaking, this
> means that activists affiliated with the more 'Aboriginal' or 'authentic'
> tradition wield a distinct political advantage.
>
> (Satterfield forthcoming: Introduction)

It would not be surprising if there are similar trends taking place in other areas (such as South America, Australia, Indonesia) where the concerns of indigenous peoples provide an authentic alternative to a dominant capitalist discourse (see Conklin and Graham 1995, Conklin 1997). But, as the Harris case demonstrates, even where this alternative is not present, nature protectionists can extend the parameters of credible public discourse simply by daring to speak from perspectives that cannot be encompassed by capitalist or scientific rationality. This has, of course, been done many times before, throughout the history of public protest in western countries. It is done by those nature protectionists who opt for direct action, instead of operating within established political systems. By raising non-capitalist and non-scientific interests within the formal process of public decision making, nature protectionists are challenging the criteria employed by that process. They are suggesting that the emotional attachments marginalized by market rationality form a proper basis for the organization of public life.

To close this chapter, it is appropriate to recall yet another Public Inquiry, one held in 1989 for the purpose of hearing objections to the Belfast Harbour Local Plan. On the agenda was the fate of the lagoons mentioned at the beginning of Chapter 6, but the comments recalled here relate to a different matter. The local Green Party had objected to the road proposals in the plan on the grounds that they accommodate the use of private cars rather than encouraging more environmentally sustainable forms of transport (Warke 1990: 121). A Green Party representative urged the government to change its transport policy, invoking our moral obligation, not only to future generations, but also to the non-human forms of life with which we share the planet. His was a lone voice, expressing commitments which do not serve market interests, challenging the capitalist hegemony in an arena designed to sustain and promote it. I felt embarrassed for him, and the body language of others present suggested that they shared my embarrassment. Did he not know the rules? Did he not know that the planning process excluded such arguments? After he had stopped speaking there was a tangible sense of relief, as the discussion returned to the more manageable terrain of science and economics. The official parameters of the decision-making process have not changed, but perhaps, if he were to make the same case today, he would be listened to with more sympathy, and, I suspect, would have other voices to support him.

CONCLUSION

Conclusions are notoriously difficult to write, but a colleague once gave me some advice that I have followed ever since. A conclusion, he suggested, should answer the question, 'What has changed, now that this book has been written?' Of course I cannot know what, if anything, will change for potential readers. I can only say what has changed for me, what I have learned as a result of writing this book.

I began with several closely related questions. What makes someone an environmentalist? What makes some people care about nature and natural things more than others do? What leads some people actively to protect nature while others seem intent on destroying it? On one level these questions are about culture. They arose out of the experience of conducting research on environmental issues in a western context. Different ways of relating to nature – protective and hostile, careless and caring – are found in the cultures of western liberal democracies. The questions I started with are asking about this cultural diversity, demanding that it be explained. On a broader level the questions are about 'the kinds of beings we humans are' (Ingold 2000b: 25). They ask what motivates people to act, what makes them care, what shapes the commitments that govern their lives? In this book I chose to explain the cultural diversity by trying to answer these broader questions. I tried to understand how western nature protectionists come to feel about, understand and act towards nature as they do, by examining how human beings in general come to feel about, understand and act towards anything. Paradoxically, this broadening of the enquiry brings a narrowing of focus, on the human being as an individual organism living in an environment and learning about that environment (and about themselves) through their engagement with it.

I also began with a strong impression, perhaps not strong enough to be called a conviction, which again came out of my experience of research on environmental issues. It seemed to me that the labelling of some nature protectionists' efforts to defend nature against economic development as 'emotional' and 'irrational' was not only unfair, in that it supported a system loaded in favour of market interests, but also scientifically unsound. It seemed to be saying that some commitments are emotional while others are not. How could this be? Developers and decision makers do not, after all, belong to a different species from nature protectionists; they even share some of their views. How could one individual's desire to build a housing estate or construct a quarry differ fundamentally from another individual's desire to protect the things threatened by these developments? At the time I did not have the arguments to substantiate the impression that accusations of emotionalism were scientifically unsound, and I hope I was ready, if not willing, to be persuaded otherwise. But the more I delved into what anthropologists, psychologists and other specialists have written about how people come to feel, think and act as they do, the more convinced I became that this impression was correct. The points that convinced me, and which I summarize below, also helped to answer my opening questions.

Each individual human being is a complex organism living in an environment (Gibson 1979). What each individual becomes during their lifetime is a product of their engagement with that environment, a process in which they learn about the world and about themselves (Neisser 1976, Ingold 2000a). Many anthropologists and social psychologists would argue that a human being's environment is essentially social, that 'human ecology *is* human society' (Croll and Parkin 1992: 13), and that each individual is therefore a product of their own social experience. This is the central assumption of the constructionist approach in social science, which, I would agree, has been extremely fruitful in helping anthropologists to understand a great deal about cultural diversity. But it is not the whole story; in fact, it misses a very important point. The environment of most human beings may be predominantly social, but to say that it is *essentially* social is to assume that human beings can only pick up information from other human beings or in contexts of human creation, and not from the non-human things in their environment. Clearly this is not the case, as demonstrated by the rare instances of children brought up by non-human animals (Armen 1976). Throughout our lives we learn from our whole environment, not just from other human beings and their products (culture).

Precisely what we learn about the world depends on how we, as individual organisms, engage with it. In other words, it depends on our personal experiences, and because each individual's combination of experiences is unique, so too is each individual's understanding of the world. This diversity of experience means that some people think of nature, or parts of nature, as composed of personal agents, while others see it as a complex of impersonal objects and mechanisms. It means that some people think of non-human animals as resources for human use, while others see them as non-human persons worthy of moral concern, or respect, or punishment. It is diversity of experience that generates diversity in perception, knowledge and understanding.

Emotions are fundamental to the process of learning. This runs against western cultural convention, in which thought and feeling (and, therefore, rationality and emotion) have been seen as separate processes. Academics have sustained this convention by studying cognition and emotion as separate phenomena. But many scholars have also challenged it. The work of Hume (1911 [1740]), James (1956 [1897]), Frank (1988), de Sousa (1990), Oatley (1992) and many other scholars has sought to deconstruct the conventional opposition between rationality and emotion (Barbalet 1998). This book continues that effort by suggesting that, whatever else they may be, emotions can usefully be seen as learning mechanisms. This view draws on the work of Damasio (1994, 1999) and those psychologists who have observed that interest and anticipation (which some psychologists refer to as basic emotions) enable us to pick up information (Neisser 1976, Izard 1991). We learn about the world by encountering things that engage our interest. In addition, memory is affected by emotional state (Rolls 1990, Christiansen 1992), so how we feel during an experience influences what we remember about it, and therefore how it affects our future thoughts, feelings and actions.

Emotions have also been treated by some scholars as essentially social phenomena (Lutz 1988, Parkinson 1995). But I am persuaded by Damasio's (1999) argument that emotions have been central to the evolution of consciousness, and that they must therefore be pre-social. As we have seen, Damasio confines the term 'emotion' to changes in the body (including the brain) of an organism which are induced by environmental or internal stimuli. As such, emotions are present in many kinds of organism, but only some are equipped to perceive their emotions, in other words, to have feelings, and only some of these are equipped to perceive feelings in themselves. Thus emotions and feelings, as well as being instrumental in our learning about the world, are also things that we learn about. We learn to feel angry, afraid, happy, guilty or sad about particular things, and because emotions can be induced unconsciously, we also discover what induces these feelings in us.

It is the things we encounter and engage with that induce emotions in us, so our emotional attachments, like our understandings of the world, are products of experience. And again, diverse personal experiences generate diverse emotional attachments. Some people learn to enjoy wild, rugged landscapes while others learn to love woodlands, or deserts, or cities. Some learn to identify and empathize with snakes, or fleas, or spiders, while others learn indifference, or fear, or revulsion. Some learn to be excited by success in sport, or by money, or political power, or the conspicuous consumption of material wealth, while others learn to be repelled by these things. Some find contentment in family relationships, while others fear commitment and responsibility.

As fully conscious beings, who not only experience feelings but also know that we do, we can use them to guide our actions. We can plan to avoid sadness and fear, and to maximize happiness. This is how emotions motivate; they identify what matters to us. Whatever we find most emotionally compelling – most exciting, most interesting, most tragic, most satisfying, most awe-inspiring, most guilt-provoking, most enjoyable – becomes what matters most, what we hold most sacred. Our emotional development as individuals, what we learn, through experience, to hold sacred, informs our actions in the world. It creates politicians eager for power or anxious to serve, it creates developers intent on the creation of wealth and prosperity, and it creates nature lovers who value natural beauty more highly than prosperity, and who fear for the future of life on earth. The arguments presented in this book lead us to conclude that none of these commitments can be more or less emotional than the others. Clearly, people will experience different strengths of feeling about the things they value. A nature lover might feel more strongly about the preservation of a mountain than a developer feels about the proposed quarry that threatens it, or vice versa. A government official might be less concerned than the members of a local community about whether a woodland is saved or lost to a road development, or about whether economic considerations matter more than ecological ones. But all these commitments are fundamentally emotional; without emotion there is no commitment, no motivation, no action.

Nor does it make sense, in terms of the arguments I have presented, to maintain that emotion is opposed to rationality. An appropriate stance to take on the conventional opposition between emotion and rationality is not merely a critical one but a radical one (Barbalet 1998). Rational thought is directed thought, related to some purpose. This means that it is motivated thought, and emotion, I have argued, is the essence of motivation. This does not mean that emotion merely supports rational thought, through, for example, its role in learning and the production and retention of knowledge. It means that, as William James argued, rationality is itself a feeling (1956 [1897]), it is emotionally constituted. It is the direction provided by emotion that makes thought rational. The opposition between rationality and emotion is a myth, in at least two senses of that term; in the popular sense that it is false, and in the anthropological sense that it is believed in and dogmatically asserted because it protects particular interests and ideologies (Robinson 1968, Milton 1996). All areas of western public discourse are characterized by this myth. We see it whenever people's attachments to non-market interests challenge the operation of the market. Nature protection is just one area of public debate in which the myth is prominently expressed, in which accusations of emotionality are used as instruments of power, as mechanisms for putting down opponents and winning arguments.

Does it matter if the opposition between emotion and rationality is a myth? It has, after all, been a very useful device for getting decisions made, for guiding public discourse away from open aggression and towards calm negotiation. But clearly, it matters to those who are disadvantaged by the myth, to those for whom non-market interests matter most, and this, I suggest, is a sizeable proportion of the population in any liberal democracy. The market systematically destroys whatever it cannot encompass. This includes, not only nature and natural things, but also health, family, friendship, spirituality, knowledge and truth. Any failure to put the things that people hold most sacred at the centre of public decision making makes democracies, at best, undemocratic.

There is another reason why it matters if public discourse is founded on myth. As we have seen, in western societies, and increasingly across the world, science is often held to be the main arbiter of truth. Science has, to some extent – though certainly not completely and to different degrees in different contexts – replaced religion in this role. Although science has often served the interests of the market, it cannot do so self-consciously and remain true to its principles, because it proceeds through systematic questioning of its own findings. It may, from time to time, fabricate myths, but it is required to question those myths. This is what science holds sacred, and it is what makes it worthy of respect. It is clearly wrong for discourses in which science is respected as an arbiter of truth to sustain a myth that is, itself, scientifically unsound.

As an anthropologist who is deeply concerned about the way my own species treats nature and natural things, I should like to be able to claim that the arguments presented in this book point to less destructive ways of engaging with the non-human world. But this would be going too far. At best I can suggest that a full recognition of the emotional basis of all our actions might help to broaden the parameters of public discourse and give non-market interests a chance of being heard and respected. But I cannot know whether, if this process takes place, nature will ultimately benefit. One thing I am convinced of: if human beings are truly a threat to life on earth, we shall have a better chance of reducing that threat if we understand as fully as possible the kinds of beings we are. This book is offered as a contribution to that effort.

NOTES

INTRODUCTION

1 'The day the oceans boiled' was shown in the UK in Channel 4's documentary series *Equinox* on 17 June 2001.

2 'Nature' has many meanings which vary with context. In western cultures it broadly refers to phenomena not produced by human beings; this and other meanings will be clarified in the book as they arise. I do not include, within the broad field of nature protection, those environmentalist concerns directed primarily at human health: concerns about air quality, water quality, chemicals in food, and so on.

3 For convenience, I use the words 'culture' and 'cultures' rather more loosely than anthropologists usually do, referring to 'human culture(s)', 'western culture(s)', 'non-western cultures', 'capitalist culture(s)', and so on, without defining these categories. This is less problematic than it might seem for, although I am seeking to explain cultural differences, I do so not by considering cultures as units of any kind, but by focusing on the relationship between individual human beings and their environment.

1 SCIENCE AND RELIGION

1 See Yearley (1992) for a discussion of this relationship.

2 Gottlieb (1996) presents a collection of environmentalist writings in which the religious component is often explicit, sometimes implicit, but always clear.

3 See Milton (1996) for a critique of the myth of 'primitive ecological wisdom'.

4 Frazer's *The golden bough* was originally published in 1890. The edition cited here is a 1994 abridgement from the second and third editions.

5 The denial of continuity between science and common sense is referred to by Atran as the 'anti-inductivist' view (Atran 1990: 247), characterized by the work of Bachelard (1965). The debate about science and common sense can be seen as part of the long-running and broader discourse about 'primitive' thought and rationality, to which many anthropologists and philosophers have contributed.

6 The 'natural' functioning of memory is also important in analyses of religious ritual (Lawson and McCauley 1990, Whitehouse 1992, McCauley 1997). Here, for the sake of brevity, I restrict the discussion to religious ideas.

7 Boyer's model also implies that the rarity of science is not necessarily an indication of its unnaturalness. He acknowledged that the ontological categories and principles to which human minds are naturally predisposed do not emerge without appropriate stimuli in the environment. On this view, human minds could be as predisposed towards scientific ideas as towards religious ideas; science could be rare because the environmental stimuli that encourage its emergence are rare.

8   It is worth commenting here on an aspect of the opposition between science and religion that is not addressed in this chapter. The distinction between religion and common sense could be seen as depending on a perceived distinction between what is 'natural' in the sense of being normal, mundane, consistent with ontological expectations, and what is 'supernatural', in the sense of strange, mysterious, inconsistent with ontological expectations. This was how Malinowski defined the distinction, which he saw as fundamental to human culture, between the sacred and the profane (Malinowski 1948: 67). I would argue, along with many anthropologists, that this distinction is insignificant and probably non-existent in most cultures, and agree with Guthrie that most peoples have not distinguished religious knowledge from secular knowledge (Guthrie 1993: 196). In contrast, a separation of the natural from the supernatural is essential to science. Lloyd (1979) noted that the work of the first philosopher scientists in ancient Greece was characterized by this distinction, while Guthrie saw it as having developed in European thought after the Reformation (Guthrie 1993: 196). Ancient Greece and post-Reformation Europe provided the two cultural contexts in which science is said to have developed.

2 THE NATURALNESS OF IDEAS

1   The issue of what constitutes personhood will recur several times in this book, particularly in Chapters 3 and 5.
2   See Milton (1996) for a discussion of this concept of culture.
3   Because I am concerned, in this chapter and the next, with how people come to know nature, I treat meaning here as a cognitive or mental phenomenon. In Chapter 6, in discussing how people come to value nature, I shall suggest a broader and more fundamental concept of meaning which places it at the centre of ecological relations.
4   I apologize for the potentially confusing use of 'nature' in at least two senses: to describe an object of human knowledge and representation, and to describe our innate ability/ tendency to know. To use a different term for either sense would misrepresent the material. I trust that it will always be clear from the context which sense is intended.
5   I am aware that the term 'innate' is less used than it once was by psychologists, but I shall use it here for the sake of simplicity.
6   I am not suggesting that those who conceptualize cognition in terms of domain-specific mechanisms necessarily regard such mechanisms as innate. An alternative view is that they are task-specific and are generated through the development of expertise (Hirschfeld and Gelman 1994: 15–16). The world of cognitive theory, like most areas of research, is a vast array of models which touch in different places (the contributions to Hirschfeld and Gelman (1994) provide a good indication of the complexity). Models in which domain-specific mechanisms are seen as innate are relevant here because they imply the proposition under examination, that particular ideas can be described as 'natural'.
7   Carey and Spelke claim that adults 'are inclined to deny personhood to apes, dolphins, and parrots, however impressive their behavioural accomplishments' (1994: 188), and therefore conclude, following Wiggins (1980), that 'person' is 'at least in part' a species concept. But this is not an illuminating statement. If a concept is something 'in part' then it must also 'in part' be something else. The evidence that people in western society frequently understand non-human animals as persons, in all the senses discussed in this chapter, is undeniable in my view.

3 KNOWING NATURE THROUGH EXPERIENCE

1   The assumption that all learning is mediated by social interaction would help to explain Boyer's (1994a) assertion that the knowledge of ontological categories

possessed by very young children is 'under-determined by experience'. If children had to wait for their fellow human beings to teach them things, either intentionally or as a by-product of social interaction, we would indeed expect their knowledge to develop much more slowly than it does. An implication of the argument presented in this chapter is that we do not need to resort to theories about innate ideas in order to explain the apparently early and effortless development of knowledge. It arises out of direct engagement with the social and non-social environment.

2   Gibson was thus in danger, in my view, of perpetuating the mind–body dualism which he sought to overthrow, for he did not demonstrate that mind and body are united in perception.

3   While the things in our environment are not mental constructs, they are, of course, physical constructs, and are 'continually under construction' (Ingold 1995: 57) by human beings, non-human animals and other forces of nature.

4   Although Neisser referred to the newborn child, there is no reason to suppose that perception starts at birth. Unborn children also engage with their environment, as every mother surely knows. This is confirmed by studies of twins, whose pre-birth environment must be more interesting and informative than that of single babies. Take an example described by Piontelli (1992: 17–18), of an 18-month-old child whose twin brother had died two weeks before birth. The child behaved as if this event had made a strong impression on him, shaking objects 'as if trying to bring them back to life'. However we interpret this behaviour, it seems clear that the child's pre-birth experience of interaction with his twin had generated expectations, anticipations, which had been left unfulfilled during the two weeks before his birth.

5   To take an interesting example, a series of films about dinosaurs, in which this approach was used, was shown on television in 1999 (*Walking with Dinosaurs*, BBC and The Discovery Channel). Models and computer animations were used to create supposedly realistic footage of dinosaurs moving around their environment, feeding, hunting, mating, fighting, and so on. In several of the programmes the adventures of a single animal formed the central story line. The fact that the animals were long extinct made the films doubly representational. In Britain, the series generated much debate in the press about whether the soap opera style obscured and distorted the scientific knowledge on which the films were claimed to have been based. Ironically, the producers' justification for this style was that they wanted to make a series of real wildlife documentaries rather than science programmes.

6   It was not always so, of course. Functionalist explanations, in the traditions of Malinowski, Durkheim and Radcliffe-Brown, were couched in terms of what institutions do rather than what persons do, but then in these approaches it was institutions, not persons, that were considered to be the main constituents of society.

4 ENJOYING NATURE

1   For a discussion of the issues surrounding 'endo-ethnography', or 'anthropology at home', see Aguilar 1981, Jackson 1987, van Ginkel 1994.

2   The main alternative to constructionist approaches in the anthropology of emotion has been psychoanalytic approaches advocated especially by Spiro (1982) and more recently by Nuckolls (1996 and 2001). The basis of these approaches is the understanding that emotions can influence actions unconsciously. I have no quarrel with this idea and, as we shall see, consider the unconscious aspects of emotions to be essential to their operation. However, psychoanalytic approaches did not seem appropriate for examining emotions which are seen, by those who experience them, as fully conscious motivating forces. For this reason, I do not consider them here. (See Figlio (1996) for a psychoanalytic perspective on emotions towards nature.)

3   I shall suggest later, in Chapter 6, that there is a sense in which emotions are similar

to meanings, but the concept of meaning employed there goes beyond the mental or cognitive (see Chapter 2, n. 3).

4   This project, entitled 'Nature conservation and public response in Northern Ireland', was conducted in 1987–88 and funded by the Leverhulme Trust. Interviewees included staff and volunteers from the Royal Society for the Protection of Birds, the Ulster Trust for Nature Conservation (now the Ulster Wildlife Trust), Conservation Volunteers (Northern Ireland) and the Belfast Urban Wildlife Group.

5   Interestingly, we often identify a physiological cause. Parents may attribute the bad temper of a child to tiredness or hunger. Skilled perceivers of their own bodies know very well the effects of hormone levels on their general mood and tendency to behave in certain ways. This shows that there is no clear line between what we normally think of as physical states and what we normally think of as emotions. And, of course, we use the word 'feeling' to describe both. We say that we feel tired, hungry or sick, just as we say we feel happy, sad or angry.

6   At this point it is worth briefly addressing what might be seen as an inconsistency in the approach presented here. On the one hand, I am arguing that our emotional responses to particular things are learned through experience. On the other hand, I am accepting the view that emotions can be unconsciously induced. It might be asked how learned responses can operate unconsciously. There are two answers to this. First, learning does not have to be a conscious process. According to the model of perception developed by Gibson and Neisser and implied in the work of Lazarus and Damasio, we continually pick up information about our environment and use it to inform our expectations, without being aware that we are doing so. Second, even when learning is a conscious process, its effects can operate unconsciously, through the effect psychologists describe as 'conditioning'. I experienced an interesting example of conditioning after returning from fieldwork in Africa some years ago. When I went to Africa I was not afraid of snakes, nor did I find it very easy to learn to fear them (despite what advocates of biophilia and domain-specific emotions might expect). But I gradually learned to take great care when walking through long grass. After returning to Ireland, where there are no snakes, I was at first surprised to discover that I could no longer take walks in the countryside without feeling tension, particularly in my legs (I feel it at this moment as I recall and record it). Happily, the effect disappeared after a few months.

7   Emotions, in Damasio's narrower sense, are part of the reality we perceive, and feelings consist of the information we pick up about our emotions. So neither can be mental constructs, in terms of the model of perception presented in Chapter 3, though, of course, feelings are used, like all information is used, in the construction of mental representations, cultural models, of our environment and ourselves.

5 IDENTIFYING WITH NATURE

1   Most world views contain contradictions, and deep ecology is no exception. If the distinction between life and non-life is a human construct, and of no importance in the wider scheme of things, it seems reasonable to ask why it is important if the Earth loses its ability to support life. My answer, presented in this chapter, is that for deep ecologists, as for other nature protectionists, perceived personhood is the strongest basis for identification with other entities; and personhood, while it can be perceived in anything (as we have seen in Chapter 3), is most easily perceived in the things conventionally regarded as living.

2   This sense of identity with other things in nature is partly responsible for a recent trend in burial in the UK (and possibly elsewhere). Instead of being buried in a conventional coffin, which prevents some agents of decomposition from getting at the body, some people are now being buried in biodegradable coffins which allow their

remains to be more quickly absorbed and 'recycled' by natural processes, helping to sustain other life forms. Trees are often chosen as memorials in preference to headstones.

3 It could be argued that Fox's instances of 'cosmologically based identification' and 'ontologically based identification' already subsume what I am describing here, that being of the same substance is essentially the same as being part of the same unfolding reality, or as having simple existence in common. But I do not think either of these ideas expresses strongly enough the sense of material identity with other entities that is evident in the work of some deep ecologists (see especially Seed *et al.* 1988).

4 Naess' response to the problem of how we can identify with entities not normally thought of as living beings was to extend his understanding of 'life' to encompass the whole of reality: 'If we can conceive of reality or the world we live in as alive in a wide, not easily defined sense then there will be no non-living beings to care for!' (1988: 27).

5 As Fox explained, his use of this term reflected the thinking of transpersonal psychologists such as Maslow, Sutich and Grof. Maslow distinguished between people who are merely good at 'self-actualization', at fulfilling their basic needs, and those who are able 'to transcend the ego, the self, the identity, to go beyond self-actualization' (Maslow, quoted in Fox 1995: 295).

6 As I quote these words, and report those of Henrietta Fourmile, I am aware of the declaration at the beginning of the volume in which they appear:

> Be advised that information contained in this volume has been provided in good faith, and for the common good of humankind, the furtherance of mutual understanding between peoples, and the preservation of all life on our planet. It is not to be used for personal or commercial gain, but be treated with respect, and used only for the purpose for which it was gifted. Anyone who reads this volume assumes the moral and ethical obligations implied by this statement.
>
> (Posey 1999: v)

I hope that my own use of it will not be considered disrespectful, the purpose of this book being to further our understanding of ourselves and other human and non-human persons.

6 VALUING NATURE: MEANING, EMOTION AND THE SACRED

1 I confess that I should not have been surprised had I been more familiar with Douglas' (1970) grid/group model of cultural diversity (see Milton 1991). The case of the Belfast Harbour lagoons is described in more detail in Milton 1990: 39–40.

2 I am grateful to Tim Ingold for pointing out the advantages of treating 'value' as a verb rather than a noun.

3 For instance, one of the most influential anthropological perspectives in the 1970s and 1980s was Barth's 'transactionalism' (which closely resembles economists' models of human interaction). Social interactions were described as 'transactions' in which values are exchanged like commodities, each party seeking to ensure that the value they gain is greater than or equal to the value they lose (Barth 1966). Recently, Nuckolls has sought ways of addressing the dual emotional/cognitive character of values through a psychoanalytic approach (Nuckolls 1996, 1998).

4 For a summary of the main philosophical arguments on animal rights see Garner 1993: 9–38. Some of Stephen Clark's main papers are available in a published collection (Clark 1997).

5 Others have pointed out that ecosystems depend on the exchange of information as well as matter and energy (see Ellen 1982: 74), and even Rappaport (1979: 158) acknowledged that 'all organisms behave in terms of meanings' (see Hornborg 1996: 53).

6 Here I do not address Durkheim's classic definition of sacred things as things that are separated from the profane, or 'set apart and forbidden' (Durkheim 1971 [1915]: 47), because it refers to how things are treated once they are understood as sacred, rather than how they come to be understood as sacred.

7 Bateson's understanding of the sacred thus appears to contain a contradiction, depending both on a holistic vision of the world and on the maintenance of a barrier between different kinds of experience.

8 This poem has, of course, been published many times. I took these lines from Quiller-Couch 1980: 655.

7 PROTECTING NATURE: WILDNESS, DIVERSITY AND PERSONHOOD

1 Damasio's distinction between emotions (as physiological processes) and feelings (as perceptions of those processes), which was found to be useful in earlier chapters, is not important here. In this chapter and the next, I use the terms 'emotion' and 'feeling' more or less interchangeably.

2 Quotations are taken from the official Wildlands Project website (www.twp.org).

3 This impression was gained from informal conversations with a few of those who had read pre-publication copies of the manuscript.

4 The protection of geological features is not unimportant, however. For instance, in the UK, some of the statutory Sites (or Areas) of Special Scientific Interest (SSSIs/ASSIs) have been designated specifically for their geological features.

5 Of these agreements, those most often invoked in the UK include: the Convention on International Trade in Endangered Species (CITES), 1973; the European Community Council Directive on the Conservation of Wild Birds, 1979 (79/409/EEC); the European Council Directive on the Conservation of Natural Habitats and of Wild Fauna and Flora, 1992 (92/43/EEC); and the United Nations Convention on Biological Diversity, 1992.

6 The point of this example is that the RSPB, one of the UK's leading conservation organizations, has been involved in conserving the white-necked picathartes, a bird of the West African rainforest (Thompson 1998).

7 Ironically, when the posters and leaflets were finally produced, they depicted an English stoat! The artist employed to draw the image was from England and did not know the difference, and the campaign organizers did not notice until it was too late.

8 By visiting the websites of NGOs operating in other countries, I tried to form an impression of whether adoption schemes for animals are a peculiarly British phenomenon. WWF, which probably have wider global coverage than any conservation NGO, offer four individually named animals for adoption on their UK website: an orang-utan, a rhino, a tiger and an elephant. WWF Canada offer a polar bear adoption scheme and WWF Australia offer turtle adoption as part of their Great Barrier Reef campaign. Interestingly, both WWF Canada and WWF Australia point out that the adoption is 'a symbolic act on your part' – 'we will not be able to introduce you to your very own turtle!' – whereas WWF(UK) apparently did not see the need to do this. WWF Germany offer a sponsorship (*Patenschaft*) scheme for two national parks and three animal species, rather than for individual animals. WDCS offer sponsorship (*Patenschaft*) for individually named orcas and dolphins on their German website but, like WWF in Canada and Australia, they refer to the relationship explicitly as 'symbolic' (*symbolische*). I could find no mention of adoption or sponsorship on the websites of the most well-known US conservation NGOs (WWF USA, the National Wildlife Federation, the Audubon Society). Nevertheless, no firm conclusions can be drawn, from this brief survey, on the popularity of adoption schemes in different western countries.

8 PROTECTING NATURE: SCIENCE AND THE SACRED

1   Because Satterfield's book has not yet been published, page numbers are not available.
2   Such groups include, for instance, international NGOs such as WWF, the World Conservation Union and Birdlife International, and national organizations such as the RSPB and the Wildlife Trusts in the UK, and the National Wildlife Federation, the Audubon Society and the Sierra Club in the USA.
3   This is not always an easy alliance. Direct activists sometimes accuse the more moderate activists of not being sufficiently committed to the cause of nature protection, and moderate activists sometimes accuse direct activists of giving environmentalism a bad name. But the overall beneficial effect of direct action, in making the moderate activists look reasonable, is widely recognized.
4   Details on the Sacred Mountain Society's case against the quarry were available on a website which posted information on their behalf (http://nativenet.uthscsa.edu/archive/nl/9302/0041.html).
5   A full account of the Harris superquarry debate is given in a book by Alastair McIntosh (McIntosh in press). Details of publications on the case are available on his website (www.AlastairMcIntosh.com).
6   The Highland Clearances took place between 1782 and 1854, when the Scottish clan chiefs evicted large numbers of their own clansmen from their land so that it could be leased to lowland sheep farmers.
7   Although the official grounds on which the quarry was rejected by the Scottish Executive were the need to protect the integrity of the NSA, there could, of course, be any number of unofficial grounds which could not be publicly acknowledged because they do not fall within the legally recognized category of 'planning matters'. These might include a deep commitment, on the part of the decision makers, to the sanctity of the Scottish landscape. They might also include a desire, by the newly constituted Scottish Executive, to assert their independence by refusing to provide road-building materials for use in England.

REFERENCES

Abram, D. (1997) *The spell of the sensuous: perception and language in a more-than-human world*, New York: Vintage Books.

Abu-Lughod, L. (1986) *Veiled sentiments: honour and poetry in a Bedouin society*, Berkeley: University of California Press.

Adams, W. M. (1996) *Future nature: a vision for conservation*, London: Earthscan.

Aguilar, J. (1981) 'Insider research: an ethnography of a debate', in D. A. Messerschmidt (ed.) *Anthropologists at home in North America: methods and issues in the study of one's own society*, Cambridge: Cambridge University Press.

Allen, P. G. (1996) 'The woman I love is a planet; the planet I love is a tree,' in R. S. Gottleib (ed.) *This sacred Earth: religion, nature, environment*, London and New York: Routledge.

Armen, J-C. (1976) *Gazelle-boy*, London: Picador.

Atran, S. (1990) *Cognitive foundations of natural history: towards an anthropology of science*, Cambridge: Cambridge University Press.

Bachelard, G. (1965) *L'activité rationaliste de la physique contemporaine*, Paris: Presses Universitaires de France.

Barbalet, J. M. (1998) *Emotion, social theory and social structure: a macrosociological approach*, Cambridge: Cambridge University Press.

Barnes, S. (2000) 'A personal view', *Birds: the magazine of the RSPB* 18, 1: 17.

Barry, J. (1999) *Rethinking green politics*, London: Sage.

Barth, F. (1966) *Models of social organization*, Royal Anthropological Institute Occasional Paper 23, London: RAI.

Bartlett, J. C., Burleson, G. and Santrock, J. W. (1982) 'Emotional mood and memory in young children', *Journal of Experimental Child Psychology* 34: 59–76.

Bateson, G. (1991) *A sacred unity: further steps to an ecology of mind*, New York: Harper-Collins.

Bateson, G. and Bateson, M. C. (1987) *Angels fear: towards an epistemology of the sacred*, New York: Macmillan.

Batten, L. A., Bibby, C. J., Clement, P., Elliot, G. D. and Porter, R. F. (1990) *Red data birds in Britain: action for rare, threatened and important species*, London: T. & A. D. Poyser.

Berglund, E. K. (1998) *Knowing nature, knowing science: an ethnography of local environmental activism*, Cambridge: White Horse Press.

Bird-David, N. (1992) 'Beyond "the original affluent society": a culturalist reformulation', *Current Anthropology* 33, 1: 25–47.

—— (1993) 'Tribal metaphorization of human–nature relatedness: a comparative analysis', in K. Milton (ed.) *Environmentalism: the view from anthropology*, London and New York: Routledge.

—— (1999) '"Animism" revisited: personhood, environment and relational epistemology', *Current Anthropology* 40, Supplement, February: 67–91.

Birdlife International (1997) 'Ruddy Duck set-back', *Birdlife in Europe* 2, 2: 1.

Boyer, P. (1994a) *The naturalness of religious ideas: a cognitive theory of religion*, Berkeley: University of California Press.

—— (1994b) 'Cognitive constraints on cultural representations: natural ontologies and religious ideas', in L. A. Hirschfeld and S. A. Gelman (eds) *Mapping the mind: domain specificity in cognition and culture*, Cambridge: Cambridge University Press.

—— (1996) 'What makes anthropomorphism natural: intuitive ontology and cultural representations', *Journal of the Royal Anthropological Institute* (NS) 2: 83–97.

Brewer, B. (1998) 'Experience and reason in perception', in A. O'Hear (ed.) *Current issues in philosophy of mind*, Cambridge: Cambridge University Press.

Briggs, J. (1970) *Never in anger*, Cambridge, MA: Harvard University Press.

Brydon, A. (n.d.) 'Artists with agency: visualizing place and the extension of modernity in Iceland', paper presented at conference on Landscapes and Memory, Anthropological Association of Ireland, Maynooth, 11–13 May 2001.

Bulmer, R. (1967) 'Why is the cassowary not a bird? A problem in zoological taxonomy among the Karam of the New Guinea Highlands', *Man* 2, 1: 5–25.

—— (1979) 'Mystical and mundane in Kalam classification of birds', in R. F. Ellen and D. Reason (eds) *Classifications in their social context*, London: Academic Press.

Burridge, K. O. L. (1969) *New Heaven, new Earth: a study of millenarian activities*, Oxford: Blackwell.

Callicott, J. B. (1982) 'Traditional American Indian and Western European attitudes toward nature: an overview', *Environmental Ethics* 4: 293–318.

—— (1994) *Earth's insights*, Berkeley: University of California Press.

Carey, S. (1985) *Conceptual change in childhood*, Cambridge, MA: MIT Press.

Carey, S. and Spelke, E. (1994) 'Domain-specific knowledge and conceptual change', in L. A. Hirschfeld and S. A. Gelman (eds) *Mapping the mind: domain specificity in cognition and culture*, Cambridge: Cambridge University Press.

Carson, R. (1956) *The sense of wonder*, London: Collins.

Cavalieri, P. and Singer, P. (eds) (1993) *The great ape project: equality beyond humanity*, London: Fourth Estate.

Chapman, A. J. and Wright, D. S. (1976) 'Social enhancement of laughter: an experimental analysis of some companion variables', *Journal of Experimental Child Psychology* 21: 201–18.

Christiansen, S. A. (1992) 'Emotional stress and eyewitness memory: a critical review', *Psychological Bulletin* 112: 284–309.

Clark, S. R. L. (1978) 'How to calculate the greater good', in R. Ryder and D. Paterson (eds) *Animal rights*, London: Centaur Press.

—— (1981) 'Awareness and self-awareness', in D. G. M. Wood-Gush, M. Dawkins and R. Ewbank (eds) *Self-awareness in domesticated animals*, Wheathampstead, Herts: Universities Federation for Animal Welfare (UFAW).

—— (1985) 'Hume, animals and the objectivity of morals', *Philosophical Quarterly* 25: 117–33.

—— (1997) *Animals and their moral standing*, London and New York: Routledge.

Cohen, J. M. and Cohen, M. J. (eds) (1960) *The Penguin Dictionary of Quotations*, Harmondsworth, Middx: Penguin Books.

Conklin, B. A. (1997) 'Body paint, feathers, and VCRs: aesthetics and authenticity in Amazonian activism', *American Ethnologist* 24, 4: 711–37.

Conklin, B. A. and Graham, L. (1995) 'The shifting middle ground: Amazonian Indians and ecopolitics', *American Anthropologist* 97: 695–710.

Cosmides, L. and Tooby, J. (1994) 'Origins of domain specificity: the evolution of functional organization', in L. A. Hirschfeld and S. A. Gelman (eds) *Mapping the mind: domain specificity in cognition and culture*, Cambridge: Cambridge University Press.

Cotgrove, S. and Duff, A. (1980) 'Environmentalism, middle-class radicalism and social change', *Sociological Review* 28: 333–51.

—— (1981) 'Environmentalism, values, and social change', *British Journal of Sociology* 32, 1: 92–110.

Croll, E. and Parkin, D. (1992) 'Anthropology, the environment and development', in E. Croll and D. Parkin (eds) *Bush base: forest farm: culture, environment and development*, London and New York: Routledge.

Damasio, A. R. (1994) *Descartes' error: emotion, reason and the human brain*, New York: G. P. Putnam's Sons.

—— (1999) *The feeling of what happens: body and emotion in the making of consciousness*, London: Heinemann.

Darwin, C. (1965 [1872]) *The expression of emotions in man and animals*, Chicago, IL: University of Chicago Press.

Dawkins, R. (1976) *The selfish gene*, Oxford: Oxford University Press.

—— (1986) *The blind watchmaker*, London: Penguin Books.

—— (1998) *Unweaving the rainbow*, London: Allen Lane, The Penguin Press.

Dennett, D. C. (1987) *The intentional stance*, Cambridge, MA: MIT Press.

Denzin, N. (1984) *On understanding emotion*, San Francisco, CA: Jossey-Bass.

de-Shalit, A. (1995) *Why posterity matters: environmental politics and future generations*, London and New York: Routledge.

de Sousa, R. (1990) *The rationality of emotion*, Cambridge, MA: MIT Press.

Devall, B. and Sessions, G. (1985) *Deep ecology: living as if nature mattered*, Layton, UT: Gibbs M. Smith.

Devall, W. B. (1970) 'Conservation: an upper-middle class social movement: a replication', *Journal of Leisure Research* 2: 23–6.

Diamond, J. (1993) 'New Guineans and their natural world', in S. R. Kellert and E. O. Wilson (eds) *The biophilia hypothesis*, Washington, DC: Island Press.

diZerega, G. (1997) 'Empathy, society, nature, and the relational self', in R. S. Gottlieb (ed.) *The ecological community*, London and New York: Routledge.

Douglas, M. (1957) 'Animals in Lele religious symbolism', *Africa* 27: 46–58.

—— (1970) *Natural symbols*, London: Cresset.

Drever, J. (1952) *A dictionary of psychology*, London: Penguin.

Dunbar, R. I. M. (1985) 'How to listen to the animals', *New Scientist* 106: 36–9.

Durkheim, E. (1971 [1915]) *The elementary forms of the religious life*, London: George Allen & Unwin.

Durrell, G. (1959) *My family and other animals*, Harmondsworth, Middlesex: Penguin Books.

Dwyer, P. D. (1996) 'The invention of nature', in R. F. Ellen and K. Fukui (eds) *Redefining nature: ecology, culture and domestication*, Oxford and Washington, DC: Berg.

Eckersley, R. (1992) *Environmentalism and political theory: towards an ecocentric approach*, London: UCL Press.

Einarsson, N. (1993) 'All animals are equal but some are cetaceans: conservation and culture conflict', in K. Milton (ed.) *Environmentalism: the view from anthropology*, ASA Monograph 32, London and New York: Routledge.

Ellen, R. F. (1982) *Environment, subsistence and system: the ecology of small-scale social formations*, Cambridge: Cambridge University Press.

—— (1986) 'What Black Elk left unsaid: on the illusory images of green primitivism', *Anthropology Today* 2, 6: 8–12.

—— (1996) 'The cognitive geometry of nature: a contextual approach', in P. Descola and G. Pálsson (eds) *Nature and society*, London and New York: Routledge.

Emde, R. N. (1980) 'Levels of meaning for infant emotions: a biosocial view', in W. A. Collins (ed.) *Development of cognition, affect and social relations: the Minnesota Symposium of Child Psychology*, vol. 13: 1–37.

Ereira, A. (1990) *The heart of the world*, London: Jonathan Cape.

Evans-Pritchard, E. E. (1936) *Witchcraft, oracles and magic among the Azande*, Oxford: Clarendon.

—— (1956) *Nuer religion*, Oxford: Clarendon.

Evernden, N. (1992) *The social creation of nature*, Baltimore, MD: Johns Hopkins University Press.

Fehr, B. and Russell, J. A. (1984) 'Concept of emotion viewed from a prototype perspective', *Journal of Experimental Psychology* 58: 203–10.

Feit, H. (1991) 'Metaphors of nature and the love of animals: animal rights supporters and James Bay Cree hunters', paper presented at the Annual Conference of the American Anthropological Association, Chicago, November.

Figlio, K. (1996) 'Knowing, loving and hating nature: a psychoanalytic view', in G. Robertson *et al.* (eds) *FutureNatural: nature, science, culture*, London and New York: Routledge.

Fodor, J. (1983) *The modularity of mind*, Cambridge, MA.: MIT Press.

Foucault, M. (1983) 'On the genealogy of ethics: an overview of work in progress', in H. Dreyfus and P. Rabinow (eds) *Beyond structuralism and hermeneutics*, Chicago, IL: Chicago University Press.

Fox, W. (1989) 'The deep ecology–ecofeminism debate and its parallels', *Environmental Ethics* 11: 5–25.

—— (1995) *Toward a transpersonal ecology: developing new foundations for environmentalism*, New York: State University of New York Press.

Frank, R. H. (1988) *Passions within reason: the strategic role of the emotions*, New York: Norton.

Frazer, J. G. (1994) *The golden bough: a study in magic and religion*, a new abridgement from the second and third editions, edited by R. Fraser, Oxford: Oxford University Press.

Garner, R. (1993) *Animals, politics and morality*, Manchester and New York: Manchester University Press.

Gaskin, J. C. A. (1984) *The quest for eternity*, New York: Penguin Books.

Geertz, C. (1973) *The interpretation of cultures*, London: Hutchinson.

—— (1983) *Local knowledge: further essays in interpretive anthropology*, New York: Basic Books.

Gibson, J. J. (1950) *The perception of the visual world*, Boston, MA: Houghton Mifflin.

—— (1966) *The senses considered as perceptual systems*, Boston, MA: Houghton Mifflin.

—— (1979) *The ecological approach to visual perception*, Boston, MA: Houghton Mifflin.

Giddens, A. (1990) *The consequences of modernity*, Cambridge: Polity Press.

Goodall, J. (1986) *The chimpanzees of Gombe: patterns of behaviour*, Cambridge, MA: Harvard University Press.

—— (1990) *Through a window: 30 years with the chimpanzees of Gombe*, London: Weidenfeld & Nicolson.

Goodenough, W. (1961) 'Comments on cultural evolution', *Daedalus* 90: 521–28.

Goodin, R. E. (1992) *Green political theory*, Cambridge: Polity Press.

Goody, J. (1961) 'Religion and ritual: the definition problem', *British Journal of Sociology* 12: 143–64.

Gopnik, A. and Wellman, H. M. (1994) 'The theory theory', in L. A. Hirschfeld and S. A. Gelman (eds) *Mapping the mind: domain specificity in cognition and culture*, Cambridge: Cambridge University Press.

Gopnik, A., Meltzoff, A. and Kuhl, P. (2000) *How babies think: the science of childhood*, London: Weidenfeld & Nicolson.

Gottlieb, R. S. (1996) *This sacred Earth: religion, nature, environment*, London and New York: Routledge.

Grahame, K. (1936 [1908]) *The wind in the willows*, London: Methuen.

Grubb, M., Koch, M., Thomson, K., Munson, A. and Sullivan, F. (1993) *The 'Earth Summit' agreements: a guide and assessment*, London: Earthscan.

Guha, R. and Martinez-Alier, J. (1997) *Varieties of environmentalism: essays North and South*, London: Earthscan.

Guthrie, S. (1993) *Faces in the clouds: a new theory of religion*, Oxford: Oxford University Press.

Hallowell, A. I. (1960) 'Ojibwa ontology, behaviour and world view', in S. Diamond (ed.) *Culture in history: essays in honour of Paul Radin*, New York: Colombia University Press.

Hannerz, U. (1990) 'Cosmopolitans and locals in world culture', in M. Featherstone (ed.) *Global culture*, London: Sage.

Harré, R. (ed.) (1986) *The social construction of emotions*, Oxford: Blackwell.

Harries-Jones, P. (1993) 'Between science and shamanism: the advocacy of environmentalism in Toronto', in K. Milton (ed.) *Environmentalism: the view from anthropology*, ASA Monograph 32, London and New York: Routledge.

Harris, G. G. (1978) *Casting out anger: religion among the Taita of Kenya*, Cambridge: Cambridge University Press.

Harry, J., Gale, R. and Hendee, J. (1969) 'Conservation: an upper-middle class social movement', *Journal of Leisure Research* 1: 246–54.

Heerwagen, J. H. and Orians, G. H. (1993) 'Humans, habitats and aesthetics', in S. R. Kellert and E. O. Wilson (eds) *The biophilia hypothesis*, Washington, DC: Island Press.

Heller, A. (1979) *A theory of feelings*, Assen, The Netherlands: Van Gorcum.

Hirschfeld, L. A. and Gelman, S. A. (1994) 'Toward a topography of mind: an introduction to domain specificity', in L. A. Hirschfeld and S. A. Gelman (eds) *Mapping the mind: domain specificity in cognition and culture*, Cambridge: Cambridge University Press.

HMSO (1995) *Biodiversity: the UK steering group report* (2 vols), London: Her Majesty's Stationery Office.

Hochschild, A. R. (1983) *The managed heart: commercialization of human feeling*, Berkeley: University of California Press.

—— (1998) 'The sociology of emotion as a way of seeing', in G. Bendelow and S. J. Williams (eds) *Emotions in social life: critical themes and contemporary issues*, London and New York: Routledge.

Holy, L. and Stuchlik, M. (1981) 'The structure of folk models', in L. Holy and M. Stuchlik (eds) *The structure of folk models*, London: Academic Press.

Hornborg, A. (1993) 'Environmentalism and identity on Cape Breton: on the social and existential conditions for criticism', in G. Dahl (ed.) *Green arguments and local subsistence*, Stockholm Studies in Social Anthropology, Stockholm University.

—— (1994) 'Environmentalism, ethnicity and sacred places: reflections on modernity, discourse and power', *Canadian Review of Sociology and Anthropology* 31, 3: 245–67.

—— (1996) 'Ecology as semiotics', in P. Descola and G. Pálsson (eds) *Nature and society*, London and New York: Routledge.

—— (1998) 'Ecological embeddedness and personhood: Have we always been capitalists?', *Anthropology Today* 14, 2: 3–5.

Horton, R. (1960) 'A definition of religion and its uses', *Journal of the Royal Anthropological Institute* 90: 201–26.

—— (1967) 'African traditional thought and western science, *Africa* 37: 50–71, 159–87.

Hughes, B. (1993) 'Stiff-tail threat', *BTO News* 185: 14.

Hughes, B. and Williams, G. (1997) 'What future for the white-headed duck?', *Ecos: A Review of Conservation* 18, 2: 15–19.

Hume, D. (1911 [1740]) *A treatise of human nature*, vol. II, London: J. M. Dent & Sons.

Ingold, T. (1992) 'Culture and the perception of the environment', in E. Croll and D. Parkin (eds) *Bush base: forest farm*, London: Routledge.

—— (1993) 'Globes and spheres: the topology of environmentalism', in K. Milton (ed.) *Environmentalism: the view from anthropology*, London and New York: Routledge.

—— (1994) 'From trust to domination: an alternative history of human–animal relations', in A. Manning and J. Serpell (eds) *Animals and human society: changing perspectives*, London and New York: Routledge.

—— (1995) 'Building, dwelling, living: how animals and people make themselves at home in the world', in M. Strathern (ed.) *Shifting contexts: transformations in anthropological knowledge*, London and New York: Routledge.

—— (1999) Comment on '"Animism" revisited: personhood, environment and relational epistemology', by N. Bird-David, *Current Anthropology* 40, Supplement, February: 67–91.

—— (2000a) *The perception of the environment: essays in livelihood, dwelling and skill*, London and New York: Routledge.

—— (2000b) Letter in *Anthropology Today*, 16, 4: 25–6.

—— (2001) 'From the transmission of representations to the education of attention', in H. Whitehouse (ed.) *The debated mind: evolutionary psychology versus ethnography*, Oxford: Berg.

Izard, C. E. (1977) *Human emotions*, New York: Plenum Press.

—— (1991) *The psychology of emotions*, New York and London: Plenum Press.

—— (1993) 'Four systems of emotion activation: cognitive and noncognitive processes', *Psychological Review* 100, 1: 68–90.

Jackson, A. (ed.) (1987) *Anthropology at home*, ASA Monograph 25, London: Tavistock.

James, W. (1884) 'What is an emotion?', *Mind* 9: 188–205.

—— (1890) *Principles of psychology*, New York: Holt.

—— (1956 [1897]) 'The sentiment of rationality', in *The will to believe and other essays in popular philosophy*, New York: Dover Publications.

Jamison, A., Eyerman, R., Cramer, J. and Læssøe, J. (1990) *The Making of the New Environmental Consciousness*, Edinburgh: Edinburgh University Press.

Jones, S. (1999) *Almost like a whale: the origin of species updated*, London: Doubleday.

Kant, I. (1785) *Groundwork of the metaphysic of morals*, in H. J. Paton (1972) *The moral law: Kant's groundwork of the metaphysic of morals*, London: Hutchinson.

Karmiloff-Smith, A. (1992) *Beyond modularity: a developmental perspective on cognitive science*, Cambridge, MA: MIT Press.

Kay, P. (1965) 'Ethnography and the theory of culture', *Bucknell Review* 19: 106–13.

Keil, F. C. (1979) *Semantic and conceptual development*, Cambridge, MA: Harvard University Press.

—— (1989) *Concepts, kinds and conceptual development*, Cambridge, MA: MIT Press.

Kellert, S. R. (1993) 'The biological basis for human values of nature', in S. R. Kellert and E. O. Wilson (eds) *The biophilia hypothesis*, Washington, DC: Island Press.

Kemper, T. D. (1987) 'How many emotions are there? Wedding the social and autonomic components', *American Journal of Sociology* 93: 263–89.

Kennedy, J. S. (1992) *The new anthropomorphism*, Cambridge: Cambridge University Press.

Kluckhohn, C. (1951) 'Values and value orientations in the theory of action', in T. Parsons and E. Shils (eds) *Toward a general theory of action*, Cambridge, MA: Harvard University Press.

Kuhn, T. S. (1970) *The structure of scientific revolutions*, Chicago, IL: University of Chicago Press.

Laird, J. D. and Apostoleris, N. H. (1996) 'Emotional self-control and self-perception: feelings are the solution, not the problem', in R. Harré and W. G. Parrott (eds) *The emotions: social, cultural and biological dimensions*, London and Thousand Oaks, CA: Sage.

Lawson, E. T. and McCauley, R. N. (1990) *Rethinking religion: connecting cognition and culture*, Cambridge: Cambridge University Press.

Lawson, T. (1996) 'Brent Duck', *Ecos: A Review of Conservation* 17, 2: 27–35.

—— (1999) 'A shot in the foot', *Guardian*, 10 February.

Lazarus, R. S. (1991) *Emotion and adaptation*, Oxford: Oxford University Press.

Leach, E. (1976) *Culture and communication*, Cambridge: Cambridge University Press.

Leavitt, J. (1996) 'Meaning and feeling in the anthropology of emotions', *American Ethnologist* 23, 3: 514–39.

Leslie, A. M. (1987) 'Pretence and representation: the origins of "theory of mind"', *Psychological Review* 94: 412–26.

—— (1994) 'ToMM, ToBY, and agency: core architecture and domain specificity', in L. A. Hirschfeld and S. A. Gelman (eds) *Mapping the mind: domain specificity in cognition and culture*, Cambridge: Cambridge University Press.

Livingston, J. (1981) *The fallacy of wildlife conservation*, Toronto: McClelland and Stewart.

Lloyd, G. E. R. (1979) *Magic, reason and experience*, Cambridge: Cambridge University Press.

Lovelock, J. (1979) *Gaia: a new look at life on Earth*, Oxford: Oxford University Press.

—— (1988) *The ages of Gaia*, Oxford: Oxford University Press.

Luhrmann, T. (1993) 'The resurgence of romanticism: contemporary neopaganism, feminist spirituality and the divinity of nature', in K. Milton (ed.) *Environmentalism: the view from anthropology*, London and New York: Routledge.

Lupton, D. (1998) *The emotional self: a sociocultural exploration*, London, and Thousand Oaks, CA: Sage.

Lutz, C. A. (1988) *Unnatural emotions: everyday sentiments on a Micronesian atoll and their challenge to western theory*, Chicago, IL, and London: University of Chicago Press.

Lutz, C. A. and Abu-Lughod, L. (eds) (1990) *Language and the politics of emotion*, Cambridge: Cambridge University Press.

Lutz, C. A. and White, G. M. (1986) 'The anthropology of emotions', *Annual Review of Anthropology* 15: 405–36.

Lyon, M. L. (1998) 'The limitations of cultural constructionism in the study of emotion', in G. Bendelow and S. J. Williams (eds) *Emotions in social life: critical themes and contemporary issues*, London and New York: Routledge.

McCauley, R. N. (1997) 'Bringing ritual to mind', in R. Fivush and E. Winograd (eds) *Essays in honour of Ulrich Neisser*, Hillsdale, NJ: Erlbaum.

—— (2000) 'Comparing the cognitive foundations of religion and science', in F. Keil and R. Wilson (eds) *Explanation and cognition*, Cambridge, MA: MIT Press.

McIntosh, A. (in press) *Soil and soul: people versus corporate power*, London: Aurum Press.

McIntosh, A., MacLeod, Revd D. and Herney, S. S. E. (1995) 'Public Inquiry on the proposed Harris superquarry: witness on the theological considerations concerning superquarrying and the integrity of creation', *Journal of Law and Religion* 11: 757–91.

McKibben, B. (1990) *The end of nature*, London: Viking Press.

Macnaghten, P. and Urry, J. (1998) *Contested natures*, London: Sage.

Macy, J. (1987) 'Faith and ecology', *Resurgence*, July–August: 18–21.

—— (1991) *World as lover, world as self*, Berkeley, CA: Parallax Press.

Malinowski, B. (1948) *Magic, science and religion and other essays*, Glencoe, IL: The Free Press.

Mandler, G. (1975) *Mind and emotions*, New York: Wiley.

Manes, C. (1990) *Green rage: radical environmentalism and the unmaking of civilization*, Boston, MA: Little, Brown & Co.

Marvin, G. (2000) 'The problem of foxes: legitimate and illegitimate killing in the English countryside', in J. Knight (ed.) *Natural enemies: people–wildlife conflicts in anthropological perspective*, London and New York: Routledge.

Mathews, F. (1991) *The ecological self*, London: Routledge.

Milton, K. (1990) *Our countryside our concern: the policy and practice of conservation in Northern Ireland*, Belfast: Northern Ireland Environment Link.

—— (1991) 'Interpreting environmental policy: a social-scientific approach', in R. Churchill, J. Gibson and L. M. Warren (eds) *Law, policy and the environment*, Oxford: Blackwell.

—— (1996) *Environmentalism and cultural theory: exploring the role of anthropology in environmental discourse*, London and New York: Routledge.

—— (1997) 'Nature, culture and biodiversity', in F. Arler and I. Svennevig (eds) *Cross-cultural protection of nature and the environment*, Odense, Denmark: Odense University Press.

—— (1998) 'Nature and the environment in indigenous and traditional cultures', in D. E. Cooper and J. A. Palmer (eds) *Spirit of the environment: religion, value and environmental concern*, London and New York: Routledge.

—— (1999) 'Nature is already sacred', *Environmental Values* 8, 4: 437–49.

—— (2000) 'Ducks out of water: nature conservation as boundary maintenance', in J. Knight (ed.) *Natural enemies: people–wildlife conflicts in anthropological perspective*, London and New York: Routledge.

Moore, N. W. (1987) *The bird of time: the science and politics of nature conservation*, Cambridge: Cambridge University Press.

Morris, B. (1994) *Anthropology of the self*, London: Pluto.

Mumford, L. (1982) *Sketches from a life*, New York: The Dial Press.

Munn, N. (1973) *Walbiri iconography: graphic representation and cultural symbolism in a Central Australian society*, Ithaca, NY: Cornell University Press.

Munro, D. (1997) 'Introduction', in D. Munro, J. F. Schumaker and S. C. Carr (eds) *Motivation and culture*, London and New York: Routledge.

Nabhan, G. P. and St Antoine, S. (1993) 'The loss of floral and faunal story: the extinction of experience', in S. R. Kellert and E. O. Wilson (eds) *The biophilia hypothesis*, Washington, DC: Island Press.

Naess, A. (1973) 'The shallow and the deep, long-range ecology movement: a summary', *Inquiry* 16: 95–100.

—— (1982) 'How my philosophy seemed to develop', in *Philosophers on their own work*, vol. 10, New York: Peter Lang.

—— (1985) 'Identification as a source of deep ecological attitudes', in M. Tobias (ed.) *Deep ecology*, San Diego, CA: Avant Books.

—— (1988) 'Self-realization: an ecological approach to being in the world', in J. Seed, J. Macy, P. Fleming and A. Naess *Thinking like a mountain: towards a council of all beings*, Philadelphia, PA: New Society Publishers.

—— (1989) *Ecology, community and lifestyle: outline of an ecosophy*, translated and edited by D. Rothenberg, Cambridge: Cambridge University Press.

Nasby, W. and Yando, R. (1982) 'Selective encoding and retrieval of affectively valent information: two cognitive consequences of children's mood states', *Journal of Personality and Social Psychology* 43, 6: 1244–53.

Neisser, U. (1976) *Cognition and reality: principles and implications of cognitive psychology*, San Francisco, CA: W. H. Freeman & Co.

—— (1988) 'Five kinds of self-knowledge', *Philosophical Psychology* 1, 1: 35–59.

Nuckolls, C. W. (1996) *The cultural dialectics of knowledge and desire*, Madison: University of Wisconsin Press.

—— (1998) *Culture: a problem that cannot be solved*, Madison: University of Wisconsin Press.

—— (2001) 'Fear of Freud', in H. Whitehouse (ed.) *The debated mind: evolutionary psychology versus ethnography*, Oxford: Berg.

Oatley, K. (1992) *Best laid schemes: the psychology of emotions*, Cambridge: Cambridge University Press.

O'Neill, J. (1993) *Ecology, policy and politics: human well-being and the natural world*, London and New York: Routledge.

Ortony, A. and Turner, T. J. (1990) 'What's basic about basic emotions?', *Psychological Review* 97: 315–31.

Osgood, C. E. (1966) 'Dimensionality of the semantic space for communication via facial expressions', *Scandinavian Journal of Psychology* 7: 1–30.

Otto, R. (1950) *The idea of the Holy*, Oxford: Oxford University Press.

Pain, G. M. (1999) *Report of Public Local Inquiry into extraction of anorthosite at Lingerbay, Isle of Harris* (vols 1–4), Edinburgh: Scottish Office Inquiry Reporters' Unit.

Palmer, J. A. (1998) 'Spiritual ideas, environmental concerns and educational practice', in D. E. Cooper and J. A. Palmer (eds) *Spirit of the environment: religion, value and environmental concern*, London and New York: Routledge.

Panskepp, J. (1982) 'Toward a general psychobiological theory of emotions', *Behavioural and Brain Sciences* 5: 407–67.

—— (1992) 'A critical role for "affective neuroscience" in resolving what is basic about basic emotions', *Psychological Review* 99, 3: 554–60.

Parkinson, B. (1995) *Ideas and realities of emotion*, London and New York: Routledge.

Parsons, T. (1951) *The social system*, New York: Free Press.

Payne, R. (1995) *Among whales*, New York: Scribner.

Payne, R. and McVay, S. (1971) 'Songs of humpback whales', *Science* 173: 585–97.

Peace, A. (forthcoming) 'Loving Leviathan: the discourse of whale watching in an Australian eco-tourist location', in J. Knight (ed.) *Animals in person: cultural contexts of human-animal intimacies*, Oxford: Berg.

Pearce, D. (ed.) (1991) *Blueprint 2: greening the world economy*, London: Earthscan.

—— (ed.) (1994) *Blueprint 3: measuring sustainable development*, London: Earthscan.

Pearce, D., Markandya, A. and Barbier, E. B. (1989) *Blueprint for a green economy*, London: Earthscan.

Piontelli, A. (1992) *From foetus to child: an observational and psychoanalytic study*, London and New York: Tavistock and Routledge.

Plutchik, R. (1982) 'A psychoevolutionary theory of emotions', *Social Science Information* 21, 4: 529–53.

Popper, K. (1965) *Conjectures and refutations: the growth of scientific knowledge*, London: Routledge & Kegan Paul.

Posey, D. A. (1998) 'The "balance sheet" and the "sacred balance": valuing the knowledge of indigenous and traditional peoples', *Worldviews: Environment, Culture, Religion* 2, 2: 91–106.

—— (ed.) (1999) *Cultural and spiritual values of biodiversity*, London: Intermediate Technology Publications, on behalf of the United Nations Environment Programme.

Quiller-Couch, A. (ed.) (1980) *The Oxford Book of English Verse 1250–1918*, London: Granada.

Rappaport, R. (1979) *Ecology, meaning and religion*, Berkeley, CA: North Atlantic Books.

Ratcliffe, D. (1997) 'The importance of the natural', *Ecos* 18, 3/4: 34–7.

Regan, T. (1983) *The case for animal rights*, London: Routledge & Kegan Paul.

Renninger, K. A. and Wozniak, R. H. (1985) 'Effect of interest on attentional shift, recognition and recall in young children', *Developmental Psychology* 21, 4: 624–32.

Richards, A. (1997) 'Chapter 1: Passionate minds', in L. Wolpert and A. Richards (eds) *Passionate Minds: the inner world of scientists*, Oxford: Oxford University Press.

Richards, P. (1993) 'Natural symbols and natural history: chimpanzees, elephants and experiments in Mende thought', in K. Milton (ed.) *Environmentalism: the view from anthropology*, London and New York: Routledge.

—— (1997) 'Common knowledge and resource conservation', in F. Arler and I. Svennevig (eds) *Cross-cultural protection of nature and the environment*, Odense: Odense University Press.

Robinson, M. (1968) '"The House of the Mighty Hero" or "The House of Enough Paddy"? Some implications of a Sinhalese Myth', in E. R. Leach (ed.) *Dialectic in practical religion*, Cambridge: Cambridge University Press.

Rolls, E. T. (1990) 'A theory of emotion, and its application to understanding the neural basis of emotion', *Cognition and Emotion* 4: 161–90.

Rolston, H. (1999) 'Ethics and the environment', in E. Baker and M. Richardson (eds) *Ethics Applied*, New York: Simon & Schuster.

Rosaldo, M. (1980) *Knowledge and passion: Ilongot notions of self and social life*, Cambridge: Cambridge University Press.

RSPB (1994) Recruitment advertisement, *BBC Wildlife Magazine* 13, 3: 11.

—— (2001a) Recruitment advertisement, *BBC Wildlife Magazine* 19, 1: 25.

—— (2001b) 'A prickly problem for Hebridean waders', *Birds* 18, 5: 63.

Satterfield, T. (forthcoming) *The anatomy of a conflict: identity, knowledge and emotion in old-growth forests*, Vancouver: University of British Columbia Press.

Schleiermacher, F. (1988) *On religion*, Cambridge: Cambridge University Press.

Schwartz, S. H. (1997) 'Values and culture', in D. Munro, J. F. Schumaker and S. C. Carr (eds) *Motivation and culture*, London and New York: Routledge.

Scott, C. (1989) 'Knowledge construction among Cree hunters: metaphors and literal understanding', *Journal de la Société des Americanistes* 75: 193–208.

Scott, P. (1990) *Observations of wildlife*, Oxford: Phaidon Press.

Seed, J. (1985) 'Anthropocentrism', in B. Devall and G. Sessions *Deep ecology: living as if nature mattered*, Layton, UT: Gibbs M. Smith.

—— (1988) 'Introduction: "To hear within ourselves the sound of the Earth crying"', in J. Seed, J. Macy, P. Fleming and A. Naess *Thinking like a mountain: towards a council of all beings*, Philadelphia, PA: New Society Publishers.

Seed, J., Macy, J., Fleming, P. and Naess, A. (1988) *Thinking like a mountain: towards a council of all beings*, Philadelphia, PA: New Society Publishers.

Shiva, V. (1993) *Monocultures of the mind: perspectives on biodiversity and biotechnology*, London: Zed Books.

Simmel, G. (1971 [1903]) 'The metropolis and mental life', in D. N. Levine (ed.) *Georg Simmel: on individuality and social forms*, Chicago, IL: University of Chicago Press.

Simmons, I. G. (1993) *Interpreting nature: cultural constructions of the environment*, London and New York: Routledge.

Singer, P. (1976) *Animal liberation*, London: Cape.

Soper, K. (1995) *What is nature? Culture, politics and the non-human*, Oxford: Blackwell.

Soulé, M. E. (1993) 'Biophilia: unanswered questions', in S. R. Kellert and E. O. Wilson (eds) *The biophilia hypothesis*, Washington, DC: Island Press.

Soulé, M. E. and Noss, R. (n.d.) 'Rewilding and diversity: complementary goals for continental conservation', on the *Wildlands Project* website (www.twp.org).

Spangler, D. (1993) 'Imagination, Gaia, and the sacredness of the Earth', in F. Hull (ed.) *Earth and spirit*, New York: The Continuum Publishing Co, reprinted in R. S. Gottlieb (ed.) (1996) *This sacred Earth: religion, nature, environment*, London and New York: Routledge.

Spelke, E. (1991) 'Physical knowledge in infancy: reflections on Piaget's theory', in S. Carey and R. Gelman (eds) *The epigenesis of mind*, Hillsdale, NJ: Erlbaum.

Sperber, D. (1975) *Rethinking symbolism*, Cambridge: Cambridge University Press.

—— (1985) 'Anthropology and psychology: towards an epidemiology of representations', *Man* (NS) 20: 73–89.

—— (1994) 'The modularity of thought and the epidemiology of representations', in L. A. Hirschfeld and S. A. Gelman (eds) *Mapping the mind: domain specificity in cognition and culture*, Cambridge: Cambridge University Press.

Spiro, M. E. (1966) 'Religion: problems of definition and explanation', in M. Banton (ed.) *Anthropological approaches to the study of religion*, London: Tavistock.

—— (1982) *Oedipus in the Trobriands*, Chicago, IL: University of Chicago Press.

Sroufe, L. A. (1979) 'Socioemotional development', in J. D. Osofsky (ed.) *Handbook of infant development*, New York: Wiley.

Steven, K. C. (1993) *Remembering Peter*, Fareham, Hants: The National Poetry Foundation.

Steward, J. (1955) *Theory of culture change*, Urbana: University of Illinois Press.

Stiles, K. (1993) 'Newsdesk: those ruddy ducks', *Wildfowl and Wetlands: The Magazine of the Wildfowl and Wetlands Trust* 108: 5–6.

Stiles, K. and Delany, S. (1993) 'Background to the 1994 ruddy duck survey', *WWT Information Sheet*, Slimbridge, Glos: Wildfowl and Wetlands Trust.

Strang, V. (1997) *Uncommon ground: cultural landscapes and environmental values*, Oxford and New York: Berg.

Strathern, M. (1988) *The gender of the gift: problems with women and problems with society in Melanesia*, Berkeley: University of California Press.

Strongman, K. T. (1996) *The psychology of emotion: theories of emotion in perspective*, New York: Wiley.

Svašek, M. (2000) 'Borders and emotions: hope and fear in the Bohemian–Bavarian frontier zone', *Ethnologia Europaea: Journal of European Ethnology* 30, 2: 111–26.

Tambiah, S. J. (1990) *Magic, science, religion and the scope of rationality*, Cambridge: Cambridge University Press.

Tanner, A. (1979) *Bringing home animals: religious ideology and mode of production of the Mistassini Cree Hunters*, St John's, Newfoundland: Institute of Social and Economic Research, Memorial University of Newfoundland.

Taylor, B. (1997) 'On sacred or secular ground? Callicott and environmental ethics', *Worldviews: Environment, Culture, Religion* 1: 99–111.

Thomas, K. (1983) *Man and the natural world: changing attitudes in England 1500–1800*, Harmondsworth, Middx: Penguin Books.

Thompson, H. S. (1998) 'White-necked picathartes *Picathartes gymnocephalus*: its ecology and conservation', *RSPB Conservation Review* 12: 93–6.

Tomkins, S. S. (1962) *Affect, imagery, consciousness*, vol. 1, New York: Springer.

Tooby, J. and Cosmides, L. (1990) 'The past explains the present: emotional adaptations and the structure of ancestral environments', *Ethology and Sociobiology* 11: 375–424.

Toren, C. (2001) 'The child in mind', in H. Whitehouse (ed.) *The debated mind: evolutionary psychology versus ethnography*, Oxford: Berg.

Tucker, M. E. (1997) 'The emerging alliance of religion and ecology', *Worldviews: Environment, Culture, Religion* 1: 3–24.

Turner, V. W. (1967) *The forest of symbols: studies in Ndembu ritual*, Ithaca, NY: Cornell University Press.

Tylor, E. B. (1871) *Primitive culture: researches into the development of mythology, philosophy, religion, art, and custom* (2 vols), London: John Murray.

UK Ruddy Duck Working Group (1995) *Information Note*, Peterborough, Cambs: Joint Nature Conservation Committee.

Ulrich, R. S. (1993) 'Biophilia, biophobia, and natural landscapes', in S. R. Kellert and E. O. Wilson (eds) *The biophilia hypothesis*, Washington, DC: Island Press.

Urry, J. (1990) *The tourist gaze*, London: Sage.

—— (1995) *Consuming places*, London and New York: Routledge.

van Ginkel, R. (1994) 'Writing culture from within: reflections on endogenous ethnography', *Etnofoor* 7, 1: 5–23.

Van Liere, K. D. and Dunlap, R. E. (1980) 'The social bases of environmental concern: a review of hypotheses, explanations and empirical evidence', *Public Opinion Quarterly* 44: 181–97.

Vidal, J. (1993) 'Hasta la vista ruddy duck', *Guardian*, 28 May.

Vogt, E. and Albert, E. (eds) (1966) *The people of Rimrock: a study of values in five cultures*, Cambridge, MA: University of Harvard Press.

von Uexküll, J. (1982) 'The theory of meaning', *Semiotica* 42, 1: 1–24.

von Uexküll, T. (1982) 'Introduction: Meaning and science in Jakob von Uexküll's concept of biology', *Semiotica* 42, 1: 1–24.

Walters, M. J. (1999) *National Wildlife*, December–January 1999. Obtained through the website of the National Wildlife Federation (http://www.nwf.org/nwf/).

Warke, F. J. (1990) *Report to the Planning Appeals Commission on a Public Inquiry into objections to Belfast Harbour Local Plan 1990–2005*, Belfast: Planning Appeals Commission.

WDCS (1991) *Why whales?*, Bath, and Lincoln, MA: Whale and Dolphin Conservation Society.

Weber, M. (1978 [1921]) *Economy and society: an outline of interpretive sociology*, Berkeley: University of California Press.

White, L. (1967) 'The historical roots of our ecological crisis', *Science* 155: 1203–7.

Whitehouse, H. (1992) 'Memorable religions: transmission, codification and change in divergent Melanesian contexts', *Man* (NS) 27: 777–97.

—— (1996) 'Jungles and computers: neuronal group selection and the epidemiology of representations', *Journal of the Royal Anthropological Institute* (NS) 2: 99–116.

—— (2001) 'Introduction', in H. Whitehouse (ed.) *The debated mind: evolutionary psychology versus ethnography*, Oxford: Berg.

Wiggins, D. (1980) *Sameness and substance*, Cambridge, MA: Harvard University Press.

Williams, S. (2001) *Emotion and social theory: corporeal reflections on the (ir)rational*, London, and Thousand Oaks, CA: Sage.

Williams, S. J. and Bendelow, G. (1998) 'Introduction: Emotions in social life: mapping the sociological terrain', in G. Bendelow and S. J. Williams (eds) *Emotions in social life: critical themes and contemporary issues*, London and New York: Routledge.

Williams, T. T. (1994) *An unspoken hunger: stories from the field*, New York: Pantheon Books.

Willis, R. (1975) *Man and beast*, St Albans, Herts: Paladin.

Wilson, E. O. (1984) *Biophilia: the human bond with other species*, Cambridge, MA: Harvard University Press.

—— (ed.) (1988) *Biodiversity*, Washington, DC: National Academy Press.

—— (1993) 'Biophilia and the conservation ethic', in S. R. Kellert and E. O. Wilson (eds) *The biophilia hypothesis*, Washington, DC: Island Press.

Winter, D. D. (1996) *Ecological psychology: healing the split between planet and self*, New York: HarperCollins.

Wolpert, L. (1992) *The unnatural nature of science*, London: Faber and Faber.

Wolpert, L. and Richards, A. (eds) (1988) *A passion for science*, Oxford: Oxford University Press.

—— (eds) (1997) *Passionate minds: the inner world of scientists*, Oxford: Oxford University Press.

Worsley, P. (1957) *The trumpet shall sound: a study of 'cargo' cults in Melanesia*, London: MacGibbon & Kee.

WWF (1986) *The new road: the bulletin of the WWF Network on Conservation and Religion*, 1, Gland, Switzerland: World Wide Fund for Nature.

Yearley, S. (1988) *Science, technology and social change*, London: Unwin Hyman.

—— (1992) *The green case: a sociology of environmental issues, arguments and politics*, London: Routledge.

INDEX

Aborigines of Australia: cosmology 102; identity 89, 105–6; story lines 101
Abram, D. 102
Abu-Lughod, L. 3, 58, 68
Adams, Bill 114, 116
adoption schemes 122–3, 157[7]n8
Africa 104
Aguilar, J. 154[4]n1
Albert, E. 93
Allen, P. G. 30
Amazonian rainforest 1
America, North: environmentalism 145; indigenous cultures 101–2; Wildlands Project 113–14, 157n2; see also Nova Scotia
Animal Aid 117, 126, 127
Animal Liberation Front 117
animals: see non-human animals
animism 37, 51, 52
anthropocentrism 5
anthropology: constructionism 1–2; cultural relativism 26; emotion 58; identity 88; symbolism 31–2; value 93–5
anthropomorphism 19–20, 21, 37
anticipatory schemata, perception 43, 44
Apostoleris, N. H. 66–7, 80
Areas of Outstanding Natural Beauty 138
Areas of Special Scientific Interest 92
Armen, J.-C. 43, 148
art values 95–6, 113
Atran, S. 13, 14, 15, 18, 22, 33, 152n5
attachments, emotional 111–12, 134, 145, 149
Australia: cosmology 102; environmental values 94, 102–3; identity 89, 105–6; story lines 101
authenticity: art 95–6; indigenous people 145; nature 113

autobiographies of environmentalists 62–3
autonomy 116–17

Bachelard, G. 152n5
badger image 118, 119
Barbalet, J. M. 4–5, 66, 130, 132, 134, 135, 141, 149, 150
Barnes, Simon 57
Barry, J. 10, 11, 30, 31
Barth, F. 156[6]n3
Bartlett, J. C. 65
Bat Conservation International 123
Bateson, G. 26, 88, 102, 103–4, 157[6]n7
Bateson, M. C. 26, 103
bats 120
Batten, L. A. 124
BBC Wildlife Magazine 122, 123
beauty: landscape 5, 61, 100; preservation 112, 129; sacredness 139–40; science 138; tourism 135; visibility 138, 139
behaviour, mutuality 49–50
behaviourism 94
Belfast Harbour lagoons 92, 146, 156n1
Bendelow, G. 3
Berglund, E. K. 10, 16, 132, 136
biocentrism 5
biodiversity 5; future generations 9; indigenous people 89; nature conservation 56, 115–16, 118; non-human animals 29; personhood 123–4, 128; protection agencies 117
biology 26, 78
biophilia 60–2
Bird-David, N. 47–8, 48, 50, 52, 53, 86, 88, 102
bird habitats 92, 129–30, 146, 156n1
Birdlife International 125
Birds magazine 57, 125

Blake, William 40
bodily changes, emotion 59, 66–7, 80, 90–1, 155n5
Born Free Foundation 117, 118
Boyer, P. 16, 17, 33, 34, 35, 36, 38, 152n7, 153[3]n1
brain damage 59, 66
Brewer, B. 42
Briggs, J. 68
Britain: foot and mouth disease 131; Future Nature Project 113, 114; see also Ireland, Northern; Scotland; Wales
British Association of Nature Conservationists 114
Brydon, A. 145
Bulmer, R. 31
burials 155–6n2
Burridge, K. O. L. 22
Bush, George W. 1

Callicott, J. B. 10, 11, 47, 102
Cape Breton Island, Nova Scotia 140–2, 145, 158n5
capitalism: emotion 134–5; global 133; hegemony 144; nature protectionism 136; quarry 143; science 53, 136, 150–1
carbon 1
Care for the Wild 117, 123
Carey, S. 35, 37, 38, 48, 153n7
caring 3–4
Carson, R. 10
cassowaries 31
Cavalieri, P. 94
Chapman, A. J. 69
children: cognitive development 17, 35, 37; experience 63–4; feral 43; sponsorship of 123; see also infants
chimpanzees 73–4, 76, 81
China 20
Christianity 10, 78, 83, 142–3; see also Presbyterianism; Sabbath observance
Christiansen, S. A. 65, 149
Clark, S. R. L. 28, 94–5, 156[6]n4
climate change 1, 51
coastal dunes 114
coffins, biodegradable 155–6n2
cognition 35, 44, 65, 153n6
cognitive development 17, 35, 37
cognitive scientists 38
Cohen, J. M. 40
Cohen, M. J. 40
Coleridge, S. T., The Rime of the Ancient Mariner 103–4

commoditization 106–7, 135
common sense 12–15, 152n5, 153n8
commonality 76, 77
conatus 84
conferences 56–7, 73, 76, 81, 110
Conklin, B. A. 141, 145
consciousness: emotion 100–1, 155n5; feelings 80; interest 64–5; past 77; self 80–1, 88, 94
conservationists 51, 57, 117; see also nature conservation
constructionism: anthropology 1–2; culture 32; emotion 3, 4, 58, 154[2]n2; environment 41, 43; experience 40–1; nature protectionism 111; psychology 58
Convention on International Trade in Endangered Species 157n5
Cosmides, L. 3, 35, 60
cosmology 102
Cotgrove, S. 68
Cree hunters 47
Croll, E. 148
culling 125–8
cultural diversity 1–2, 92, 147
cultural relativism 26
culture 152n3; constructionist 32; conventions 41; identity 142; nature 57; relational epistemology 48; science 20; symbolism 98–9; see also western culture

Daily Telegraph 127
Damasio, A. R. 4, 24, 61, 66, 67, 155n6; brain damage 59, 66; emotion/feeling 67, 80, 88, 99–100, 149, 157n1; emotions 4, 5, 69, 80, 82, 90, 155n7, 157n1; feelings 79, 80, 81, 157n1
Darwin, C. 59
Dawkins, R. 20, 47, 52, 84
de-Shalit, A. 95
de Sousa, R. 5, 148–9
decision making: direct action 133; emotion 24; feelings 129–30; science 137
decontextualizing process 106, 108
deep ecology 5–6, 155n1; commonality 77; identification 56, 74–6, 78–9, 82; Naess 63; nature/well-being 91; personhood 29; re-enchantment of nature 10; self-realization 83, 84, 85; transpersonal 83–4
Delany, S. 127, 128

Dennett, D. C. 20
Denzin, N. 61
Descartes, René 5, 21, 24
destruction 57, 75
Devall, B. 29
Devall, W. B. 68
Diamond, J. 62
Digital Terrain Model 138
dinosaurs 154n5
direct action 132, 133, 158n3
divine power 28, 30
diZerega, G. 88
domains 34–5; cognition 153n6; emotion
    60–2; experiential 61; learning 35, 48;
    mapping across 37; ontological 61
Douglas, M. 32, 156n1
Drever, J. 58
ducks 125–6
Duff, A. 68
Dunbar, R. I. M. 52
dunes 114
Dunlap, R. E. 68
Durkheim, É. 12, 16, 154n6, 157[6]n6
Durrell, Gerald 63
Dwyer, P. D. 102

Earth: divine will 30; as mother 31, 32,
    38; see also Gaia
Earth First! 133
Eckersley, R. 95
eco-drama 127
ecological self 47, 83, 84
ecology 4, 53–4, 74
economics/science 53
ecosystems: energy transfer 98–9;
    exchange of information 156[6]n5;
    identification 82; self-realization 29;
    self-regulating 30, 84–5; suffering 51
education 47, 58
Einarsson, N. 31, 32, 46
Ellen, R. F. 16, 17, 90, 112, 156[6]n5
Emde, R. N. 59, 61
emotion 3–4, 58–60, 65, 68–9;
    anthropology 58; attachments
    111–12, 134, 145, 149; bodily changes
    59, 66–7, 80, 90–1, 155n5; capitalism
    134–5; cognition 65; constructionism
    3, 4, 58, 154[2]n2; Damasio 4, 5, 69,
    80, 82, 90; decision making 24;
    domain-specificity 60–2; facial
    expressions 66–7, 118; feelings 67,
    79–81, 88, 99–100, 149, 157n1; gender
    130, 131–2; interest 65; James 66–7;

knowledge 58; learning 66, 148–9,
    150, 155n6; meaning 98–101,
    154–5n3; nature 55–6, 61; perception
    59, 66, 155n7; personhood 27, 86;
    rationality 4–5, 21–4, 111, 128, 130–3,
    148–50; religion 22–3, 87; sacredness
    101–5; science 23; sociology 58;
    unconscious 100–1, 155n5; value
    93–4; western culture 56, 111, 131
empathy 74–5, 81–3
enjoyment of nature 56, 70–2, 86–7
environment 47; affordances 42–3;
    constructionism 41, 43; enspirited
    102; experience 40; humanity 10, 61,
    148; identity 89; individuals 148;
    meaning 100; perception 42;
    technology 10
environmental philosophy 95
environmentalism: autobiographies 62–3;
    cultural diversity 1–2; North America
    145; political power 51; science 136;
    values 74, 94, 102–3
Ereira, A. 10
erosion 114
ethnography 56, 68
Evans-Pritchard, E. E. 31, 104
Evernden, N. 97, 112
evolution theory 18
evolutionary psychology 35
experience 69; children 63–4;
    constructionism 40–1; domain 61;
    environment 40; infants 38;
    knowledge 34, 41; learning 70–2;
    memories 57; nature 56–7, 62–4;
    sharing 69–70; social/non-social 41,
    43–4; subjective 88
exploitation 10, 29, 53, 119
extinction of species 51, 58, 61
eye contact 118, 121

facial expression 66–7, 118
feelings: consciousness 80; Damasio 79,
    80, 81; decision making 129–30;
    emotion 67, 79–81, 88, 99–100, 149,
    157n1; knowledge 103; perceptions
    67; rules 69
Fehr, B. 86
Feit, H. 116
feminists 132
Figlio, K. 154[2]n2
Findhorn Foundation 73, 110
fleas 75, 76, 82
Fodor, J. 35

foot and mouth disease 131
'For the Love of Nature?' conference 73,
76, 81, 110
forests 131, 136; *see also* rainforests
fostering 123
Foucault, M. 61
Fourmile, Henrietta 89, 156[5]n6
Fox, W. 29, 83, 115, 156[5]n5;
cosmologically-based identification
156n3; deep ecology 74, 82;
identification 74, 76, 77, 78, 82;
ontologically-based identification
156n3; personally-based identification
88–9, 90, 118; personhood 84;
subjective experiences 88
fox-hunting 50, 86–7
Frank, R. H. 5, 148–9
Frazer, J. G. 11–12, 19, 152[2]n4
Friends of the Earth 118
friendship 120, 121
future generations arguments 9, 95
Future Nature Project 113, 114

Gaia theory 30, 31, 38, 51, 82, 84
Garner, R. 28
Gaskin, J. C. A. 22
Geertz, C. 13, 22, 32
Gelman, S. A. 34–5, 153n6
gender/emotion 130, 131–2
genes, selfish 20, 52, 84
Gibson, J. J. 42–3, 43, 44, 45, 47, 67, 88,
148, 154[3]n2, 155n6
Giddens, A. 106
global capitalism 133
global warming 1
globalism 108
Goodall, Jane 20, 52, 73, 76, 81
Goodenough, W. 32
Goodin, R. E. 95–7, 97–8, 105, 112, 113
Goody, J. 16, 19
Gopnik, A. 36, 38, 45
gorillas 111
Gottlieb, R. S. 10, 152[2]n2
Graham, L. 145
Grahame, Kenneth 122
Green Party 146
green theory of value 95–7
Greenpeace 29, 119, 133
Grof, S. 156[5]n5
Grubb, M. 29, 115
Guha, R. 63
Guthrie, S. 16, 19, 21, 22–3, 33, 50–1,
153n8

Hallowell, A. I. 47
Hannerz, U. 106, 108
Harré, R. 3, 58
Harries-Jones, P. 127
Harris, G. G. 104
Harris quarry 137–9, 142–4, 158n6;
cultural identity 142; Presbyterian
tradition 142–3; sacredness 144
Harry, J. 68
Hebrides: Harris quarry 137–9, 142–4;
hedgehogs 124–5, 126
hedgehogs 124–5, 126
Heerwagen, J. H. 61
Heller, A. 134
Herney, Chief Sulian Stone Eagle 142,
143, 144
hierarchical reductionism 52
Hirschfeld, L. A. 34–5, 153n6
HMSO 115
Hochschild, A. R. 3, 4, 66, 69
Holy, L. 32
Hornborg, A. 98–9, 105, 106, 107, 140,
141, 145, 156[6]n5
Horton, R. 13, 14, 15, 16, 20
Hughes, B. 125, 126
human nature 17, 73
humanity: environment 10, 61, 148;
nature 2, 96; non-human animals 116
Hume, David 5, 148–9
humpback whales 119–20
hunter-gatherers 10; cognitive modules
35; moral obligations 10; personalized
understandings of nature 102–3;
personhood 47; relational
epistemology 47
hunting 50, 86–7, 102
hybridization 125–6, 126

Iceland 145
ideas, natural/unnatural 25, 38–9
identification: chimpanzees 73–4;
cosmologically based 78, 82, 156n3;
deep ecology 56, 74–6, 78–9, 82;
ecosystems 82; Fox 74, 76, 77, 78, 82;
Gaia 82; identity 77–8, 78; identity-
based 79, 85; morality 75; Naess 73,
76, 78, 156n4; ontologically based 78,
82, 156n3; person-based 79, 82, 87,
110–11, 115, 118; personally based 79,
87, 88–9, 90, 118, 122; personhood
81–3; self-realization 83–5; similarity
79; western culture 79
identity: Aborigines 89, 105–6;

anthropology 88; cultural 142; environment 89; global 106, 107–8; identification 77–8; local 106, 107–8; personal 105–6; self-realization 105–6, 109
inanimate objects: *see* living/non-living things
indigenous people: authenticity 145; biodiversity 89; sacredness 141–2; spirituality 101–2
indigenous species 113
individuality 120, 148
infants: experience 38; mother—child interaction 46; unborn 154n4
Ingold, T. 1, 2, 32, 38, 40, 41, 42, 44, 48, 50, 52, 53, 88, 102, 116, 147, 148, 154[3]n3, 156[6]n2
innate learning 34–5, 37, 40
intentionality 27, 28; divine power 28; Gaia 30; non-human animals 82; personhood 28–9, 36, 85; religion 19
interconnectedness 84
interest: conflicting 124; consciousness 64–5; emotion 65
international agreements 115, 157n5
International Fund for Animal Welfare 117
International Whaling Commission 29
International Wildlife Coalition 123
interpersonal relationships 70, 86
interpersonal self 45, 46, 47
intersubjectivity 46, 111
intuitive ontology 33–4, 39
Ireland, Northern: Belfast Harbour lagoons 92, 146, 156n1; gender stereotypes 130; Killyleagh 129; land use planning 135
Izard, C. E. 58–9, 59, 61, 64–5, 66, 149

Jackson, A. 154n1
James, William: emotion 58, 66–7, 81; interest 64; rationality 5, 148–9, 150
Jamison, A. 6
Jones, S. 18

Kalam, cassowaries 31
Kale, Herb 58
Kant, Immanuel 5, 74
Karmiloff-Smith, A. 44
Kay, P. 32
Keil, F. C. 17, 37, 38
Kellert, S. R. 60, 61
Kelly Rock 140–2

Kelly's Mountain 140–2, 145
Kemper, T. D. 59, 64
Kennedy, J. S. 19, 20, 21, 28, 37, 50, 52
Killyleagh, Northern Ireland 129
kinship 94
Kluckhohn, Clyde 93, 94
Kluscap's Mountain 140–2, 145
knowledge: ecology 53–4; emotion 58; experience 34, 41; feeling 103; perception 42–4, 64; psychology 42; religious/secular 153n8; representation 31, 32, 40–1
Kuhn, T. S. 13
Kyoto agreement 1

Laird, J. D. 66–7, 80
land use planning 135
landscape: beauty 5, 61, 100; enspirited 104–5; visual assessment 139
Lange, Harry 58
language use 20; *see also* metaphor
Lawson, E. T. 19–20, 21, 22, 152n6
Lawson, T. 126, 127
Lazarus, R. S. 58, 65, 155n6
Leach, E. 31
League Against Cruel Sports 126
learning: domains 35, 48; education 47; emotion 66, 148–9, 150, 155n6; experience 70–2; innate 34–5, 37, 40; modules 35, 36, 37; social interaction 41, 153–4n1
Leavitt, J. 3–4, 4, 58
Leslie, A. M. 27, 36, 45
Lilongula, Ruth 89, 90, 105
lion image 118
lioness 121
living/non-living things 17–18, 37, 47–8, 61
Livingston, J. 76, 77
Lloyd, G. E. R. 153n8
localism 108
logging of yew trees 131
love of nature 24, 57–8
Lovelock, J. 30, 84
Luhrmann, T. 51
Lupton, D. 3
Lutz, C. A. 3, 4, 23, 58, 68, 86, 130, 131, 132, 149
Lyon, M. L. 4, 58

McCauley, R. N. 15, 18, 19–20, 20, 21, 22, 34, 152n6
McIntosh, Alastair 142–4, 158n6

McKibben, B. 8, 97–8, 100, 112
MacLeod, Donald 142–4
Macnaghten, P. 68
McVay, S. 119
Macy, J. 10, 76, 77
magic 11–12
Malinowski, B.: *Magic, science and religion*
   12–13; magic/science 11–12; science
   15, 22; science/religion 153n8, 154n6
Mandler, G. 59
Manes, C. 10
marginalization 132, 145
market interests: *see* capitalism
Martinez-Alier, J. 63
Marvin, G. 86
Maslow, A.H. 156[5]n5
Mathews, F. 29, 84, 85
meaning: emotion 98–101, 154–5n3;
   environment 100; nature 96–7,
   152n2; value 98, 100; von Uexkül 99
memories 57, 65–6, 77, 152n6
metaphor 20, 31, 77
methane 1
Mi'kmaq Studies 129, 140–2
Milton, K. 47, 51, 90, 96, 97, 108, 113,
   126, 150, 152[2]n3, 153n2, 156n1
mind/body dualism 21, 24, 154n2
mind/perception 79
mind theory 27, 36, 37
modernity 108
modules 35, 36, 37
money 106–7
Moore, Norman 63
moral arguments: future generations 95;
   obligation 10; whaling 29–30
moral status 28
morality 10, 61, 74, 75
Morris, B. 88
mother–child interaction 46
motivation 92–3, 94, 98
mud-flats 129–30
Mumford, L. 63
Munn, N. 101
Munro, D. 94, 98
mutuality of behaviour 49–50

Nabhan, G. P. 61
Naess, Arne: childhood experience 63;
   empathy 74–5, 82–3; identification
   73, 76, 78, 156[5]n4; self-realization
   88; well-being 91
Nasby, W. 65
National Parks 138

National Scenic Area 137–9, 138, 142,
   158n8
National Wildlife 58
natural ideas 25, 38–9
natural processes 50–1, 97, 114
naturalness 33–4, 58–60, 113
nature 24, 57–8; anthropocentrism 5;
   authenticity 113; culture 57;
   education 58; emotion 55–6, 61;
   enjoyment of 56, 70–2, 86–7;
   experiences 56–7, 62–4;
   giving/receiving 53; humanity 2, 96;
   meaning 96–7, 152n2; personhood
   27–8, 44; qualities 112; re-
   enchantment 10, 30; religion 33,
   142–3; as resources 29, 115; science
   52–3; understanding of 19, 21, 23, 27,
   30, 51–4, 102–3; well-being 91;
   wildness 97, 112–13, 114
Nature Conservancy 63
nature conservation: Belfast Harbour 92;
   biodiversity 56, 115–16, 118;
   conferences 56–7; culling 126–8;
   science 9–10, 128
nature/nurture debate 17, 25, 34
nature protectionism 5–6, 24; capitalism
   136; constructionism 111; emotion 3,
   4; emotion/rationality 133; moral
   status 28; qualities of nature 112;
   religion 10–11; representation 31;
   resource-based arguments 29–30;
   science 9–10
Nayaka 47–8
Neisser, U. 42–6, 43, 44, 45–6, 49–50, 64,
   67, 68, 88, 99, 148, 149, 154[3]n4,
   155n6
neopaganism 51
non-human animals: autonomy 116–17;
   behaviour 20; conflicting interests
   124; and humans 116; images 118,
   119; information 48–9; intentionality
   82; perception 48–9; personhood
   26–7, 30, 41, 46–7, 49–50, 86, 110,
   115, 153n7; personification 36, 38;
   resources 41; rights organizations 117;
   self-consciousness 94; sentience 94;
   suffering 94; value 29, 95
non-literality 31
Noss, R. 114
Nova Scotia 140–2, 143
Nuckolls, C. W. 93, 98, 154[2]n2,
   156[6]n3
Nuer twins 31

nurture: *see* nature/nurture debate

Oatley, K. 5, 148–9
objectivity 20, 136
ocean warming 1
O'Neill, J. 95
Ordnance Survey map data 138
Orians, G. H. 61
Ortony, A. 59
Osgood, C. E. 64
otters 55
Otto, R. 22
ozone depletion 51

Pain, G. M. 137, 138, 139, 140, 142, 143–4
Palmer, J. A. 63, 70
panda image 118
Panskepp, J. 59
Parkin, D. 148
Parkinson, B. 4, 68, 69, 86, 149
Parsons, T. 93
past, consciousness of 77
Payne, R. 119
Peace, A. 135
Pearce, D. 107
perception: anticipatory schemata 43, 44; Bateson 26; cognition 44; emotion 59, 66, 155n7; environment 42; feelings 67; knowledge 42–4, 64; mind 79; Neisser 99; non-human animals 48–9; personhood 47–8, 79; self 45, 66–8; transformation 42–3; unborn child 154n4; visual 42
peregrines 124
personalism 20–1
personhood: biodiversity 123–4, 128; deep ecology 29; emotion 27, 86; enjoyment of nature 86–7; Fox 84; hunter-gatherer cultures 47; identification 81–3; individuality 120; intentionality 28–9, 36, 85; life 47–8, 61; moral status 28; natural idea 33–4; natural processes 50–1; nature 27–8, 44; non-human animals 26–7, 30, 41, 46–7, 49–50, 86, 110, 115, 153n7; perception 47–8, 79; relational epistemology 47, 86; self 80–1, 85; self-realization 115; species 48; western culture 88; whales 30
personification 36, 38, 39, 44
philosophy 94–5
Piaget, Jean 44

Piontelli, A. 154n4
Plutchik, R. 64
pollution 51
Popper, K. 13
Posey, D. A. 89, 92, 101, 105, 156n6
positivism 3, 4
Potter, Beatrix 125
poverty alleviation 123
predictability 37
Presbyterian tradition 142–3
preservation of beauty 112, 129
protection agencies 117
psychology 35, 42, 58, 94
Public Inquiries 137–9, 142–4, 146

quarries: Cape Breton Island 140–2, 145, 158n5; capitalism 143; Harris 137–9, 142–4, 158n6
Quiller-Couch, A. 157[6]n8

Radcliffe-Brown, A. R. 154n6
radical approach, emotion/rationality 5
rainforests 1, 135
Rappaport, R. 98, 106, 107, 108, 156[6]n5
Ratcliffe, D. 113
rational calculability 134
rationality/emotion 4–5, 21–4, 111, 128, 130–3, 148–50
re-enchantment of nature 10, 30
reality 87–8
Redland Aggregates Ltd 137–9
reductionism, hierarchical 52
reflexes 99–100
Regan, T. 28, 94
relational epistemology 48, 52–3; Bateson 103; culture 48; hunter-gatherer cultures 47; personhood 47, 86; religion 50–1
religion 15–16, 18; anthropomorphism 19–20; Boyer 34; common sense 12–15, 153n8; emotion 22–3, 87; intention 19; knowledge 153n8; magic 11–12; natural 16–19, 23, 37; nature 33, 142–3; nature protectionism 10–11; Presbyterianism 142–3; relational epistemology 50–1; Sabbath observance 142, 144; science 8–11, 15–19, 153n8; understanding 21, 23
Renninger, K. A. 65
Reporter, Public Enquiry 143–4
representation: knowledge 31, 32, 40–1; literal 77; metaphoric 77; nature protectionism 31; whaling 32

resources: forests 136; nature as 29–30, 115; non-human animals 41
Richards, A. 136
Richards, Alison 23
Richards, P. 13, 88
rights organizations 117
Rio Earth Summit 10
robins 121
Robinson, M. 150
rocks 85
Roineabhal mountain 137–9, 142–4
Rolls, E. T. 65, 149
Rolston, H. 83
Rosaldo, M. 68
roseate terns 124
Royal Society for the Prevention of Cruelty to Animals 117, 123
Royal Society for the Protection of Birds 117, 121, 123–4, 126, 127
ruddy ducks 125–6, 127
Russell, J. A. 86

Sabbath observance 142, 144
Sacred Mountain Society 140, 158n5
sacredness: Bateson 157n7; beauty 139–40; Durkheim 157n6; emotion 101–5; forests 136; Harris quarry 144; indigenous people 141–2; spirituality 102; value 104; western culture 141–2
St Antoine 61
Satterfield, T. 131–2, 132, 136, 145, 158n1
Save Kelly's Mountain Society 140, 141
Schleiermacher, F. 22
Schwartz, S. H. 94
Schweitzer, Albert 75
science 136; beauty 138; capitalism 53, 136, 150–1; common sense 12–15, 152n5; counter-intuitiveness 18; culture 20; decision making 137; economics 53; emotion 23; magic 11–12; nature 52–3; nature conservation 9–10, 128; nature protectionism 9–10; objectivity 20, 136; personalism 20–1; religion 8–11, 15–19, 153n8; truth 30–1; understanding 16–19, 21, 23
Scotland: Harris quarry 137–9, 142–4, 158n6; hedgehogs 124–5, 126; National Scenic Areas 138; Nova Scotia 143; Scottish Executive 137, 143–4, 158n8; Scottish Natural Heritage 137–9

Scott, C. 10, 47
Scott, P. 63
Scott, Sir Peter 62–3
Scottish Executive 137, 143–4, 158n8
Scottish Natural Heritage 137–9
Sea Shepherd 133
Seed, J. 10, 76, 77, 156[5]n3
self: consciousness 80–1, 88, 94; ecological 47, 83, 84; empirical 83; extended 84; interpersonal 45, 46, 47; perception 45, 66–8; personhood 80–1, 85; transpersonal 83, 84: see personhood
self-knowledge 88
self-realization: deep ecology 83, 84, 85; ecosystem 29; identification 83–5; identity 105–6, 109; Naess 88; personhood 115
self-regulating systems 30, 84–5
sentience 94
Sessions, G. 29
Shiva, V. 106, 108
similarity: commonality 76, 77; empathy 81–2; facial expressions 118; identification 79; kinship 94
Simmel, G. 134
Simmons, I. G. 68
Singer, P. 28, 94
Sites of Special Scientific Interest 138
social constructions 41, 87–8
social interaction 41, 153–4n1
social sciences 5
sociology 58
Solomon Islands 89
Soper, K. 112
soul 111
Soulé, M. E. 60, 114
Spangler, D. 10
species: extinction 51, 58, 61; flagship 118; indigenous 113; keystone 114; personhood 48
species conservation agencies 117
Spelke, E. 35, 37, 38, 48, 153n7
Sperber, D. 17, 32, 35, 62
Spinoza, B. 84
spirituality 101–2, 104–5
Spiro, M. E. 16, 19, 154[2]n2
sponsorship, Wildfowl and Wetlands Trust 122
Sroufe, L. A. 59
Steven, Kenneth C. 55
Steward, J. 41
Stiles, K. 125, 126, 127, 128
stoat 119, 157[7]n7

Strang, V. 94, 101, 102, 105–6
Strathern, M. 27, 88
Strongman, K. T. 65
Stuchlik, M. 32
subjectivity 20, 56, 79, 88
subsistence hunters 50
suffering 51, 94
Sutich, A.J. 156[5]n5
Svašek, M. 66
symbolism 14, 31–2, 46, 98–9

Tambiah, S. J. 12, 20
Tanner, A. 10, 47, 53, 102
Taylor, B. 11
technology 10
terns 124
Thomas, K. 68
Thompson, H. S. 157[7]n6
Tomkins, S. S. 61
Tooby, J. 3, 35, 60
Toren, C. 23
tourism 30, 135
transactionalism 156[6]n3
transformation 42–3
transpersonal 83–4, 156[5]n5
truth, scientific 30–1
Tucker, M. E. 10
Turi, Johan Mathis 92
Turner, T. J. 59
Turner, V. W. 32
twins 31, 154n4
Tylor, E. B. 11–12, 16, 20

UK Ruddy Duck Working Group 125, 127
Ulrich, R. S. 60, 61
Ulster Wildlife Trust 119
UN Biodiversity Convention 115, 157n5
unconscious 100–1, 155n5
understanding of nature 19, 21, 23, 27, 30,
    51–4, 102–3
Urry, J. 68

value: anthropology 93–5; cathected 93;
    emotion 93–4; environmentalism 74,
    94, 102–3; green theory 95–7; meaning
    98, 100; motivation 94, 98; non-
    human animals 29, 95; philosophy
    93–5; psychology 94; sacredness 104;
    shared 111
van Ginkel, R. 154n1
Van Liere, K. D. 68
Vidal, J. 126
visibility/beauty 138, 139

Vogt, E. 93
von Uexküll, J. 98, 99
von Uexküll, T. 79

Wader Recovery Project 125
Wales 124
Walters, Mark Jerome 57–8, 58, 61
Warke, F. J. 145
water voles 121–2
Waterways Trust 121–2
Watson, Paul 133
WDCS 30
Weber, Max 5, 12, 134
well-being from nature 91
Wellman, H. M. 36, 38, 45
western culture: emotion 56, 111, 131;
    identification 79; personhood 88;
    sacredness 141–2
Whale and Dolphin Conservation Society
    117, 119, 122–3
whales 30, 46, 119–20
whaling: campaigns against 46;
    exploitation 119; moral arguments
    29–30; representations 32
White, G. M. 3
White, L. 10
white-headed ducks 125–6, 127
Whitehouse, H. 34, 44, 65, 152n6
Wiggins, D. 153n7
wilderness 63, 113–14
Wildfowl and Wetlands Trust 62, 117,
    122, 126, 127
Wildlands Project, North America
    113–14, 157n2
wildlife documentaries 50, 154n5
wildlife products 110, 120–1
Wildlife Trusts 117, 118, 119
wildness 97, 112–13, 114
Williams, G. 125, 126
Williams, S. 3, 130
Williams, S. J. 3
Williams, Terry Tempest 131
Willis, R. 32
Wilson, E. O. 60–2, 115
Winter, D. D. 21, 118, 131
Wolpert, L. 13, 15, 16, 20, 82, 97, 136
women, social constructions 41
World Society for the Protection of
    Animals 117
World Vision 123
World Wide Fund for Nature 10, 62–3,
    117, 118, 157[7]n8
Worsley, P. 22

Wozniak, R. H. 65
Wright, D. S. 69

Yando, R. 65
Yearley, S. 11, 152[2]n1

yew trees 131

Zen Buddhism 78
Zone of Visual Influence technique
    138